What might be possible if society were to design for peace?

Black Lives Matter Harlem
Street Mural ▶ p. 120

Conflict Kitchen ▶ p. 164

IRANIAN
TAKEOUT

Cynthia E. Smith

HarassMap ▶ p. 174

COOPER
HEWITT

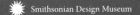 Smithsonian Design Museum

New York

Designing Peace

Building a Better Future Now

Contents

Musings on Peace

John Paul Lederach

John Paul Lederach is Professor Emeritus of International Peacebuilding at the University of Notre Dame and currently serves as a Senior Fellow with the foundation Humanity United. A practitioner-scholar he has engaged with and written widely about conflict transformation and peacebuilding in many of the settings explored in this volume. He currently serves on the Advisory Council to the Colombian Truth Commission.

I

We sat in roofless church in the East Coast region of Nicaragua.

The burnt vigas offering open skies above us were not by original design.

They fell in fragile placement when mortars destroyed mortar.

A standing bell tower and a foot-pushed pump organ brought us to attention.

Pieces around a war puzzle assembled.

People watched, mum and curious.

In this place of deep division and irreplaceable loss, some noise and rumors of peace had brought them in from the surrounding bush.

The call to order started with words of an aged poet.

> *Truth and Mercy have met together.*
> *Justice and Peace have kissed.*

II

Some months later in that year of 1987, I asked a few community leaders to enact a conversation if these words became people.

What if Sister Truth walked around your village, what might she say if she encountered, say, Brother Justice or Sister Mercy? What would each be worried about? What would each say they needed from the other? What would each ask of you?

At the conclusion of the impromptu drama, when Truth, Mercy, Justice, and Peace had all spoken and now stood face-to-face in a tight circle, I wondered aloud what we might call their gathering.

A voice rang out.

This place where they meet is called reconciliation.

III

The works curated throughout this volume trace out to care and healing. They invite us into surprise, a chance to turn and look again.

The pursuit of peace always leads us into the swirling confusion and harm of conflict knowing that healing cannot open toward understanding without imagination and curiosity.

If you cannot imagine that the well-being of your grandchildren is tied to the well-being of your enemy's grandchildren, Sister Peace will never speak.

Such imagination will take a carefully curated passageway.

That odd twist of phrase back in Nicaragua's East Coast still rings paradoxically true.

Reconciliation shapes a container, a place of encounter.

Encounter requires paths converging and circling.

Paths cut through fog only with a sense of horizon.

Horizons are always within sight but just beyond touch, requiring yet more encounters along the way.

Along-the-way.

Peace sits and circles around over and again.

IV
Peace works at the edge.

Peace shapes the liminal space between humans being human in search of their humanity.

Because peace lives at the edge, we experience an impermanence of place.

Displaced. Internally displaced persons, IDPs, became an acronym for the unintended spoiling broil of war.

People in search of place.

The search for belonging remains the rarest and mostly unnamed resource sought by the human species.

In the face of division and conflict, we are all *internally* displaced persons.

V
We pontificate, pronounce, and propose about peace. We are good with words in that way.

But peace works defy words because they speak into the unspeakable.

Peace works require us to stop, to notice unexpected passageways.

The question peace poses: How do we stay open to what is not fully known?

It takes a passageway—this portico—to imagine something rooted in the world of hurt and harm around us that gives birth to that which does not yet exist.

Peace works: To curate serendipitous design that opens pathways into our rehumanization; the craft acknowledgment and repair across division and harm; to carve the containers of belonging.

VI
Advice for all those who enter here.

Turn these pages slowly.

Walk these passageways with care.

Stop and take note.

People's lives will evoke.

Places will invite.

Prepare to be touched by beauty and surprise.

In this place, in this gallery of possibility, images and words offer a portal to where people imagined the encounter and shaped anew the living of their shared humanity.

They are truly the poets of place and belonging.

VII
Peace works (n).

Peace works (v).

Writing on the facade of the library at the Ritsona refugee and asylum-seeker camp, north of Athens, 2017.

Foreword

Ruki Neuhold-Ravikumar

Design signifies intent. As a twenty-first-century museum, Cooper Hewitt, Smithsonian Design Museum interprets design not only in terms of its form and function, but also in relation to its impact on the communities in which it is implemented. The tension between positive intentions and unintended consequences become apparent when our teams unpack complex topics. Our publications present audiences with ways to see themselves, and they ignite, we hope, moments of joy, reflection, and action. With *Designing Peace: Building a Better Future Now*, we aim to serve as a provocateur, resource, and partner, encouraging dialogue and inspiring those who seek to build a more just and peaceful world.

This book and its companion exhibition explore the many aspects of peace, its temporal nature, and the multiple ways in which it is experienced. They pose questions about design's role in bringing the world closer to peace in its various definitions and forms. How might design facilitate trust while also acknowledging harm? How might design, with its visionary potential, provide tools to arrest violence but also to frame an architecture of peace? Cynthia E. Smith, the museum's curator of socially responsible design, has considered the challenges to peace globally, learning from the refugees forced to leave their homes worldwide, from local organizations fighting injustice and exclusion, and from communities experiencing domestic and societal violence, among many others. She met with and listened to design practitioners and artists active in the field of humanitarian design and conducted interviews with individuals instrumental in peacebuilding and design, and encountered a wide range of ideas and approaches concerning what "full humanity" and "disobedient peace" might look like.

Ruki Neuhold-Ravikumar is the acting director of Cooper Hewitt, Smithsonian Design Museum.

We are deeply grateful to Cynthia for taking conversations about design at Cooper Hewitt to a place they have not gone before.

Design is collaborative, and many people contributed to the success of this project. We are grateful to James Goggin and Shan James of Practise for giving a physical form to the systems and ideas that make up this book, for designing with us, and for providing our readers with a resource that captures what hope may look like in a multiplicity of lives. We thank Eric Höweler, Jonathan Fournier, and Karl Heckman of Höweler + Yoon Architecture, in collaboration with Yoonjai Choi and Ken Meier of Common Name, for their exemplary exhibition and graphic design, and the whole team at Cooper Hewitt for exemplifying the generosity, democracy, and spirit of community that animates design and for responding to the call to make the museum a place of activism and change. We gratefully acknowledge the international Advisory Committee of leading scholars, innovators, and implementors in the fields of peacebuilding and design who generously shared key insights as we honed the project's direction. Recognition and gratitude are due as well to our Board of Trustees, for believing in Cooper Hewitt's commitment to expanding the discourse on designing for peace. And a deep thank you to trustees Karen A. Phillips and Keith Yamashita, for your generosity of valuable time and resources. Finally, we thank you, our readers and visitors, for finding ways to enact peace in your own lives.

Designing Peace would not have been possible without the generous support of the Ford Foundation and the vision of its president, Darren Walker. We are grateful to trustees Lisa Roberts and David Seltzer for their major support of this project. Immense thanks are also due to the Lily Auchincloss Foundation and to trustee Helen Hintz and Edward Hintz, and to the museum's Barbara and Morton Mandel Design Gallery Endowment Fund for its generous support. We are deeply appreciative of the gifts provided by Agnes Gund, the Cooper Hewitt Master's Program Fund, the Netherland-America Foundation, and the New York State Council on the Arts with the support of the Office of the Governor and the New York State Legislature.

The central courtyard of the Ritsona refugee and asylum-seeker camp, Greece, 2017.

Designing Peace

Preface

Darren Walker

Today the world is in conflict. There is no doubt that we live in a time of existential risks. Indeed, in this difficult moment, the very act of designing peace may seem futile, even foolish. Global inequities cast millions into poverty and sickness. Outbursts of extremism threaten to boil over. Climate catastrophes exacerbate existing tensions. Rampant militarization and rising investment in arms make violence feel likely, if not inevitable.

All of this, and more, compels many to dream of peace as an absence: as the lull between conflicts, a quelled national security threat, the elimination of a deadly virus. But as this collection illustrates, lasting peace is more than a negative space. Peace is a sturdy construction, intentionally designed to have less inequity and injustice—a place where people actively choose to live thoughtfully and collaboratively, together.

Designing Peace: Building a Better Future Now offers a provocative glimpse into how design can help foster these conditions. It acknowledges the fact that *all* members of the design community—activists, artists, architects, academics, app developers, and so many more—have a crucial role to play in laying the foundation for a verdant world, ripe with peace.

As you peruse this selection of designs, essays, and artworks, you will be introduced to new lexicons that identify and caution against hate speech, and design installations that cement a city's unearthed histories into the public record. You will learn about apps supporting land-restoration efforts in sub-Saharan Africa and graphic novels that facilitate conversations about extremist recruitment in Tunisia. In each of these efforts to reimagine and reshape public space, community resources, and our collective consciousness, we all can find hope in a moment of seeming hopelessness—and, perhaps, find a road map toward solutions that are both practical and visionary, by design.

Right now we need creative thinking—and creative people—more than ever. I am grateful to Cooper Hewitt, Smithsonian Design Museum for continuously elevating the need for creativity in social impact—for surfacing, naming, and framing this opportunity to spark and sustain social progress. I am proud that, over the course of our long-standing partnership, the Ford Foundation has played a small role in sustaining that work. And I am delighted to see this beautiful book come to fruition.

I hope you find in these pages the inspiration to imagine a rich and lasting peace—and the tools with which to go forth and build it.

Darren Walker is President of the Ford Foundation.

Designing the Future Now

Cynthia E. Smith

Recognition of the inherent dignity and of the
equal and inalienable rights of all members
of the human family is the foundation of freedom,
justice, and peace in the world.
— Preamble, Universal Declaration of
Human Rights, 1948

I stood at the entrance to a citizen-run refugee camp
on Lesbos (Lesvos), a small Greek island of roughly one
hundred thousand residents near Turkey. This did not
look like a typical United Nations refugee camp, with
row upon row of uniform white tents.[1] Several orange
life jackets strung along a fence spelled out in large,
black letters the hopeful message "SAFE PASSAGE."
These repurposed vests had been abandoned along
with thousands of others by migrants who had successfully made the treacherous eight-mile (twelve-
kilometer) voyage across the Aegean Sea from Turkey.
Collected by island residents, they testify to the
courage needed to leave one's home—to flee conflict,
persecution, and poverty—and embark on an uncertain
journey in search of safety and a better future.

Beyond welcoming signage, I could see busy
open-air workshops, people heading to medical and
legal clinics, living quarters surrounded by gardens,
gathering spaces with sheltering tree canopies, and
buildings emblazoned with large murals. In 2012, when
refugees began arriving—five thousand a day at the
peak—local residents took over an empty former

children's summer camp called Pipka and established an
open refugee camp in solidarity with the new arrivals.[2]
Over the following eight years, it provided a dignified
reception for the most vulnerable and offered medical
and legal assistance along with language and job
training for refugees and locals alike.[3]

The Pipka solidarity camp exemplifies the efforts
of a growing global movement to counter mounting
discord and uncertainty and envision and build a far
more peaceful future. From neighborhoods to global
networks, people are challenging institutions and
structures forged through inequity, injustice, and
dominance, and they are using the principles, strategies,
and practices of design to do so.[4] They are researching
and modeling another world, one with inclusive, participatory societies that value equity, justice, creativity,
and mutual cooperation, that respect our interdependent living and nonliving ecosystems, that are free from
danger, exclusion, violence, and fear, and that are
accepting of different voices, behaviors, views, and
cultural and gender expressions.

My previous research has resulted in a set of
exhibitions, programs, and publications that explore
how design—at every scale, in all parts of the world—
can address some of our most vexing issues. In an
era of growing uncertainty and chaos and escalating
environmental damage and socioeconomic inequity,
amplified by increasing extremism and nationalism,
I began this current exploration by asking what might
be possible if society were to design for peace.

The work of designing peace is being undertaken
all around the world, and it is extremely diverse, as
exemplified by the work gathered in this compilation.[5]
Organized here by a series of questions about the
potential of design to foster peace, the work ranges
from theoretical explorations to practical solutions,
reflecting the scale and scope of the practice across
geographies and cultures. Separately, design and
peacebuilding are dynamic processes that use engagement, trust building, communication, iteration, and

Cynthia E. Smith is Cooper Hewitt, Smithsonian
Design Museum's Curator of Socially Responsible
Design. She integrates her training as an industrial
designer with her advocacy on human rights and social
justice issues, organizing a humanitarian-focused
design exhibition and publication series, serving on
international design juries, and lecturing widely on
socially responsible design.

an understanding of context to facilitate positive change. Combined, they offer matchless opportunities for the formulation and implementation of transformative responses to dire situations and unjust systems. As a whole, *Designing Peace* explores the ways in which we might collectively pool our creative forces to envision the future we want to live in—and to take action to create it.

Defining Peace

Peace is not a static condition but a dynamic and complex process that can be built, nurtured, and achieved in a multitude of ways, in different contexts, and at various physical scales—from interpersonal, local, and community levels to national, international, global, and even interterrestrial dimensions. Peace can be internally or externally focused. It can be fragile or sustainable. As an ideal, peace can inspire and clarify principles. In 1956 the American civil rights leader Martin Luther King Jr. said, "True peace is not merely the absence of . . . tension, but the presence of justice."[6] Johan Galtung, the founder of peace studies, described negative and positive forms of peace in 1964, in the first issue of the *Journal of Peace Research*. Negative peace, he wrote, is defined by what is not there: the absence of violence and of war. Positive peace is defined by what is there: the presence of social justice, of equality, and of harmonious social relations.[7]

The Institute for Economics and Peace, an Australian think tank, publishes an annual Positive Peace Index that tracks key drivers of peace by country. It further expands the definition of positive peace, describing it as an active condition that comprises "the attitudes, institutions, and structures which create and sustain peaceful societies."[8] Alternately, the research organization Everyday Peace Indicators takes a bottom-up, participatory approach in which communities define and measure peace for themselves.[9]

Activists and scholars point to a gendered dimension of peace. For Helen Kezie-Nwoha, an African feminist peace activist, one key aspect of "feminist peace" is the absence of structural violence—pervasive forms of violence built into social structures and institutions.[10] Feminist peace and conflict theory also points to the interconnectedness of violence of every type, whether domestic, societal, state-based, or interstate.[11] Canadian pacifist and feminist Ursula Franklin articulated a connection between peace, escalating militarization, and human experience, defining peace "not as the absence of war, but as the presence of justice and the absence of fear."[12] Rosario Padilla, a Philippines-based women's peace activist, calls for a "genuine peace," which she defines as a state in which the majority of the world—women—can live their full humanity without oppression and repression.[13]

Not a passive concept, peace can destabilize by subverting the status quo.[14] To counter injustice in his native Mexico, peace researcher Pietro Patella introduced the concept of "disobedient peace." He outlines an engaged peace process that collectively builds knowledge, questions the normalized social order and blind obedience to authority, develops a moral and social identity, and calls attention to injustice through acts of defiance, disobedience, and noncooperation with inhumane social orders.[15]

Life jackets spell out "SAFE PASSAGE," a hopeful message to all who enter the Pipka solidarity refugee camp on the Greek island of Lesbos, 2017.

United Nations Sustainable Development Goal 16: Peace, Justice, and Strong Institutions

Targets

16.1 Significantly reduce all forms of violence and related death rates everywhere

16.2 End abuse, exploitation, trafficking, and all forms of violence against and torture of children

16.3 Promote the rule of law at the national and international levels and ensure equal access to justice for all

16.4 By 2030, significantly reduce illicit financial and arms flows, strengthen the recovery and return of stolen assets, and combat all forms of organized crime

16.5 Substantially reduce corruption and bribery in all their forms

16.6 Develop effective, accountable, and transparent institutions at all levels

16.7 Ensure responsive, inclusive, participatory, and representative decision making at all levels

16.8 Broaden and strengthen the participation of developing countries in the institutions of global governance

16.9 By 2030, provide legal identity for all, including birth registration

16.10 Ensure public access to information and protect fundamental freedoms, in accordance with national legislation and international agreements

16.A Strengthen relevant national institutions, including through international cooperation, for building capacity at all levels, in particular in developing countries, to prevent violence and combat terrorism and crime

16.B Promote and enforce nondiscriminatory laws and policies for sustainable development

Securing Our Collective Future

There are dozens of ongoing conflicts around the world, including internal insurgencies, civil wars, long-standing armed standoffs, and new territorial disputes.[16] Yet most of humanity values peace; it is one of our most sought-after human conditions. Internationally, Goal 16 of the United Nations Sustainable Development Goals (SDGs) calls directly for peace, justice, and strong institutions. More broadly, the SDGs outline a pathway to greater peacefulness worldwide through the elimination of hunger and poverty, improvements in health and education, the building of more resilient cities and infrastructure, the fostering of innovation, action on climate change, and more. Even a small diversion of the estimated $1.9 trillion in annual global military spending could mean a huge reinvestment in the peace initiatives delineated in the SDG blueprint.[17]

At the opposite end of the scale, organizations like Peace Direct support the power of local action. Their research has shown that community-based efforts involving excluded groups, including women, youth, displaced people, refugees, sexual minorities, and ex-combatants, contribute significantly to a more durable peace.[18] Elevating local knowledge—geographic, cultural, Indigenous—and coupling it with open dialogue builds trust and strong relationships, which are paramount in creating a more just and inclusive peace.[19]

A shift in perspectives, priorities, and approaches is urgently required at every level in many disciplines, including design, if we are to secure our collective future. Of the multitude of questions that arise around the potential of designing for peace, here are several to consider.

How Can Design Support Humane Forms of Peace and Security?

Humane forms of peace and security may be achieved only by expanding our aspirations beyond the military definition of security promulgated by nation-states to encompass a condition characterized by respect for human dignity, cultural identity, and the environment, and in which individuals are valued and protected and their basic needs are met. Design efforts that bring people together, creating dialogue across difference, are paramount in this approach. In the Netherlands, the **Startblok Elzenhagen** housing development—an innovative model for co-living—was designed specifically to build community between newly arrived young refugees and local youth. To facilitate conversations among returning child combatants, their families, and their communities in the Democratic Republic of the Congo, a team of researchers and community members used the technique of **body mapping** to visually express the impacts of war and begin a collective healing process. In the United States, a Boston-based design studio created **Social Emergency Response Centers**, pop-up crisis centers that bring communities together for

Peacebuilding vs. Military Spending in the United States

In 2020 the United States directed a massive $718 billion[A] to military spending, more than three times that of any other nation, while allocating only $2.1 billion[B] toward peacebuilding.

mutual aid during social rather than natural disasters. At an urban scale, as refugees settle in cities around the world, design can contribute to reinvigorated and inclusive neighborhoods, as architects Håvard Breivik-Khan and Tone Selmer-Olsen explain in their essay in this volume (see pp. 40–43).

Design approaches that incorporate participatory involvement and local values are critical to creating a more lasting and compassionate form of peace. To authentically reflect the experience of Tunisian youth, a local comic book design collective collaborated with young people on the graphic novel series **The Adventures of Daly**, building awareness about extremist recruitment. **Oceanix City**, a modular floating-settlement concept, is adaptable to hyperlocal conditions, considering the social, political, environmental, and economic aspects of each site. The success of the Colombian government's **Christmas Operations**— guerrilla demobilization campaigns designed by a Bogotá-based creative agency—was due to their use of hyperspecific cultural material and their collaboration with friends and family members of the fighters.

Instigating empathy and embedding values in such works is essential. The digital game **Papers, Please** stimulates compassion in its players for border inspectors and migrants alike; it is one example from a growing creative movement aimed at driving real-world change through immersive media and social-impact games. As architect Michael Murphy describes, monuments and memorials are key sites of empathy and identification; the most powerful memorials, those that honor and connect with individual stories while also evoking the multitude of lives lost, will also be those that contribute the most to peace (pp. 26–33). For-profit companies can also participate in peace-forward design, researchers Jason Miklian and Kristian Hoelscher assert. By incorporating peace and development expertise into early design phases, technology companies may not only avoid unintended negative consequences but also create ethical, peace-positive products (pp. 68–71). And as urbanist Toni L. Griffin explains, the design of cities may contribute significantly to the cultivation of peace: she outlines a dozen values that help communities in redesigning their cities for "greater access, agency, ownership, beauty, diversity, and empowerment" (pp. 36–39).

Collaborative research and design teams are documenting and exposing activity in hard-to-reach locales to advance international dialogue on security and peace. Beth Simmons, Michael Kenwick, and Dillon Horwitz analyze satellite imagery collected over decades to reveal the steady thickening of international borders (pp. 58–65). The public-facing online tool **Island Tracker** reveals artificial island building and construction on disputed reefs and islets in the South China Sea. The **Teeter-Totter Wall** brought worldwide attention to

Body mapping enables former child soldiers and their families and communities to visually communicate the depth of their experiences, beginning a process of collective healing, Democratic Republic of the Congo, 2011.

the US-Mexico border wall, temporarily transforming a small section of the barrier from a place of separation and intolerance to one of dignity and hope for families on both sides.

How Can Design Address the Root Causes of Conflict?

Design can play a significant and active role in addressing underlying sources of division well before conflict arises. This urgent work requires the engagement of science, technology, and culture to create opportunities for less traditional forms of mediation, such as cultural diplomacy, which builds relations between divergent groups through sports, language, ideas, and the arts.[20] **CONIFA**— a global soccer federation of around sixty teams representing stateless people, minority groups, and states unaffiliated with FIFA (the sport's major international governing body)—builds bridges worldwide, with its players acting as informal ambassadors during its convenings. To provide an international forum for stateless, blacklisted, and autonomist groups, Dutch artist Jonas Staal develops alternative parliaments around the world (pp. 74–81), melding art and politics in projects such as the **New World Summit – Rojava** in Syria. Michael Adlerstein argues that the UN Security Council Chamber, the room in which many of the world's conflicts are discussed, has become obsolete. Designed before the emergence of our current borderless, Earth-threatening issues, he writes, it should be replaced with a new Climate Change Chamber (pp. 86–91). Similarly, science diplomacy, "an international, interdisciplinary, and inclusive (holistic) process, involving informed decisionmaking to balance national interests and common interests for the benefit of all," provides opportunities to work together on pressing global concerns.[21] One site of concern is the Arctic Ocean, as melting polar ice exposes new sea

Rojava's "People's Parliament" under construction, Dêrik, Canton Cizîrê, Rojava, 2015. Part of the project New World Summit—Rojava, the structure is both a symbol of the stateless democracy's ideal of collective self-representation and a forum for its day-to-day practice.

routes and vast oil and gas reserves. The scientific and technology-based working groups of the Arctic Council provide research and partner with the region's Indigenous people to inform environmental protections and sustainable development for this area of overlapping interests.[22] In sub-Saharan Africa, the **Regreening Africa** smartphone app enables local farmers to easily record and share their land-restoration efforts as citizen scientists in collaborative efforts to counter land degradation.

Aiming to transform mainstream narratives, collaborative teams of designers, artists, architects, and peace researchers are taking an active role in illuminating the invisible systems that counter peace efforts, from social media to supply chains. Anticipating conflict over resource mining on the Moon, a France-based design studio created **Astropolitics**, a map that visualizes and critiques the intertwined technological-industrial-economic systems of the Earth and its satellite. Another group documented and designed **Rare Earthenware**, ceramic vessels composed of toxic mud gathered from a remote mine tailings lake in China, embodying the hidden costs of high-technology products, including green technology. **Hate Speech Lexicons**, a series of handbooks developed to combat inflammatory language in the media, identify offensive terms in countries around the world and offer alternative words and phrases.

Working across disciplines, architects are examining the politics of the built environment and proposing design interventions that disrupt convention. Responding to the recent "bathroom wars" in the

United States, the design and research initiative **Stalled!** seeks to transform gender-segregated restrooms into inclusive public spaces. Noting that India's war histories are as much about peace as about aggression, Mumbai-based architects responded to a competition brief for a national war museum with a design for a **Peace Pavilion**. And in Denmark, rather than a monument to war and its heroes, the proposed **House of Peace** is an interactive landmark floating in the city harbor, welcoming visitors from around the world.

Frameworks for the attainment and maintenance of free, just, and peaceful societies are foundational in confronting inequity and building resilience. In California,

instructors at a renowned design school used one such framing document to initiate a dialogue on human rights, asking students to visualize the ideals it expresses in **Universal Declaration of Human Rights Posters**. Another system, the **Positive Peace Index**, identifies the socioeconomic factors essential for durable peace. It has been put into practical use by local groups and international organizations.

How Can Design Engage Creative Confrontation?

Not all conflict is damaging. When it engages with unjust systems, conflict can be transformative, creating space for debate among various voices and viewpoints and catalyzing positive change. Provocative creative actions by designers, artists, and activists have brought new attention to entrenched issues. Nadine Bloch and Andrew Boyd assembled the Beautiful Trouble Toolbox, a set of core tactics, principles, and theoretical concepts by more than seventy artists and activists that can be used in imaginative ways to propel creative activism (pp. 116–119). In New York, the **Black Lives Matter Harlem Street Mural** makes a strong visual statement of protest against police killings of Black Americans and in affirmation of the value of Black lives, as do similar murals in communities across the country and around the world. As an alternative to confrontational street protest, London's **Art the Arms Fair** presents art events that expose the international arms trade and expand the discourse on its role in contemporary society. With a view to harsh realities on the ground, one art collective incorporates discarded bullet casings into woven rugs called **Maps (Bullet Rug Series)**, which offer evidence of international arms-trafficking routes, secret military interventions, and lethal weaponry design. And, as

Caroline O'Connell explains, in Northern Ireland during the period known as the Troubles, collaborative textile making was harnessed to express a united stance for peace by women from the communities on both sides of the conflict (pp. 126–129).

Visual symbols can activate global movements by communicating across divides. Lee Davis writes about an effort to create a set of universal graphic symbols in the late 1960s, with the goal of reducing confusion and conflict brought on by increasing globalization (pp. 132–135). More recently, a Uruguayan graphic designer created a new **World Peace Symbol**, devoid of the problematic meanings associated with previous signs. Another visual design, the **Extinction Symbol**, is simple, replicable, and easily deployed in a multitude of contexts. Incorporating the image of an hourglass, it signifies the urgent need for action in the face of accelerating plant and animal species extinctions.

How Can Design Embrace Truth and Dignity in a Search for Peace and Justice?

Design can play a vital function in elevating the universal and aspirational values of truth and dignity, which are fundamental in attaining peace and justice. Realizing justice can mean engaging all of society in a dialogue about the past and reckoning with legacies of abuse, elevating those voices left out—from the historically marginalized to transnational communities of risk— while ensuring that everyone's essential needs are met.[23] The redressing of past wrongs can take different forms, including memorialization, institutional reform, prosecution, commemoration, reparation, and truth and reconciliation commissions.[24] While more than forty truth commissions have been formed around the world since Argentina's National Commission on the

Letters from the Black Lives Matter Harlem Street Mural, designed and painted by artists Thomas Heath (MA), Dianne Smith (TT), and Joyous Pierce (ER), a bold declaration along a busy New York boulevard, 2020.

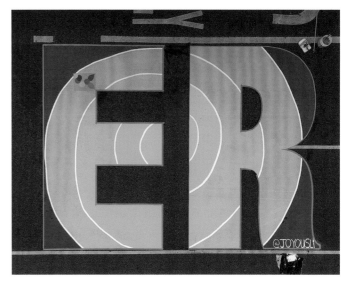

urges practitioners to "develop a 'prophetic aesthetic' to counter the colonial malaise so that we can remember and develop new futures from the power of the past."[25] **My Ancestors' Garden**, his landscape design for the International African American Museum in Charleston, South Carolina, brings to light historical realities that have been long obscured. A research team based primarily in London uses advanced architectural and spatial analysis to counter social, political, and environmental injustices. Its investigative project **The Murder of Halit Yozgat** exposed long-denied racism in Germany's security services.

The creation of forums for silenced voices is critical in the pursuit of truth and dignity. Activist Binalakshmi Nepram advocates for elevating the voices of women living in forgotten conflict zones and of the millions of Indigenous people living in ecological hotspots, emphasizing the importance of bringing them to the fore in peace efforts and especially at the negotiating table (pp. 150–155). The quarterly broadsheet **The Chronic**, produced to counter harmful external perspectives and generate new knowledge by Africans for Africans, is an accessible venue for writing, mapping, illustrating, and exploring the complexities, innovations, and dreams of people across the continent. In New Orleans, as Jim Crow–era Confederate monuments came down, a collective of designers, artists, urbanists, and educators invited city residents to imagine new public markers.

Disappearance of Persons was created in 1983, some argue for a complete reimagining of the prevailing international systems and institutions. South Africa–based political scientist Everisto Benyera makes a case for an international reparation model that will finally bring colonialism to an end, transforming nation-states into citizen-states characterized by the drive for life, not power; peace, not war; inclusivity, not difference; and survival for all, not just the fittest (pp. 142–143).

Design can give tangible form to concealed histories and prejudices and demand a reckoning with truth and justice. Landscape architect Walter Hood

At Conflict Kitchen, food is taste tested with members of the local Palestinian community, Pittsburgh, 2014.
Serving the cuisines of nations the United States was in conflict with helped people discover their shared humanity.

Their project **Paper Monuments** facilitated, collected, and shared residents' designs, disseminating under-told stories of the city.

Design can also facilitate creative platforms for knowledge exchange. Aiming to stimulate discussions beyond divisive political rhetoric and media headlines, **Conflict Kitchen**, a temporary takeout restaurant in Pittsburgh, served food and information from nations the United States was in conflict with. The Argentinean design team Iconoclasistas uses maps—appropriating a principal tool used by those in power to seize territory and plunder resources—to visualize their critical interrogations, which they provide as free downloads to further creative activism (pp. 156–159). And in Turkey, local women established a collective kitchen in solidarity with newly arriving Syrian migrant women. Merve Bedir, an architect and member of the group, illustrates and enumerates the shared values of the kitchen, which include collective belonging, justice, learning together, and unconditional hospitality (pp. 166–169).

A worker sews at the Safe Passage Bags Workshop at the Mosaik Support Center in Mytilene, Greece, 2017. The center, run by Lesvos Solidarity, brings refugees together with local residents, providing a range of services as well as a way to make a living.

How Can Design Facilitate the Transition From Instability to Peace?

The establishment of a sustainable peace, one that is transformative, long-term, and beneficial to all segments of society, requires an acknowledgment that "development, peace and security, and human rights are interlinked and mutually reinforcing," as the UN General Assembly has affirmed.[26] Nobel Peace Prize laureate Ellen Johnson Sirleaf stresses that durable peace also requires the involvement of women, those on the margins, and youth at every stage of negotiation, creation, and maintenance.[27] Interdisciplinary design can play a significant role in bringing together disparate stakeholders and disciplines, engaging all sectors in this multifaceted approach to sustainable peace.

Architects, urban designers, and landscape architects propose alternative futures for postwar cities and conflicted landscapes, aiming to transform conflict into renewal. Peacekeeping—a contradictory concept, in that it generally involves the deployment of military forces—can create new insecurities within the populations it is meant to safeguard. It is turned on its head in **BLUE: The Architecture of UN Peace Missions**, a bold proposal that calls for typically closed and temporary peacekeeping bases to open up to the local civilian population, providing services and remaining in use after the peacekeepers depart. Using 3D scanning, digital modeling, and recycled rubble, **Recoding Post-War Syria** is a new methodology for regenerating damaged post-conflict cities into advanced urban environments, starting with Damascus. A mixed-use tower in Beirut, **Stone Garden**, signals belonging for its refugee construction workers (whose handwork is visible in the building's striated facade) and healing and renewal for its architect, who experienced the city in the aftermath of war. At a transnational level, in the **Korea Remade** studio, landscape design students envisioned a unified Korean peninsula, erasing borders, removing land mines, facilitating human resettlement, and instituting a complex reorganization of the landscape. A Middle East environmental peacebuilding organization teamed with two design schools to encourage cross-border cooperation in protecting a shared resource, proposing designs for a **Jordan River Peace Park** spanning the Israel-Jordan border.

As a record number of people around the world are displaced from their homes, numerous migration-focused initiatives are incorporating innovative design and technology into their humanitarian responses.[28] Most people fleeing conflict and disaster take few possessions other than a mobile phone. The **RefAid** mobile app allows migrants to use their phones to identify nearby services and geolocate them on a map, transforming the delivery of aid. In response to the millions fleeing Venezuela, **Casa Azul** resource centers, located along popular migration routes, were designed to be clearly identifiable as welcoming and safe spaces offering humanitarian services, including culture and beauty as essential healing tools. To expand critical access to information and educational resources in remote locations, such as refugee or displaced people's camps, an international nonprofit engaged a prominent industrial designer to create **Ideas Box**, a durable, portable library and pop-up multimedia center that is easily shipped and deployed. Residents of Lesbos founded the **Safe Passage Bags Workshop** at the Pipka solidarity refugee camp on the small Greek island. In addition to providing training and employment for migrants and locals, the workshop sends an important message to the world about the right to safe passage.

Gender equity is the top predictor of the peacefulness of a society, urban planner Chelina Odbert writes, but with women underrepresented in the design and planning professions (and their use patterns erroneously assumed to be the same as men's), they are often left with an inefficient and dangerous set of options when it comes to urban public space (pp. 176–181). Responding to this reality in Cairo, four young women designed **HarassMap**, a location-based reporting system for the sexual harassment and assault of women that provides researchers around the world with a pool of anonymized, crowd-sourced raw data, a tool for instigating social and policy change. In the project **Designing for Dignity**, an industrial design and systems design student team reimagined Oslo's sexual violence prevention and response structures, centering the needs of survivors by mapping and improving the service touchpoints they encounter on their journey through the medical and justice systems.

For the hanged and beaten.
For the shot, drowned, and burned.
For the tortured, tormented,
and terrorized.
For those abandoned by the rule of law.
We will remember.
With hope because hopelessness is the enemy of justice.
With courage because peace requires bravery.
With persistence because justice is a constant struggle.
With faith because we shall overcome.

— National Memorial for Peace and Justice, Montgomery, Alabama

Imagining the Future Now

We stood together silently. Above, in rows stretching out ahead and behind us, hung hundreds of memorials to the more than four thousand African Americans lynched in the United States. Each six-foot-tall Corten steel pillar, approximately the size of a person, was etched with a county name and the dates of the acts of racial terrorism that had occurred there, along with the names of the victims. As we moved outside and down the hill, duplicate monuments, laid out horizontally on the ground like caskets, sat ready, waiting for the counties to claim them and bring them home to confront what had happened in their communities.

We had come to the National Memorial for Peace and Justice from the nearby Legacy Museum, where the direct connection between American slavery, the

tyranny of lynching and Jim Crow segregation, and the current mass incarceration of Black people is clarified and brought to life. It is fitting that the museum and the memorial are located in Montgomery, Alabama, the city that launched both the civil rights movement and the Confederacy. It signals that even in this conflicted locale we can move forward together toward truth, justice, and reconciliation if we honestly confront the legacy of slavery and racial injustice. The two physical spaces, part of a broader initiative that aims to end mass incarceration, challenge racial and economic injustice, and protect basic human rights for the most vulnerable, exemplify a growing movement to envision, design, and build the future we want to live in now.

This concept of prefigurative intervention has roots in the civil rights movement, in which peaceful activists presented an alternative to the injustice they experienced daily, modeling their aims in advance of achieving them.[29] If humans are to survive as a global community, peace activist John Paul Lederach writes, we must find ways to foster moral imagination: the capacity to recognize turning points and possibilities, to venture down unknown paths and create what does not yet exist. This means admitting that our current response modes—in which domination provides the only security against being dominated, "us" is pitted against "them," and violence is the default defense—are failing us. It is necessary to cultivate an interdependent web of relationships and honor its complexity, trust that creative and meaningful change is possible, and seek constructive engagement with the people and things we fear most and least understand.[30]

In response to increasingly urgent social, environmental, and economic inequities, divisions, and crises, a myriad of inspired creative partnerships are surfacing around the world. Designers, architects, and artists are collaborating with disenfranchised youth and stateless people, international aid agencies and community groups, athletes and scientists, and think tanks and foundations, both in their local communities and across international borders. *Designing Peace* asks us to join with these creative efforts to confront injustice and to imagine new narratives. To build inclusive, participatory societies that value equity and justice, truth and dignity, creativity and mutual cooperation, beauty and difference, and agency and empowerment, and that nurture respect for each other and for our entire ecosystem. To envision a world that is accepting of multiple voices, behaviors, views, and expressions. To begin designing peace, now.

→ The National Memorial for Peace and Justice in Montgomery, Alabama, comprises more than eight hundred Corten steel monuments, one for each US county in which a racial terror lynching took place.

1   Currently, more than 26 million refugees (migrants who have been granted international protections because they can't return to their home country due to threats of persecution) and 48 million internally displaced people (uprooted within their home countries) are living in semipermanent camps with limited access to work and education. Many of these camps, built quickly to serve an urgent need, host hundreds of thousands of people. Among the world's largest refugee camps are the Kutupalong-Balukhali expansion site in Bangladesh; the Bidi Bidi refugee camp in Uganda; the Dadaab and Kakuma refugee camps in Kenya; the Azraq and Za'atari refugee camps in Jordan; the Nyarugusu, Nduta, and Mtendeli refugee camps in Tanzania;and the Kebribeyah, Aw-barre, and Sheder refugee camps in Ethiopia. "Refugee Camps," USA for UNHCR, https://www.unrefugees.org/refugee-facts/camps/.

2   The organizing group Lesvos Solidarity describes its model of solidarity as promoting "equality, trust, justice, respect for each other and for the environment, creativity, empowerment, and active participation." "Vision," Lesvos Solidarity, https://lesvossolidarity.org/en/who-we-are/mission-and-vision.

3   The camp was closed by the Greek government in October 2020. "Greece: Well-Run PIKPA Camp Evicted While Situation on Islands and Mainland Continue to Deteriorate," *ECRE Weekly Bulletin*, November 6, 2020, https://ecre.org/greece-well-run-pikpa-camp-evicted-while-situation-on-islands-and-mainland-continue-to-deteriorate/.

4   Caroline Hill, Michelle Molitor, and Christine Ortiz of the Equity Design Collaborative assert that "racism and inequity are products of design. They can be redesigned." In their article of that name, they write of "our moral imperative to live in the future we desire to create," one of three foundational beliefs required to make such a transformation.

The other two are "innovation's need for inclusion and intentional design" and "the indistinguishable relationship between the past and the present." Hill, Molitor, and Ortiz, "Racism and Inequity Are Products of Design. They Can Be Redesigned," November 15, 2016, https://medium.com/equity-design/racism-and-inequity-are-products-of-design-they-can-be-redesigned-12188363cc6a.

5   This publication is part of a larger project that includes the exhibition *Designing Peace* at Cooper Hewitt, Smithsonian Design Museum, New York, June 10, 2022, through September 4, 2023.

6   Martin Luther King Jr., "'When Peace Becomes Obnoxious,' Sermon Delivered on 18 March 1956 at Dexter Avenue Baptist Church," in *The Papers of Martin Luther King, Jr.* 3, *Birth of a New Age, December 1955–December 1956,* ed. Clayborne Carson et al. (Berkeley, Calif.: University of California Press, 1992), 208.

7   Johan Galtung, "An Editorial," *Journal of Peace Research* 1, no. 1 (1964): 1–4.

8   "What Is Positive Peace?," Institute for Economics and Peace, https://www.economicsandpeace.org/about/faqs/.

9   "The Everyday Peace Indicator research approach is a new means of understanding and tracking changes in difficult-to-measure concepts like peace, reconciliation, governance, and violent extremism. Instead of outside experts and scholars developing indicators of success, communities themselves are asked to establish their own everyday indicators. . . . This approach is driven by the premise that communities affected by war know best what peace means to them and therefore should be the primary source of information on peacebuilding effectiveness." "What Is the Everyday Peace Indicators Approach?," Everyday Peace Indicators, https://www.everydaypeaceindicators.org/how-does-epi-work.

10   Helen Kezie-Nwoha, "What Feminist Peace Means in Changing Contexts of Conflicts," *African Feminism*, June 28, 2019, https://africanfeminism.com/what-feminist-peace-means-in-changing-contexts-of-conflicts/. For a further definition of structural violence, see Galtung, "Violence, Peace, and Peace Research," *Journal of Peace Research* 6, no. 3 (1969): 167–91.

11   Annette Weber summarizes feminist peace and conflict theory in an unpublished 2006 essay. Weber, "Feminist Peace and Conflict Theory," https://www.uibk.ac.at/peacestudies/downloads/peacelibrary/feministpeace.pdf.

12   Ursula Franklin, interview by Anna Maria Tremonti, *The Current*, CBC Radio, May 6, 2010, in *Ursula Franklin Speaks: Thoughts and Afterthoughts*, ed. Sarah Jane Freeman (Montreal: McGill-Queen's University Press, 2014), n.p.

13   Rosario Padilla, "Feminist Perspective on Peace and Security in the 21st Century," Transnational Institute (TNI), July 18, 2005, https://www.tni.org/en/article/feminist-perspective-on-peace-and-security-in-the-21st-century.

14   Catia Cecilia Confortini makes this observation in "What Is Feminist Peace?," Chapter 1 of *Intelligent Compassion: The Women's International League for Peace and Freedom and Feminist Peace* (New York: Oxford University Press, 2012), 7, pointing to the scholarship of J. Ann Tickner: "Feminist Perspectives on Peace and World Security," in *Peace and World Security Studies: A Curriculum Guide*, 6th ed., ed. Michael T. Klare (Boulder, CO: Lynne Rienner, 1993), 43–54; and "Introducing Feminist Perspectives into Peace and World Security Courses," *Women's Studies Quarterly* 23, no. 3 (Fall 1995), 48–57.

15   Pietro Ameglio Patella, "Paz desobediente: No-cooperación hacia las órdenes inhumanas," *Polisemia* 14, no. 26 (2019): 1–26. For an analysis of Patella's work in English, see "Disobedient Peace as a Form of Non-Cooperation with an Inhumane Social

Order," *Peace Science Digest*, May 19, 2020, https://peacesciencedigest.org/disobedient-peace-as-a-form-of-non-cooperation-with-an-inhumane-social-order/.

16 According to the Uppsala Conflict Data Program, a key provider of data on armed conflicts, in 2020 there were over 160 conflicts worldwide: fifty-six examples of state-based armed conflict, over seventy deemed non-state violence, and more than forty categorized as one-sided violence against civilians. See UCDP conflict tracker, https://ucdp.uu.se/encyclopedia.

17 Nan Tian, Diego Lopes da Silva, and Alexandra Kuimova, "Military Spending and the Achievement of the 2030 Agenda for Sustainable Development," *United Nations Office for Disarmament Affairs Occasional Papers*, no. 35 (April 2020): 21–29.

18 *Local Peacebuilding: What Works and Why*, Peace Direct and the Alliance for Peacebuilding, summary report, June 2019, https://www.peacedirect.org/us/wp-content/uploads/sites/2/2019/07/P890-PD-Peacebuilding-effectiveness-report_V6.pdf.

19 For more on the value of local peacebuilding knowledge, see "Local, National, and International Peacebuilding," special issue, *Peace Science Digest*, October 2020.

20 For more information about this form of mediation, see "What Is Cultural Diplomacy? What Is Soft Power?," Institute for Cultural Diplomacy, https://www.culturaldiplomacy.org/index php?en_abouticd.

21 Paul Arthur Berkman, "Science Diplomacy and Its Engine of Informed Decisionmaking: Operating through Our Global Pandemic with Humanity," *Hague Journal of Diplomacy* 15, 2020: 435.

22 Trevor Haynes, "Science Diplomacy: Collaboration in a Rapidly Changing World," *Science Policy* (blog), Harvard University Graduate School of Arts and Sciences, October 12, 2018, https://sitn.hms.harvard.edu/flash/2018/science-diplomacy-collaboration-rapidly-changing-world/.

23 For more on the role of memory and truth in building sustainable peace, see Fernando Travesí, "Repairing the Past: What the United States Can Learn from the Global Transitional Justice Movement," International Center for Transitional Justice, July 15, 2021, https://www.ictj.org/news/repairing-past-what-united-states-can-learn-global-transitional-justice-movement.

24 For a discussion of the potential of these forms of justice in the United States, see Christina Lu, "Does America Need a Truth and Reconciliation Commission?," *Foreign Policy*, April 29, 2021, https://foreignpolicy.com/2021/04/29/united-states-transitional-justice-truth-reconciliation-commission/.

25 Walter Hood, introduction to Hood and Grace Mitchell Tada, eds., *Black Landscapes Matter* (Charlottesville, VA: University of Virginia Press, 2020), 8.

26 UN General Assembly, Resolution 70/262, Review of the United Nations Peacebuilding Architecture, A/RES/70/262 (May 12, 2016), https://www.un.org/en/development/desa/population/migration/generalassembly/docs/globalcompact/A_RES_70_262.pdf.

27 "Like women, youth must be included in peacebuilding and post-conflict efforts. Not only do they deserve to have a say in peace, as they are affected by conflict, but youth often offer bold new solutions and innovations. They are a resource and can provide valuable support and fresh ideas to traditional peacekeeping efforts. Experience has taught me that those on the margins must be included for lasting peace to be achieved." Ellen Johnson Sirleaf, Morning *Plenary Speaker Address*, October 2, 2019, PeaceCon 2019, Washington, DC.

28 When tallied in mid-2021, 84 million people worldwide had been displaced from their homes by persecution, conflict, violence, human rights violations, or events seriously disturbing public order—the greatest number on record. Sixty-eight percent of them came from just five countries: Syria, Venezuela, Afghanistan, South Sudan, and Myanmar. It is reported that 48 million were internally displaced, 26.6 million were refugees (the most ever reported), 4.4 million were asylum seekers, and 3.9 million were Venezuelans displaced abroad. In addition, 4.3 million stateless people were reported (although the true figure is estimated to be much higher). Refugee Data Finder, United Nations High Commissioner for Refugees, https://www.unhcr.org/refugee-statistics/.

29 "Prefigurative Politics," Beautiful Trouble, https://www.beautifultrouble.org/toolbox/#/tool/prefigurative-politics. See also Andrew Boyd and Dave Oswald Mitchell, eds., *Beautiful Trouble: A Toolbox for Revolution* (New York: Or Books, 2016).

30 John Paul Lederach, *The Moral Imagination: The Art and Soul of Building Peace* (Oxford, UK: Oxford University Press, 2005), 172–73.

A Defense Budget Overview, United States Department of Defense Fiscal Year 2020 Budget Request, Appendix A, Table A-2 DoD Total, https://comptroller.defense.gov/Portals/45/Documents/defbudget/fy2020/fy2020_Budget_Request_Overview_Book.pdf

B Peacebuilding spending included funding for the Complex Crises Fund, the Human Rights and Democracy Fund (State Department), the Democracy Fund (USAID), Reconciliation Programs (Conflict Management and Mitigation, USAID), Transition Initiatives, the US Institute of Peace, the Atrocities Prevention Fund, the Prevention and Stabilization Fund, and contributions to international organizations. Ursala Knudsen-Latta, "Congress Supports Peacebuilding in FY2020 Spending Package," Friends Committee on National Legislation, December 17, 2019, https://www.fcnl.org/updates/2019-12/congress-supports-peacebuilding-fy2020-spending-package.

How can design support humane forms of peace and security?

Startblok Elzenhagen ▶ p. 44

Teeter-Totter Wall ▶ p. 64

An Architecture of Peace

Michael Murphy

In the aftermath of the 2016 Pulse nightclub massacre in Orlando, Florida, the American poet laureate Richard Blanco drafted a poem to the slain. Titled "One Pulse— One Poem," his text framed the tributes left to the victims as living offerings, intimate details that locate a human life in all its uniqueness amid the infinitely vast, seemingly unsolvable societal crisis of gun violence in America. He wrote:

> Set the page ablaze
> with the anger in the hollow ache of our bones—
> anger for the new hate, same as the old kind of hate
> for the wrong skin color, for the accent in a voice,
> for the love of those we're not supposed to love.
> Anger for the voice of politics armed with lies, fear
> that holds democracy at gunpoint. But let's not
> end here. Turn the poem, find details for the love
> of the lives lost, still alive in photos—spread them
> on the table, give us their wish-filled eyes glowing
> over birthday candles, their unfinished sand castles,
> their training wheels, Mickey Mouse ears, tiaras.
> Show their blemished yearbook faces, silver-teeth
> smiles and stiff prom poses, their tasseled caps
> and gowns, their first true loves. And then share
> their very last selfies. Let's place each memory
> like a star, the light of their past reaching us now,
> and always, reminding us to keep writing until
> we never need to write a poem like this again.

Blanco's list: the Mickey Mouse ears, tiaras, and photographs are the artifacts of lives. He asks us to see these objects as active, talismanic agents in our own transformational understanding of atrocity. When these charged objects, embodied with a human legacy, are placed in the right context and given space, they transcend time and culture and register a deeper impulse: the demand for us to contribute.[1]

A lone gunman killed forty-nine people and injured fifty-three others at Pulse in an attack that garnered international condemnation. Pulse was an established gay nightclub whose clientele largely identified with LGBTQ+ communities, and the conventional "thoughts and prayers" response to yet another American mass shooting shifted into a global call for solidarity with queer communities. The nightclub grounds, on Orange Avenue south of downtown Orlando, immediately became a memorial site where thousands of tribute objects were left. The owners of the nightclub began to collect and catalog these objects only days after the shooting, acknowledging their historic significance and the importance of documenting the moment with care. The nightclub owners and organizers from the community are developing a new permanent memorial to mark the site of the atrocity and a museum to preserve and display the tributes left at the site.

This memorial and museum are a necessary repository of things, of the very real and weathered tributes left on the front lawn at Pulse and the digital proclamations from the global community acknowledging the trauma and expressing solidarity. They are also part of a larger memorial movement happening around the world. Designers, artists, and architects are being called on as spatial experts to create locations of memory that will also serve greater social aspirations and transform society holistically toward peaceful outcomes.

But how does our experience at such sites of memory change us? How is the design of the memorial an

Michael Murphy is the founding principal and executive director of MASS Design Group.

How can design support humane forms of peace and security?

agent in a transformational journey? How do we, in Blanco's words, "place each memory like a star, the light of their past reaching us now, and always, reminding us to keep writing until we never need to write a poem like this again"? How do memorials counter violence and create peace?

The Violence Triangle

The Norwegian sociologist and peace studies scholar Johan Galtung argues that in order to advocate for peace, we must first understand violence at different scales. Galtung's triangle model articulates three types of violence: direct, structural, and cultural. Direct violence is physical or emotional injury inflicted by one person on another. It is personal, and its time scale is momentary. Galtung calls it an "event."[2] Structural violence, on the other hand, is a process, created by systems that inflict damage over time. It can last for generations and manifests itself in phenomena such as malnutrition, inadequate access to health care or housing, and inequalities in policing and sentencing. Cultural violence is perpetrated by one culture against another based on ideological justifications—religious, linguistic, artistic, or scientific—that can be used to legitimize injury in the name of belief.[3]

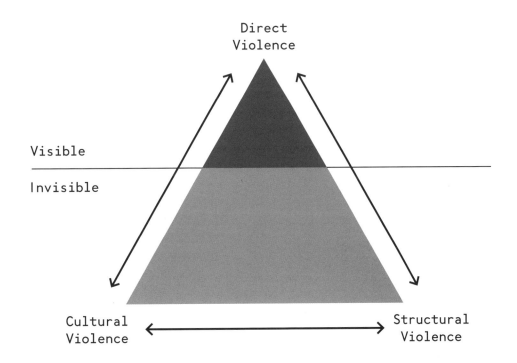

Johan Galtung, Conflict Triangle, 1969

Rendering of the monument Our Destiny, Our Democracy, honoring Congressperson Shirley Chisholm, planned for Prospect Park in Brooklyn, New York. Designed by Amanda Williams and Olalekan Jeyifous, 2019.

Memorial Typologies

All memorials *act* in some way, some subtly and some less so, but their effectiveness in creating peace or opposing violence can be difficult to determine. Galtung's triangle provides a pathway for analysis. Among memorials, typologies align with the three types of violence he identified: memorials that *mark*—address direct violence; those that *provoke*—address structural violence; and those that *evoke*—address cultural violence. The first category is the most common. These are physical markers of historic events or people, and they typically take the form of didactic signage or the renaming of places. Statues and sculptures are three-dimensional markers. Their power, by design, is to emit an air of undebatable historical fact. They create a unique event, and they have been perceived both as causing harm—Confederate monuments, for example (pp. 30–31)—and as promoting reparative healing, like the memorial to the groundbreaking lawmaker Shirley Chisholm planned for Brooklyn's Prospect Park, designed by Olalekan Jeyifous and Amanda Williams.

The second category, memorials that provoke, are those that demand a response—often tactile, participatory engagement. The AIDS Memorial Quilt is a striking example. It demands engagement from the public, namely the contribution of panels in honor of loved ones who have died. In this way the quilt is a participatory memorial. It is also both permanent (it weighs fifty-four tons) and adaptive, as it may be reconfigured to fit various display locations. Many credit the AIDS Memorial Quilt with the passage of beneficial congressional legislation regarding AIDS and with influencing a narrative shift nationally in the discussion of the disease. As an act of advocacy, it has led to lifesaving structural change in American law, policy, and justice.

Memorials in the third category, those that evoke, are often more spatial and experiential. A visitor goes on a journey through the memorial, a passage that enables the gradual absorption of ideas. Evocative memorials stimulate the visitor not just to acknowledge information but also to act on it. To experience the memorial is to take part in a ritualistic truth telling, an experience akin to cultural production and hence linked, in our rubric, with the amelioration of cultural violence. An evocative memorial works toward peace by catalyzing new cultural institutions and providing tools for cultural rituals that are physical and tactile rather than merely conceptual or historical.

How can design support humane forms of peace and security?

Two Approaches to Memorializing the Holocaust

The Memorial to the Murdered Jews of Europe (MMJE), designed by architect Peter Eisenman and completed in 2005, is intended to create a journey of indeterminate direction. A field of tomblike concrete slabs, the memorial is essentially a landscape of unmarked boxes, a labyrinth of multiple experiences, that leaves the visitor self-directed and disoriented. By design, it pulls the user in: the ground descends slowly, suggesting the hidden atrocities the Nazi regime was able to facilitate in plain site. The memorial resists the inclination to shape a didactic narrative journey. It is non-hierarchical: it has no singular entrance or exit, and visitors must choose their own paths and thus their own interpretations.

My own experience at the Berlin memorial was haunting but also perverse. I watched adult visitors navigate solemnly through the labyrinth of forms as they would through a cemetery: silent, cautious, respectful. But I also saw children using the space as a playground, jumping from one slab to another. Was this dual interpretation deliberate or even, possibly, the point of Eisenman's design? I found the ambiguity troubling. I was not sure I had the tools I needed to decode this work. It was clear that the field of slabs evoked a sense of infinite, inconceivable loss. But who were the people? What were their stories? And then I noticed a design choice which specified this ambiguity:

the sea of slabs are unmarked—no names, dates, stories, or intimate characteristics. There is a haunting museum of stories on the site, below ground, but it is not integral to the memorial itself. The MMJE evokes and provokes, but it does not clearly mark. Some see this indeterminacy as powerful, and some fault it for promoting problematic outcomes, such as children dancing on symbols of death.

The MMJE contrasts sharply with another memorial on the streets of Berlin, and in other cities in Germany: the *Stolpersteine*, or "stumbling blocks." Designed by German artist Gunter Demnig, these small brass plaques are inserted among the cobblestones on streets and sidewalks. Each bears the name of a Jewish victim of the Nazis who lived at that location. On my first encounter with these brass plaques, on a drizzly day in Hameln, in Lower Saxony, I literally tripped over one of them while walking on Bäckerstraße. As I slipped, I was forced to look down at the sidewalk, where three cobblestone-sized markers were laid, one each for Moritz Blankenberg, Lotte Blankenberg, and Elise Blankenberg. Each was inscribed with their date of birth and date of escape, internment, deportation, and murder. I read their names and then I looked up at the house in front of me. I now saw the building, with its historic architecture, exposed wood rafters, and contemporary storefront window displays, as a site of murder, occupation, and theft. The invisible was made

Memorial to the Murdered Jews of Europe, Berlin. Designed by Peter Eisenman, 1998–2005.

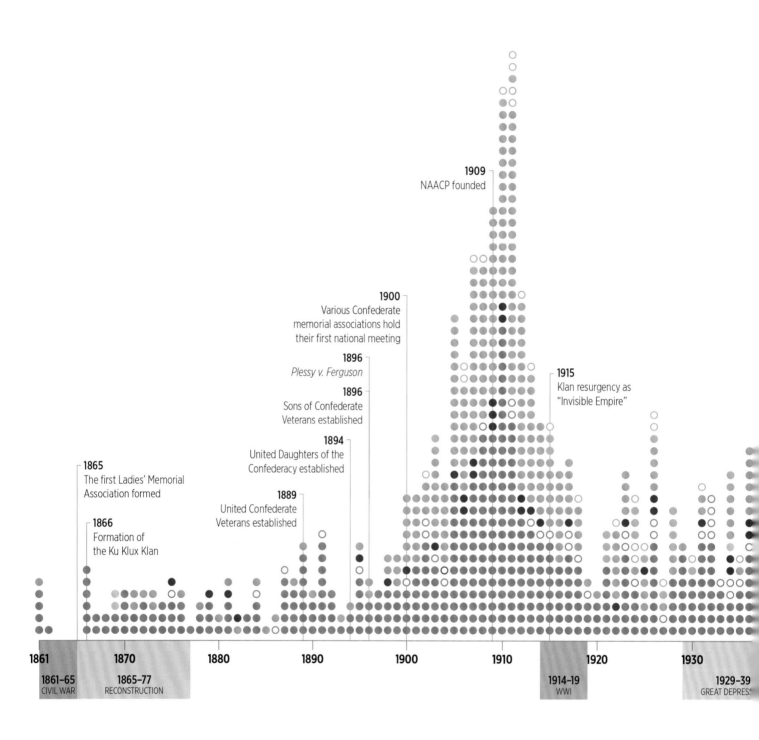

1909
NAACP founded

1900
Various Confederate
memorial associations hold
their first national meeting

1896
Plessy v. Ferguson

1896
Sons of Confederate
Veterans established

1915
Klan resurgency as
"Invisible Empire"

1894
United Daughters of the
Confederacy established

1865
The first Ladies' Memorial
Association formed

1889
United Confederate
Veterans established

1866
Formation of
the Ku Klux Klan

| 1861 | 1870 | 1880 | 1890 | 1900 | 1910 | 1920 | 1930 |

1861–65
CIVIL WAR

1865–77
RECONSTRUCTION

1914–19
WWI

1929–39
GREAT DEPRES*

A chart from the Southern Poverty Law Center's 2019 "Whose Heritage?" report indicates a sharp increase in the prevalence of Confederate symbolism and monuments between 1900 and 1920 and again from the mid-1950s through the 1960s.

How can design support humane forms of peace and security?

WHOSE HERITAGE?
153 YEARS OF CONFEDERATE ICONOGRAPHY

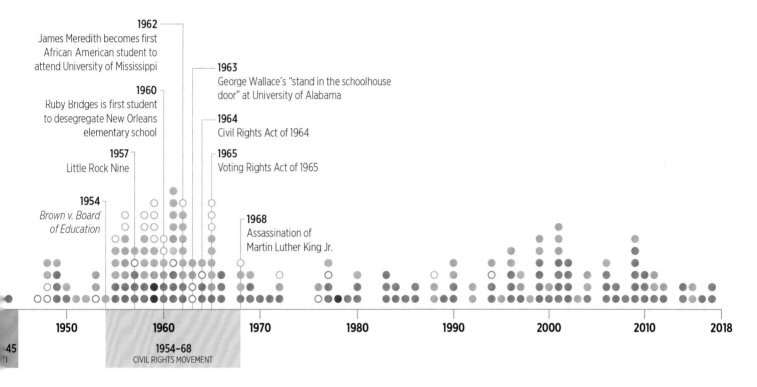

1962
James Meredith becomes first
African American student to
attend University of Mississippi

1963
George Wallace's "stand in the schoolhouse
door" at University of Alabama

1960
Ruby Bridges is first student
to desegregate New Orleans
elementary school

1964
Civil Rights Act of 1964

1957
Little Rock Nine

1965
Voting Rights Act of 1965

1954
*Brown v. Board
of Education*

1968
Assassination of
Martin Luther King Jr.

1950   1960   1970   1980   1990   2000   2010   2018

45

1954–68
CIVIL RIGHTS MOVEMENT

● SCHOOLS
● MONUMENTS ON COURTHOUSE GROUNDS
● ROADS
● MONUMENTS ON OTHER GOVERNMENT OFFICE GROUNDS
● OTHER SITES (INCLUDING MONUMENTS)

*This chart does not include monuments or other symbols for which the dedication dates are unknown.
The hollow circles indicate the dedication dates for symbols that now have been removed from public spaces.

visible; I could sense the layering of history, with all its complexity and indeterminacy. In that moment, I experienced Moritz, Lotte, and Elise as memorable, personable, and relatable. I understood that if conditions were different, I too might have been a victim.

The Intimate and the Infinite

This is the realm of the intimate, where memorials connect a unique maker or object to an understanding of a life in all its humanity and individuation. The Stolpersteine do not tell us the full story of the Blankenbergs, but they supply us with enough data to locate ourselves in their condition (and to search for more information, if we so desire). They mark, and as we stumble on them; they also evoke—in this case, something sinister, a horror that is neither recorded or visible. They allow us to read the built landscape differently and force us to wonder what other stories may be hiding in plain sight. The Stolpersteine do not provoke a specific action, but they stimulate questioning: are there others, and if so where, and how many? As a memorial, they connect the viewer to one family or one group and do not try to convey the paralyzing enormity of the inconceivably large number of victims of the Holocaust.

Conversely, Eisenman's memorial attempts to compose an image of the whole. The field, a gridded topography when viewed from above, a new landscape exhumed from the earth, suggests a labyrinth. The visitor here does not stumble into knowledge and empathy but is instead lost, discomfited, in search of answers and direction. This is the realm of the infinite, where an attempt to count the uncountable links individual loss to a greater shared loss. The infinite is transmuted through form into an experience, humanizing and historicizing death in something bigger than the self. The goal of the MMJE is cultural reckoning. Specifically naming *European* Jews and sitting at the center of Berlin, the Nazi party's base, it makes a culture-wide demand: the nation and the continent must never forget the atrocity of the Holocaust. At its core, the memorial seeks a transformational outcome that is best explained by Michel Foucault: "The strategic adversary is fascism . . . the fascism in us all, in our heads and in our everyday behavior, the fascism that causes us to love power, to desire the very thing that dominates and exploits us."[4]

Gun Violence Memorial Project, National Building Museum, Washington, DC, 2021. Designed by MASS Design Group in collaboration with artist Hank Willis Thomas and gun violence prevention organizations Purpose Over Pain and Everytown for Gun Safety, with local community-based organizations across the country.

Successful memorials navigate between the intimate and the infinite. They do not all have to mark, provoke, and evoke, but very effective ones might do all three. In the experiential flicker created by the memorial, a pathway for a shared human journey is revealed. Through the individual story, we surrender to the magnitude of shared loss. Each loss is our loss. If in this process we are given the tools to engage, the rituals to enact, the stories to hear, and the spaces in which to hear them, we may find that memorials are active contributors to cultural transformation—and are thus a tool for peace.

A Memorial to Gun Violence

In 2018 I was approached by two Chicago women who had lost sons to street shootings. Pamela Bosley and Annette Nance-Holt asked if it might be possible to create a memorial to victims of gun violence in the United States. With my design colleagues and collaborative partner, the artist Hank Willis Thomas, I wondered what it would take to memorialize the victims of an ongoing epidemic in which a hundred people are killed every day.

The AIDS Memorial Quilt teaches us that participation and collectivism in memorial making can be a potent force in manifesting political change. The quilt revealed the magnitude—the weight and breadth and physical volume—of the loss, and was thus a potent indictment of the broken systems that allowed it to occur. In the 1987 display of the quilt on the National Mall, ninety-two thousand panels covered the entirety of the nation's front lawn, linking the infinite and the intimate together in one vast, collective exercise in public mourning. Without it, would structural change have been possible (p. 127)? This was peacemaking through place making. To make peace, we must create a space for it.

What kind of space could contain and communicate the epidemic of gun violence? What forms might signal both the total volume of its casualties to date and the ever-increasing and ongoing toll? The frame of the memorial is the essential design idea, and it must both register and oscillate between the intimate and the infinite. We designed a glass house made of seven hundred transparent "bricks," one for every gun victim killed in the United States in a week. Fifty-two houses will be placed on the National Mall to evoke one full year of gun deaths. For every brick, we've collected an object, representing a life, to be contained within it. There are thirty-six thousand stories, thirty-six thousand lives, thirty-six thousand narratives to record, tell, and acknowledge.

We must see to believe, but it is not only the view of the glass houses on the Mall that will convince us. It is also entering the house, staring at the object, hearing a story. Capturing, in all its breadth, one lost life, and understanding that it could be yours. This is where we hope to break through. In creating a temporary city, and in forcing visitors to see each object within as representing a victim, we might catalyze cultural change. But the real goal is structural: to enact policy changes that American policy makers are currently too afraid to propose.

It is not enough to mark. It is not enough to represent. It is not enough to create a journey through undefined space. It is only in evoking empathy, through both the intimate and the infinite, that we can transcend a culture of violence. This is the task set for designers, artists, and architects—to create empathy, to effect change, to build peace in our world.

1   In Jewish tradition, for example, visitors leave stones atop gravesites to mark visitation and acknowledgment. The word for "stone" in Hebrew—eben (אבן)—is etymologically tied to an idea of generational legacy. It is a compound of the words for "father"—aba (אב)—and "son"—ben (בן). Within the word for stone is a rich description of its living properties, the ability to carry on legacy from one generation to the next.

2   Johan Galtung, Peace by Peaceful Means (London, Sage Publications, 1996), 199.

3   Ibid, 196.

4   Michel Foucault, preface to Gilles Deleuze and Félix Guattari, Anti-Oedipus: Capitalism and Schizophrenia, trans. Robert Hurley, Mark Seem, and Helen R. Lane (New York: Viking, 1977), xiii.

Social Emergency Response Centers

Designers
Kenneth Bailey, Soledad Boyd, Lori Lobenstine, Ayako Maruyama, Design Studio for Social Intervention (United States)

Collaborators
Local artists, photographers, volunteers (Canada, Serbia, United States)

Locations
Canada, Serbia, United States (Arkansas, Connecticut, District of Columbia, Georgia, Illinois, Massachusetts, Mississippi, New Jersey, New Mexico, Oregon)

Years 2016–present

Posters for Social Emergency Response Centers label the four key activities: Making, Cooking, Healing, and Plotting.

SERC kits comprise a mailing tube containing posters, custom face masks, buttons, stencils, zines, and signage designed to support groups hosting centers in their communities.

The Boston-based Design Studio for Social Intervention has created a disaster-response center that is intended to be deployed not in the aftermath of a hurricane or earthquake but rather for people facing numerous social emergencies—state-sanctioned violence, oil spills, gentrification, and more—currently in progress. Packed and sent in a mailing tube, the Social Emergency Response Center (SERC) kit contains all the elements needed to build what the designers have described as "temporary, pop-up spaces that help us move from rage and despair into collective, radical action."

Easily replicable materials—templates, stencils, signs, posters, buttons, and zines—provide the framework for community-focused activities and workshops. Early on, the designers determined that the kit's users would benefit from clear emergency procedures—

similar to the "Stop, drop, and roll" fire drill. A reimagined drill, included in the kit, instructs SERC participants to "Stop, look around, gather your people; Drop fear, anxiety, assumptions; Roll out new ideas, roll together." A "Tracking the Storm" timeline identifies social emergencies and asks participants to share how they have been impacted, and a handbook offers guidance in creating a welcoming and safe place for communal making and cooking—support for healing and for plotting the future. Selected locations must be accessible, visible, near public transit, and can range in size from a small bookstore to a large health center. Led by activists and artists, SERCs are creative spaces and a practical solution. Their goal is to bring people into community to collectively imagine how to build a stronger, more just democracy.

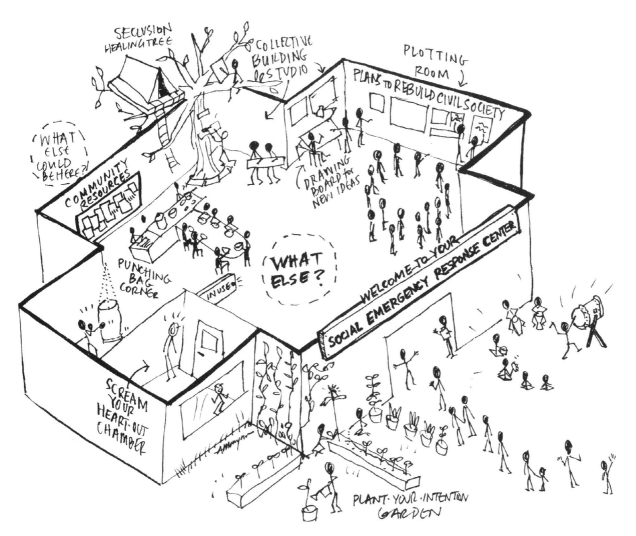

Social Emergency Response Centers may be customized to offer
activities and spaces that function and feel genuine for each community.
Drawing by Ayako Maruyama, 2016.

A SERC healing activity features Move Baby Move founder Aaron Palmer guiding a chair yoga
and mindful breathing session during the PolicyLink Equity Summit, Chicago, 2017.

Imagining the Just City

Toni L. Griffin

Toni L. Griffin is the director of the Just City Lab and a professor in Practice of Urban Planning at Harvard Graduate School of Design.

The Just City Lab investigates the definition of urban justice and the "just city," examining how design and planning contribute to the conditions of justice and injustice in cities, neighborhoods, and the public realm. The lab has been developing and testing a set of core principles, values, and metrics to assess and evaluate design's role in achieving urban justice. It also researches design practices that exemplify the achievement of the just city and its values.

Would we design better places if we put equality, equity, or inclusion first? If a community articulated what it stood for, what it believed in, what it aspired to be—as a city, as a neighborhood—would it have a better chance of creating and sustaining a more healthy, vibrant place with positive economic, health, civic, cultural, and environmental conditions? Imagine that race, income, education, and employment inequality, and the resulting segregation, isolation, and fear, could be addressed by planning and designing for greater access, agency, ownership, beauty, diversity, and empowerment. Now imagine a just city—a city with neighborhoods and public spaces that were designed to thrive through a value-based strategy for urban stabilization, revitalization, and transformation.

The Just City Index: Values Indicators

ACCEPTANCE

Belonging Being accepted and comfortable in a setting despite age, gender, race, sexuality, or income

Empathy Exercising the ability to recognize and understand the feeling and point of view of another

Inclusion The acceptance of difference and the intention to involve diverse opinions, attitudes, and behaviors

Reconciliation The process of finding a way to make two different ideas, facts, or points of view coexist or be true at the same time

Respect A mutually earned and shared honoring of different voices, opinions, behaviors, and cultural expressions

Tolerance The acceptance of difference

Trust To promote a confidence earned through the demonstration of fulfilling commitments and promises made among people and institutions

ASPIRATION

Creative Innovation Nurturing ingenuity in problem solving and intervention

Delight Creating places, spaces, and processes that promote happiness and joy

Happiness A state of well-being that brings about joy, contentment, or ease

Hope The possibility of fulfillment of a desire, aspiration, outcome, or happiness

Inspiration The result of creative thinking and collaboration that has the potential to produce new and innovative outcomes

CHOICE

Diversity An intentional state of mixed people, institutions, and cultural norms

Spontaneity To allow for the unplanned, where individuals or groups can self-create processes, interventions, or activities

DEMOCRACY

Conflict The acceptance of disagreement or opposition in pursuit of necessary change or improvement

How can design support humane forms of peace and security?

Debate Providing forums for the discussion of different voices and points of view

Protest The act of objection or disapproval in the form of public demonstration

Voice Allowing different points of view and cultural norms to help shape decision making

ENGAGEMENT

Community A group of individuals or collective groups having shared or common interests

Cooperation The process by which individuals or collective groups work together to do something

Participation The active engagement of individuals and community members in matters, both formal and informal, affecting social and spatial well-being

Togetherness A sense of solidarity within and across populations

FAIRNESS

Equality The provision of equal or equivalent distribution, status, rights, power, and amenity

Equity The distribution of material and non-material goods in a manner that brings the greatest benefit required to any particular community

Merit A good quality, feature, process, or outcome that deserves to be praised and assigned worth or value

Transparency The openness of process, rules, rights, and procedures through the sharing of knowledge and information

IDENTITY

Authenticity The recognition and promotion of physical and social characteristics that are genuine to a particular place or culture

Beauty Everyone's right to well-made, well-designed environments

Character Features or attributes used to separate distinguishable qualities of place

Pride A respect and admiration arising from feeling good and confident about some act, space, place, or relationship

Spirituality The presence of places and attitudes that support religious expression, practice, and belief

Vitality An energetic, integrated community with opportunities for and support of cultural, civic, and economic involvement

MOBILITY

Access The convenient proximity to, quality of, or connectivity to basic needs, amenities, choices, and decisions

Connectivity The physical and social networks that tie places and people together, providing contact and opportunity for social well-being

POWER

Accountability The acceptance of responsibility by individuals or collective groups to contribute to the creation and maintenance of just conditions for all

Agency Enabling the confidence, rights, and status of individuals or groups to act on behalf of their own interests

Empowerment To give formal authority or power to a person or collective group by promoting action or influence

Representation A balance of a community's desires, representative of its diversity, are present in the decision-making process

RESILIENCE

Adaptability The ability to change or be changed in order to fit or work better in some situation or for some purpose

Durability The ability of all social and spatial systems to remain strong and in good condition over a long period of time

Sustainability The quality of not being harmful to social or spatial well-being or depleting resources, and thereby supporting long-term balance

RIGHTS

Freedom The ability to act or speak freely without threat of external restriction

Knowledge The ability to gain information or awareness through education and/or experience

Ownership The ability to have a stake in the property, process, outcome

WELFARE

Healthiness A state of complete physical, mental, and social well-being that supports the absence of disease or infirmity

Prosperity The condition of being successful or thriving in terms of social, economic, civic, cultural, and health indicators

Protection The state of being kept from harm or loss in social or spatial conditions

Safety An environment that minimizes physical and emotional vulnerability and threats to well-being

Security Social and spatial conditions that support freedom from danger, exclusion, and harm

The Adventures of Daly Graphic Novels

Designers
Moez Tabia (drawings), Abir Guesmi (scenarios and dialogues), Lab 619 (Tunisia)

Collaborators
Hilde Deman, Wissem Missaoui, Bouraoui Ouni, Zeineb Saidani, Search for Common Ground–Tunisia (Tunisia)

Locations
Tunisia (Tunis, Kasserine, Gafsa, Siliana, Kef)

Years 2017–18

To prevent continued violent extremist recruitment, which threatened especially vulnerable and marginalized Tunisian youth, a frontline peacebuilding organization partnered with a local experimental comic book design collective. Their twelve-month graphic novel campaign, The Adventures of Daly, used five comic books based on different characters—an unemployed young man, a female university student and sexual-assault survivor, an employed single woman, a withdrawn male computer geek, and eight residents of a multi-unit building—as a launching point for discussions around alternatives to violence.

With Tunisia as the largest exporter of terrorist fighters in the world, the peacebuilding team Search for Common Ground–Tunisia organized focus groups and conducted interviews with local stakeholders in five Tunisian communities to learn about the factors driving radicalization. These regional dialogues resulted in ten potential comic storylines, which the group passed to the comic collective Lab 619 to develop in collaboration with Tunisian youth. The story for the first book was directly informed by the experiences of the young collaborators, mirroring actual events—a fictionalization that allowed the team to be specific while addressing sensitive topics—and the graphics, stories, and dialogue (in Tunisian dialect) were reviewed and edited by youth to further ensure that they resonated. To extend the project's reach, Search for Common Ground–Tunisia brought the books to a comics convention in Tunis, where they taught attendees about using graphic novels to prevent extremism. Partner organizations trained youth to facilitate community discussions on the themes raised by the series.

The five Adventures of Daly graphic novels. Left to right: *Daly* (دالي), *Amal* (أمل), *Soulayma* (سليمة), *Kods* (كدس), and *The Building* or *Al-Imara* (العمارة).

Graphic novels such as *Soulayma* (pictured) are used as an entry point for facilitated youth-to-youth discussions about marginalization within communities, Enfidha, Tunisia, 2020.

Excerpts from *The Building* or *Al-Imara* help frame a discussion at a youth center, Enfidha, Tunisia, 2020.

In Transit Studio

Håvard Breivik-Khan and Tone Selmer-Olsen

Håvard Breivik-Khan is an architect and researcher. He is a cofounder of and teacher at the In Transit Studio at the Oslo School of Architecture and Design. **Tone Selmer-Olsen** is an architect, researcher, and assistant professor at the Oslo School of Architecture and Design. She is a cofounder of and teacher at the In Transit Studio at the Oslo School of Architecture and Design.

How do mobility and migration inform the way we shape our cities? How can the design of social infrastructure and new ways of living contribute to diverse, tolerant, and inclusive neighborhoods? How can we plan for and facilitate social life in our communities? In Transit is a design studio, founded in 2016 at the Oslo School of Architecture and Design for architecture and urbanism students from all over the world, that is devoted to collaborative knowledge production on the subjects of displacement, urbanization, and space. The studio explores mobility and migration in the age of urbanization, proposing local, spatial, and site-specific solutions. The aim of the studio is to develop a variety of residential forms that consider different lengths of stay, models of ownership, cultural backgrounds, and immigration statuses, promoting social infrastructure through easily accessible common and public spaces.

Unfinished Athens The design facilitates construction by inhabitants, beginning with a prefabricated kitchen and bathroom cores, along with integrated infrastructure such as water and electricity. Drawing by David Kelly, 2016.

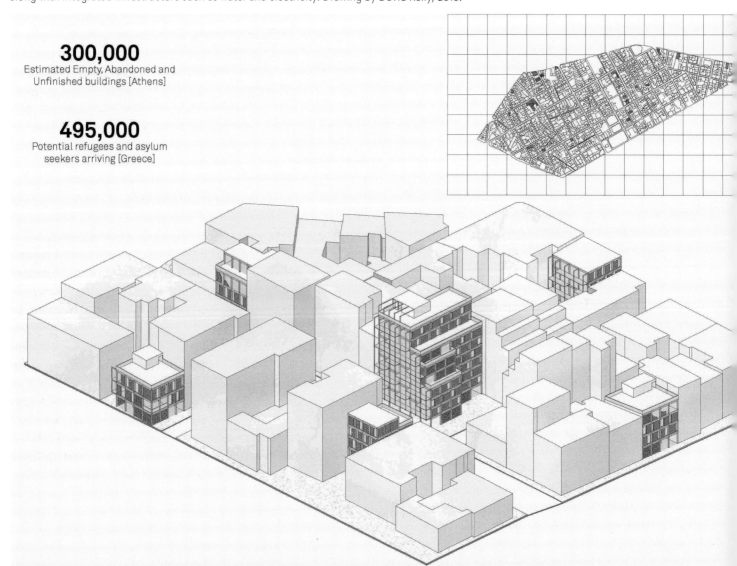

300,000
Estimated Empty, Abandoned and Unfinished buildings [Athens]

495,000
Potential refugees and asylum seekers arriving [Greece]

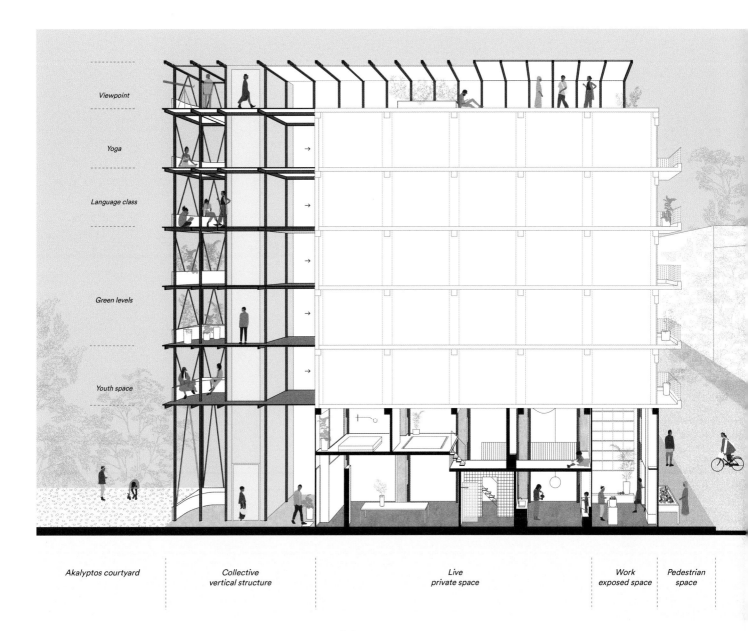

Viewpoint

Yoga

Language class

Green levels

Youth space

| Akalyptos courtyard | Collective vertical structure | Live private space | Work exposed space | Pedestrian space |

Structures for Current and Potential Citizens of Thessaloniki A new steel support system structurally improves the decaying buildings and activates unused spaces to create new live/work apartments and common areas for new arrivals. Drawing by Kaja Strand Ellingson, 2018.

← **Unfinished Athens** David Kelly, Athens, Greece, 2016

This project investigates the possibility of inhabiting abandoned concrete structures, rehabilitating the scars of economic collapse to provide homes to unhoused Greeks and to refugees. There are an estimated three hundred thousand empty, unfinished, or abandoned structures in Athens alone, relics of the 2007–08 financial crisis. Housing refugees in these structures is an opportunity to reinvigorate the communal and economic situations within struggling communities at a microscale.

↑ **Structures for Current and Potential Citizens of Thessaloniki** Kaja Strand Ellingsen, Thessaloniki, Greece, 2018

This plan proposes a strategy for resettling refugees currently living in temporary camps outside the northern Greek city of Thessaloniki by moving them into the city center, providing opportunities for employment and cultural integration and supporting and revitalizing a neighborhood in need of upgrading. There are a large number of decaying and vacant buildings in Xirokrini, a multicultural neighborhood in western Thessaloniki. Their empty ground floors and the other unused spaces in the neighborhood present an opportunity to be transformed into common structures for current and future citizens. This project proposes a scalable urban and structural strategy that rethinks public spaces by opening up the ground floors of all the buildings in the neighborhood.

Growing Tøyen A large greenhouse with public functions and temporary accommodation units is equipped with infrastructure and integrated furniture. The greenhouse provides a physical framework in which the living units can be installed according to the fluctuating needs and quantity of arrivals. At the same time, the permanent structure functions as a meeting place for neighborhood residents year-round. Drawing by Kevin Benny Kuriakose, Victor Carpintero Ferran, and Heini Hiukka, 2016.

↑ **Growing Tøyen**
Kevin Benny Kuriakose, Victor Carpintero Ferran, and Heini Hiukka, Oslo, Norway, 2016

Many reception centers for asylum seekers are located in remote areas, secluded from their surroundings and far from urban centers, commercial offerings, and public life. Growing Tøyen—an urban strategy for a neighborhood in Oslo—proposes a different kind of reception facility, with a design that ensures a high degree of livability while maintaining the capacity to accommodate many people with short notice. It was important that the design combine temporary and permanent housing for new arrivals with interventions that would be attractive for the entire Tøyen neighborhood. The project incorporates the needs of the existing population, with safe public spaces and low-threshold recreational and cultural offerings.

→ **Entrepreneurship Hub for All**
Ingrid Hove Viljoen and Olav Bog Vikane, Thessaloniki, Greece, 2018

The markets of Thessaloniki are key to the identity of the city: they are where local residents, tourists, and newcomers meet, exchanging goods and sharing ideas. The 2007–09 global financial crisis devastated these local markets along with the Greek economy, and many booths remain empty and unused. This project involves the design of a new type of marketplace: an entrepreneurship hub. This distribution and production center combines workspaces with residential apartments, creating a platform where everyone in the community, including new arrivals, may build new skills, acquire knowledge, and produce and participate in the economy.

How can design support humane forms of peace and security?

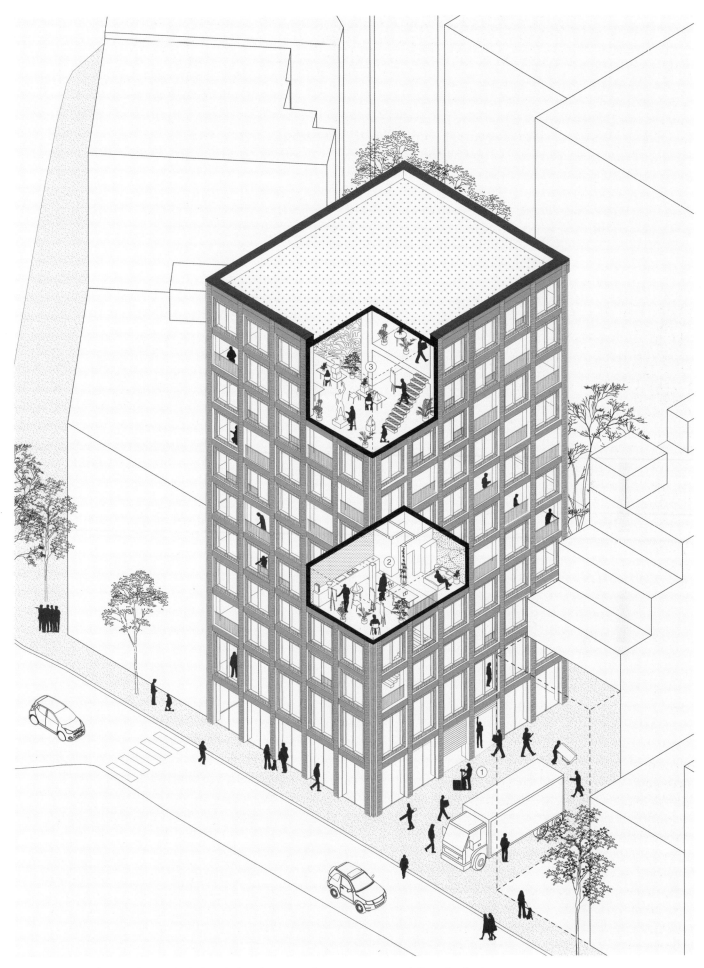

Entrepreneurship Hub for All The hub includes a basement for storage, a ground-floor distribution space, second-floor classrooms, and production and workshop spaces in every living unit throughout the building. Drawing by Ingrid Hove Viljoen and Olav Bog Vikan, 2018.

Startblok Elzenhagen

Designer
MUST Urbanism (Netherlands)

Collaborators
De Key and Eigen Haard housing organizations,
Municipality of Amsterdam (Netherlands)

Location Amsterdam, Netherlands

Year 2018

Startblok Elzenhagen offers a new model for co-living in the increasingly diverse city of Amsterdam. The affordable-housing block was designed to create community among Dutch youth and young refugees who have recently received residence permits. The young people, ages eighteen to twenty-eight, live together while they work and attend school, learning and helping each other as they begin life in the vibrant city.

Built on a former sports grounds, the housing block comprises 540 affordable units organized around its hallways. To build social cohesion, the ten to fifteen individual apartments lining each corridor share common amenities and spaces for socializing and other activities, like self-organized language or sports classes. The complex is self-managed by the tenants,

who, for a reduction in rent, can join the various support teams that maintain a safe and livable environment.

This is the second of three housing developments by MUST, and the team learned with each iteration. As urban designers they approached the physical and social design of the housing complex as a city—a system of connections and interactions between people of different backgrounds—by providing a variety of shared public spaces, such as communal grassy areas. When the complex's big lawns failed—no one was using them—they reconsidered their overall design. In the new iteration, paths and seating remain, but the group spaces moved indoors, adjacent to the well-traveled hallways. Adding large balconies on each floor, they created spaces analogous to small neighborhood streets, where numerous chance encounters could occur.

Residents' interests determine how the shared spaces are used.
Some are transformed into gardens and others are simply a place to relax.

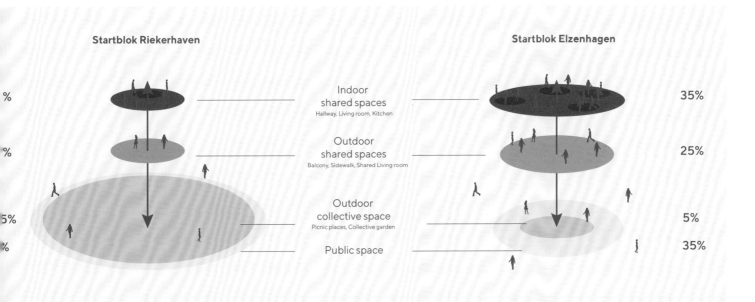

Startblok Riekerhaven   **Startblok Elzenhagen**

| | Indoor shared spaces | |
| | Hallway, Living room, Kitchen | 35% |

| | Outdoor shared spaces | |
| | Balcony, Sidewalk, Shared Living room | 25% |

| | Outdoor collective space | |
| | Picnic places, Collective garden | 5% |

| | Public space | 35% |

Residents at Startblok Elzenhagen intermingle more readily in indoor shared spaces—the hallway, living room, and kitchen—than large outdoor collective spaces. Drawing by MUST Urbanism, 2021.

Designed for reuse after fifteen years, each Startblok building occupies a standard footprint. Plantings can continue to grow after the temporary housing is relocated.

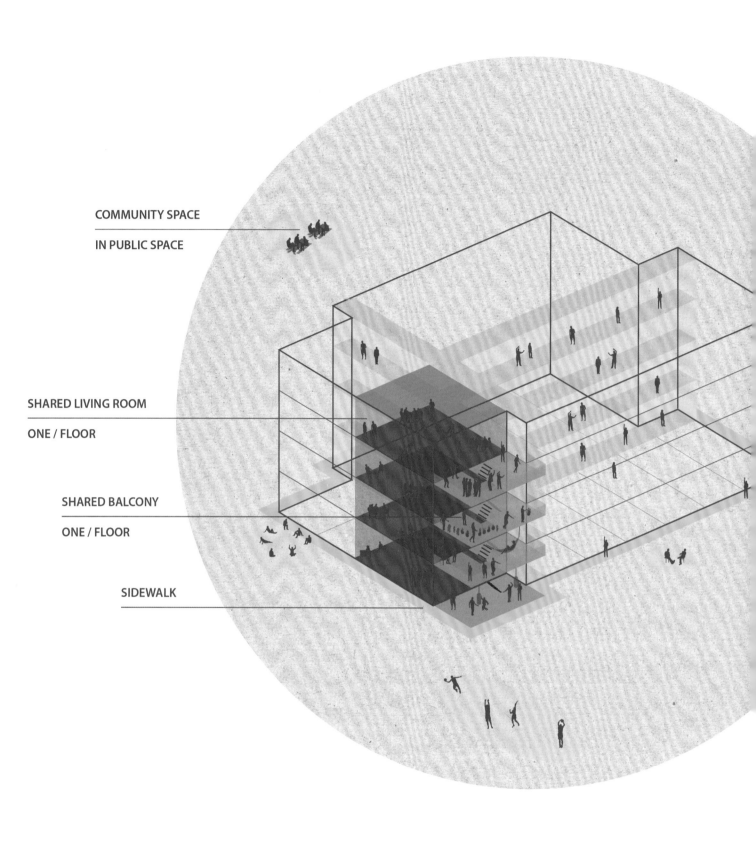

COMMUNITY SPACE

IN PUBLIC SPACE

SHARED LIVING ROOM

ONE / FLOOR

SHARED BALCONY

ONE / FLOOR

SIDEWALK

MUST Urbanism explored the housing's physical and social
design to create spaces for connection and interaction similar
to the way cities function. Drawing by MUST Urbanism, 2021.

How can design support humane forms of peace and security?

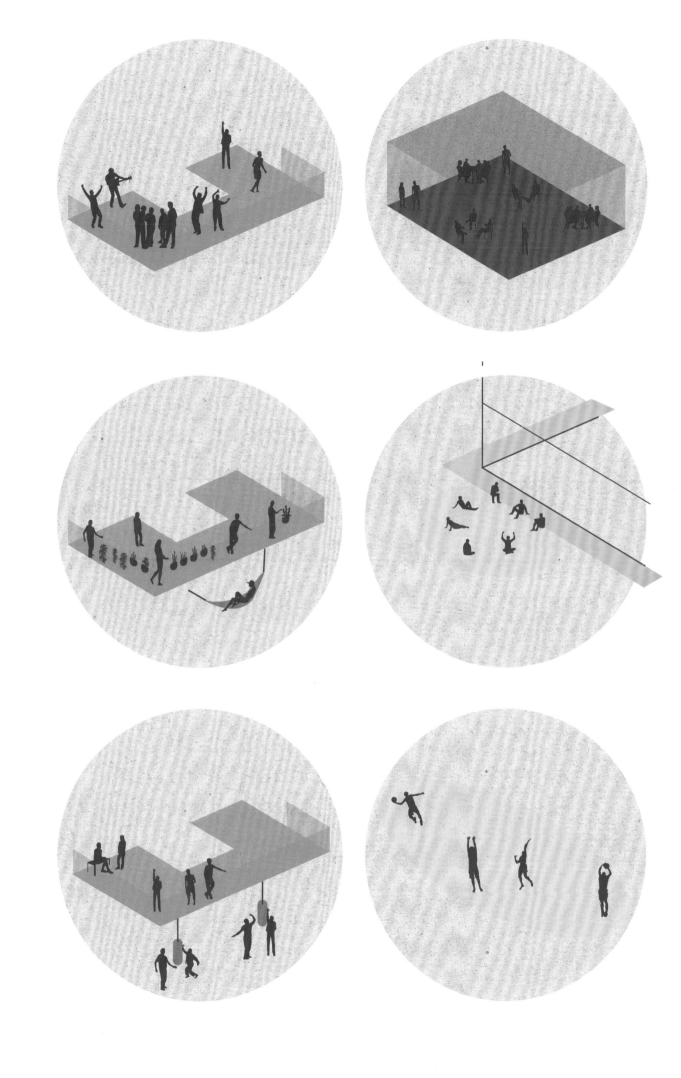

Oceanix City

Designer
Bjarke Ingels Group (Denmark)

Collaborators Center for Zero Waste Design, Dickson Despommier, Global Coral Reef Alliance, MIT Center for Ocean Engineering, Sherwood Design Engineers (United States); Mobility in Chain (Italy); Studio Other Spaces, Transsolar KlimaEngineering (Germany)

Location Global

Year 2019

Oceanix City is an adaptable, sustainable, scalable, and affordable floating city that could be deployed on the ocean near coastal megacities. Rendering by BIG-Bjarke Ingels Group, 2019.

Because of global warming, 90 percent of the world's largest cities will experience higher sea levels by 2050. The resulting flooding and coastal erosion will destroy homes and infrastructure, displacing millions and fueling tensions. Seeking bold ideas to this urgent threat, UN-Habitat turned to architects, engineers, scientists, and innovators, convening a global round-table to explore the viability of floating entire cities.

One proposal is Oceanix City, a reimagined urban design based on the United Nation's Sustainable Development Goals. This modular floating settlement, conceived by an international design team, consists of a grouping of prefabricated and flexible mixed-use neighborhoods located offshore near areas impacted by sea-level rise. The design integrates compact city systems into interlocking platforms that could support ten thousand people before scaling up. Sustainable and resilient infrastructure—wind and water turbines for energy, desalination and rain collection for fresh water, composting and anaerobic digesters to manage waste, aeroponics and ocean farming for food production, and locally sourced bamboo and modular construction for shelter—make the communities self-sustaining. Artificial reef structures, able to withstand severe storms, anchor the platforms and restore local marine habitats. The neighborhood's hexagonal shape accommodates diverse city configurations, which can be modified to adapt to local geography, culture, and socioeconomic structures. As much a public provocation as a design concept, this bold proposal asks the global community to consider how we might live together in a future defined by a warming planet. Oceanix City is a call to designers and the public that audacious action is urgently needed.

Mixed-Use Neighborhood

Oceanix City's modular hexagonal neighborhoods are designed for mixed use, including farming, energy production, recreation, work, and commerce. Drawing by BIG – Bjarke Ingels Group, 2019.

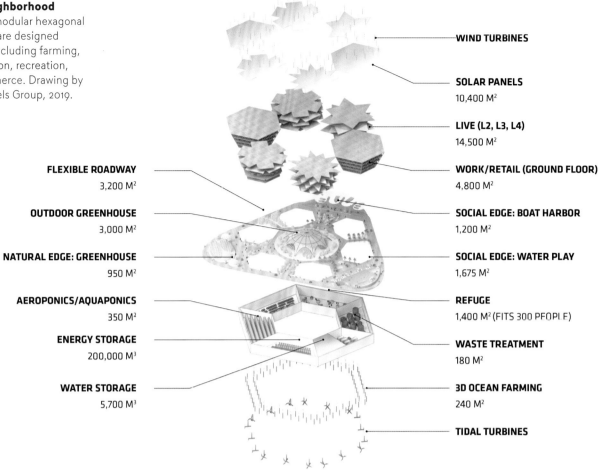

WIND TURBINES

SOLAR PANELS
10,400 M²

LIVE (L2, L3, L4)
14,500 M²

WORK/RETAIL (GROUND FLOOR)
4,800 M²

SOCIAL EDGE: BOAT HARBOR
1,200 M²

SOCIAL EDGE: WATER PLAY
1,675 M²

REFUGE
1,400 M² (FITS 300 PEOPLE)

WASTE TREATMENT
180 M²

3D OCEAN FARMING
240 M²

TIDAL TURBINES

FLEXIBLE ROADWAY
3,200 M²

OUTDOOR GREENHOUSE
3,000 M²

NATURAL EDGE: GREENHOUSE
950 M²

AEROPONICS/AQUAPONICS
350 M²

ENERGY STORAGE
200,000 M³

WATER STORAGE
5,700 M³

Beneath the floating platforms, biorock reefs, seaweed, and oyster, mussel, scallop, and clam farming clean the water and accelerate ecosystem regeneration. Rendering by BIG-Bjarke Ingels Group, 2019.

Christmas Operations

Designer
MullenLowe SSP3 (Bogotá, Colombia)

Campaigns
Operation Christmas (2010), Rivers of Light (2011),
Operation Bethlehem (2012), Mother's Voice (2013)

Collaborator
Colombian Ministry of Defense's Program of
Humanitarian Attention to the Demobilized

Location Colombia

Years 2010–13

With the goal of ending its country's decades-long internal conflicts, Colombia's Ministry of Defense engaged a Bogotá-based advertising agency to design a campaign to persuade the rebel soldiers of the FARC (Revolutionary Armed Forces of Colombia) to lay down their arms and return home. Learning that demobilizations spiked around Christmas, the creative team determined to bring the spirit of the season to the insurgents with Operation Christmas. Trees in ten rebel-held zones were decorated with thousands of blue lights. When a motion sensor was activated, banners were illuminated, reading "Demobilize. At Christmas, everything is possible."

Following that successful operation they brought the campaign to the jungle's waterways with the Rivers of Light campaign. Close to seven thousand glowing orbs were floated down rivers, filled with personal homecoming messages written by local citizens and friends and families of the fighters.

To counter the increasing desertions, the FARC moved its fighters deeper into the jungle. In response, Operation Bethlehem lit the way home with glow-in-the-dark stickers on delivery vehicles, food packaging, and tree trunks; illuminated riverside billboards and pathways with lights dropped from helicopters; and beacons beamed light from village plazas.

The next year, Mother's Voice featured the mothers of fighters with a commercial, song, and posters featuring childhood photographs of soldiers. A message of homecoming was sent: "Before being a guerrilla fighter, you are my child. This Christmas I wait for you at home." In addition to increasing demobilization, the Christmas campaigns helped shift public perception of the returning guerrillas, humanizing them: they were still a part of a family.

Rivers of Light, 2011 A note, placed inside a floating orb in the Rivers of Light campaign, is addressed to *guerrilleros* (guerrillas) and opens with *"Saludo, Amigos"* ("Hello, friends"), Solano, Colombia.

How can design support humane forms of peace and security?

Rivers of Light, 2011 During the Rivers of Light campaign, glowing orbs are deployed three miles upstream from FARC rebel bases, Caquetá River, Colombia.

Mother's Voice, 2013 To protect the guerrillas' identities the Mother's Voice posters used childhood photographs only the soldiers would recognize. Each poster declared, "Before you are a guerrilla fighter, you are my daughter [my son]."

Mother's Voice, 2013 A young woman holds a photo of her brother, who was recruited by the FARC (Revolutionary Armed Forces of Colombia), San Vicente del Caguán, Colombia.

ANTES DE SER GUERRILLERO,
ERES MI HIJO.

ESTA NAVIDAD TE ESPERO EN CASA.
DESMOVILÍZATE. EN NAVIDAD TODO ES POSIBLE.

Body Mapping

Mapmakers
Former child soldiers, family and community members
of former child soldiers

Collaborators Harvard Humanitarian Initiative,
Eastern Congo Initiative (United States) with Appui
à la Communication Interculturelle et à l'Autopro-
motion Rurale, Association des Jeunes pour le Développement Intégré-Kalundu, Caritas Bunia, Équipe
d'Éducation et d'Encadrement des Traumatisés de
Nyiragongo, Groupe d'Actions et d'Appui pour un
Développement Endogène, Projet de Réinsertion
des Enfants Ex-combattants et Autres Vulnérables-
Hope in Action (Democratic Republic of the Congo)

Location
Democratic Republic of the Congo

Years 2011–13

Mothers of former child soldiers add to a body map depicting the effects of war on the children of Uvira, South Kivu Province, Democratic Republic of the Congo, 2011.

The Democratic Republic of the Congo has one of the highest numbers of child soldiers in the world. Over fifty thousand have returned home during the seventeen years the United Nations has been keeping track. Physical and emotional trauma can make it difficult for the children to rebuild their lives and relationships. To learn directly about their experiences, a team of researchers and community partners used body mapping—a participatory action research method that acknowledges that those suffering from trauma are the experts on it—to visually express the physical, psychological, and social impacts of war and child soldiering.

Groups of former child combatants and their family and community members mapped the seen and unseen factors they confront as they collectively attempt to rebuild their lives. Using a life-sized outline of a human body on a large sheet of paper, together they illustrated phenomena that impacted them individually and collectively before, during, and after war. The images reveal their memories and identities and the physical, psychological, and social effects of their experiences. On one map, hunger was portrayed as a knife in the stomach. On another, rocks in the chest symbolized "a heavy heart."

Ten maps were made in seven communities, resulting in concrete recommendations to improve the children's reintegration experiences. The mappings also provided opportunity to generate connections and conversation. The community partners collected, laminated, and assembled all the maps, taking them—on foot and by motorcycle—to every community that participated, continuing the ongoing process of healing.

Detail of the Uvira body map, portraying the rejection, distrust, and fear former child soldiers face from their communities. Notes (not shown) describe destruction by child soldiers, which creates a lack of harmony in the community and among family members.

The Uvira body map illustrates the impacts of war on underage combatants of both genders, female (left half) and male (right half), Uvira, South Kivu Province, Democratic Republic of the Congo, 2011.

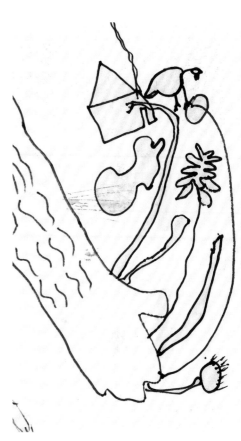

Detail of the Uvira body map, showing a child soldier's hand holding goods that are commonly pillaged: a house, a chicken, and crops.

Island Tracker

Designers
Gregory B. Poling, Paul Franz, Center for Strategic
and International Studies (United States)

Collaborators
Alison Bours, William Colson, Conor Cronin, Sarah
Grace, Tucker Harris, Leeza Luncheon, Serven Maraghi,
Harrison Prétat, Jacqueline Schrag, Emily Tiemeyer,
Center for Strategic and International Studies
(United States)

Location
South China Sea

Years 2014–present

In recent years, as tensions have grown in the South China Sea, one of the world's most disputed waterways, the Center for Strategic and International Studies (CSIS) developed and designed an innovative public-facing online tool. Island Tracker, part of the Washington-based think tank's Asia Maritime Transparency Initiative, uses easily attained commercial satellite imagery to track artificial island building and construction projects, such as new airstrips and ports, on almost seventy disputed reefs and islets claimed by China, Malaysia, the Philippines, Taiwan, and Vietnam. Providing transparency and clarity on these complex events at sea, the interactive database collects detailed information, including before and after imagery.

Designed to dissuade aggressive behavior and force unlawful actors to operate in full view of the world, while managing disputes more peacefully and equitably,

the initiative and its Tracker have proved instrumental in international discussions on militarization in the South China Sea. Combining high-resolution satellite images with commercial vessel tracking data, satellite-based radar imagery, and light-detection sensors, the team has identified fishing, oil and gas, law enforcement, and military vessels—all evidence of activity that heightens tensions in the disputed waters. The ongoing work prevents miscalculations and generates opportunities for collective action that favors regional stability.

The accessible platform is part of a larger effort by CSIS to expand policy discourse to a wide audience, including policy makers and the public alike. It was developed in its iDeas Lab, where experts partner with designers and developers to use digital tools to communicate policy solutions and strategies for the world's complex challenges.

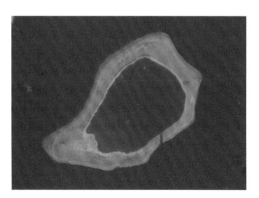

2014 The submerged Subi Reef before China's land reclamation begins, Spratly Islands, South China Sea.

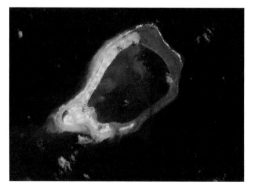

2015 Dredgers at work reclaiming land on Subi Reef, Spratly Islands, South China Sea.

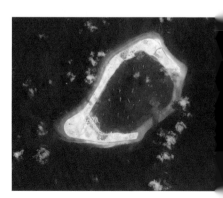

2015 Subi Reef after land reclamation, Spratly Islands, South China Sea.

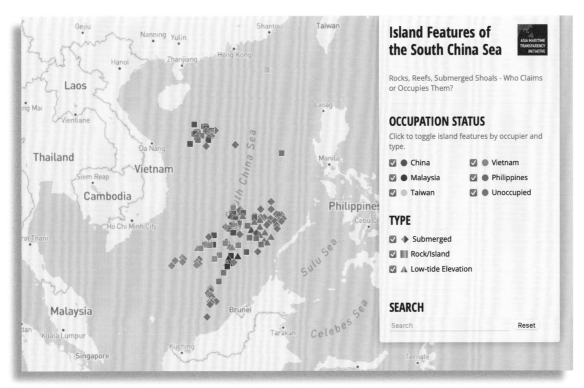

An interactive online map by the Asia Maritime Transparency Initiative identifies rocks, reefs, and submerged shoals in the South China Sea and the nations that claim them.

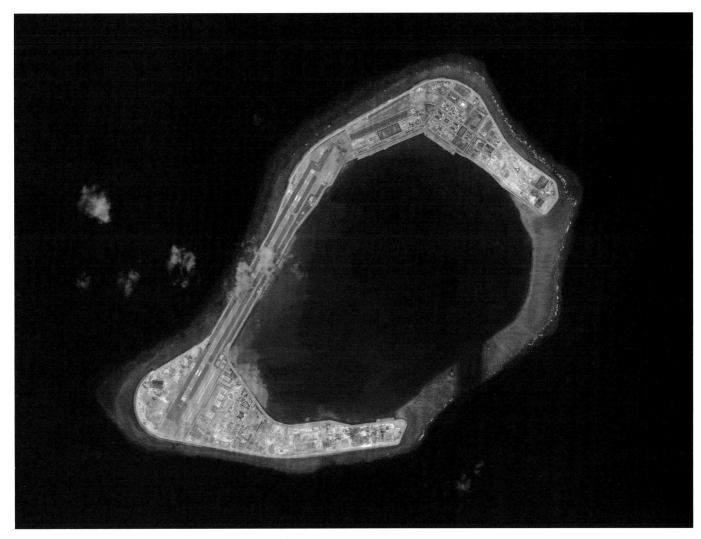

2020 China's outpost at Subi Reef with military infrastructure complete, Spratly Islands, South China Sea.

Borders and Boundaries

Beth Simmons, Michael Kenwick, and Dillon Horwitz

The Borders and Boundaries research team is engaged in an ongoing effort to systematically identify, record, and analyze every international land-border crossing visible in publicly available satellite imagery from 1990 to the present. By tapping into multiple global mapping networks, as well as collections of geotagged, ground-level photographs, we have compiled a first-of-its-kind database showing change over time in official state presence at land ports of entry. We work with the premise that the construction and maintenance of built infrastructure at international crossing points shows a government's commitment to the control and filtration of its borders. The team's ability to document and classify tangible signs, symbols, systems, and structures at ports of entry signifies how physically "present" a state is at its borders. An analysis of the data suggests that for at least the past three decades, there has been a steady "thickening" of international borders, as evidenced by an increasing incidence of official infrastructure at land-crossing points.* This buildup of infrastructure at officially designated crossing points signals a government's authority to assert control, its inclination to create logistical power, and its desire to affect the psychological experience of border crossers. Our maps, diagrams, and other data-driven visuals use coordinate-based, temporally specific observations to illustrate the spatial implications of rising political, economic, and social anxieties in an era of globalization. A responsible approach to fostering an international dialogue about ways to build a sustainable peace will include, in part, an acknowledgment of the reality of the phenomenon of border thickening, and a subsequent review of where and how it is unfolding. The accompanying images provide a starting point for this conversation.

Beth Simmons is the Andrea Mitchell University Professor of Law, Political Science, and Business Ethics at the University of Pennsylvania. Simmons is a principal investigator and director of the Borders and Boundaries research team, with expertise in the political theory of borders. **Michael Kenwick** is a Professor in the Department of Political Science, Rutgers University. Kenwick is a principal investigator on the Borders and Boundaries research team, with expertise in border politics and quantitative research methodology. **Dillon Horwitz** is a Master of Architecture candidate at the School of Architecture, Princeton University. On the Borders and Boundaries research team, Horwitz reviewed and analyzed satellite imagery to identify official state infrastructure at international land ports of entry and assisted in the development of satellite-image coding processes.

* Clear satellite imagery is not publicly accessible for all countries within this full time frame, so our analysis is limited for certain states. Images are most consistently available for countries in North America and parts of Europe, while a less frequent visual record of official border structures can be constructed for other regions of the world. High-altitude imagery from the 1990s is sparse, as well as for much of Africa, and yet even in these locations, the available evidence indicates that borders have thickened over time (albeit from a less built-up starting condition as compared to the amount of infrastructure at crossings in other parts of the world).

How can design support humane forms of peace and security?

The desire to connect is often accompanied by the state's even stronger desire to filter who and what is allowed to enter its territory at its international border crossings. Before the passage of the North American Free Trade Agreement in 1995, traffic through the US-Mexican border at Laredo/Nuevo Laredo was moderate. As trade between the countries has grown, supported by an increasing network of connective infrastructure, border security concerns have also risen, a reality which is clearly evidenced in the elaborate systems of inspection and control that have been installed at this busy crossing. The following time-series collection of images from a single crossing demonstrates change over time, highlighting the build up of infrastructure over the course of multiple years.

A series of aerial images of the International Land Port of Entry (border-crossing point) at the US-Mexico border, recording change from 1995 through 2018. Nuevo Laredo, Tamaulipas, Mexico, at left / Laredo, Texas, United States, at right. (All images: US Geological Survey. Source: Google Earth, at 27.5972898, -99.536867)

2016

2017

2018

Observable Indicators of Low Commitment

- Border crossings are devoid of barriers and inspection stations

- Borders lack fences and walls intended to prevent the movement of people or goods

- Border zones lack police, military and border patrol presence

Observable Indicators of High Commitment

- States erect physical infrastructure to filter and block movements at border crossings

- Walls and physical barriers are present between formal border-crossing points

- Border zones have police, military, and border patrol presence

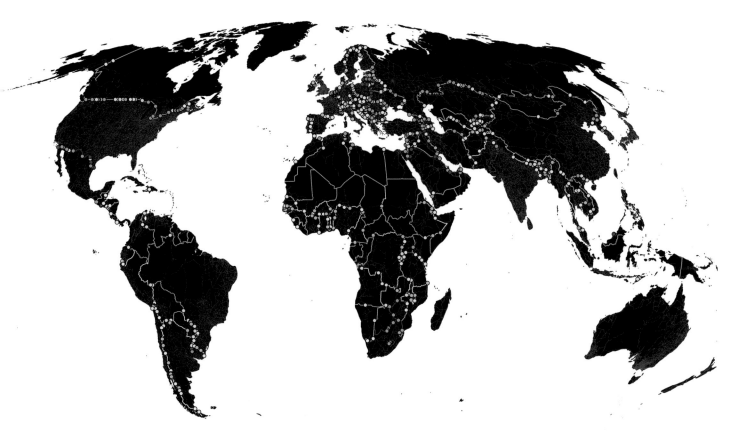

Border Crossings in 2018 This map displays data on border orientation—the state's presence—as of 2018. Every dot represents a border crossing, a place on earth where a major road (represented by the network of thinner gray lines) crosses an international border. The color of the borders reflects the average border orientation score for the two countries.

The clues of a significant global shift in spatial fragmentation are hidden in plain sight. By imposing a digital political map of the world (showing each country's borders) over a global map of major road networks, it is possible to precisely pinpoint land ports of entry worldwide. The team initially took a "top-down" perspective, using Google Earth to zoom in on international border crossings. Using carefully specified criteria, researchers examined the area around precise latitude and longitude coordinates for each land port of entry, recording the presence and number of official buildings, gates or barriers that could potentially block traffic, covered areas indicative of all-weather inspection commitments, and pull-out lanes where detailed state-authorized inspections can take place. Categorically, all of these structural and organizational interventions fall under the label of "border barriers." Our observations were aggregated into a continuum of what we call border orientation, or a state's commitment to the spatial display of capacities to control the terms of penetration of its national borders. These efforts to filter entry range from low (open border orientation, coded green) to moderate (intermediate border orientation, coded yellow) to high (controlling border orientation, coded red).

Teeter-Totter Wall

Designers
Ronald Rael, Virginia San Fratello
(United States)

Collaborators
Colectivo Chopeke (Mexico)

Fabricators
Taller Herrería (Mexico)

Location
Anapra, Chihuahua, Mexico; Sunland Park,
New Mexico, United States

Year 2019

For less than an hour on July 28, 2019, two communities long separated by an imposing steel wall came together to play on oversize teeter-totters spanning the US-Mexico border. Designed in the United States and fabricated in Mexico, the three units were painted high-contrast pink, prompted by the memorials to murdered women in Ciudad Juárez, where there is an ongoing femicide epidemic. Transported to a site just west of the city, the beams were inserted between the border wall's vertical slats by the design-build team, while others attached the banana-style bike seats and handlebars from the US side.

Children and adults on both sides immediately commenced to ride the see-saws. The wall's role as an emblematic fulcrum for US-Mexico relations—whether human relations, politics, or economics—was made literal: actions taken on one side directly impacted those on the other side. In the process, the site was transformed into a space of hope and joy, highlighting the potential of the borderlands as a place where women and children might live with dignity, despite the xenophobia and violence perpetuated by the wall.

The installation, designed by Oakland-based architecture studio Rael San Fratello, realized one of Ronald Rael's Borderwall as Architecture drawings, a project initiated in 2009 that studied alternative wall and cross-border activations—music making on a xylophone wall, binational horseracing along the fence, the growing of greenhouse crops, the conservation of wildlife migration routes—through a series of architectural propositions. The multi-year exploration imagined dismantling the seven hundred miles of border wall and reassembling cross-border economic, cultural, and historical connections.

Sketch for the Teeter-Totter Wall.
Drawing by Rael San Fratello, 2019.

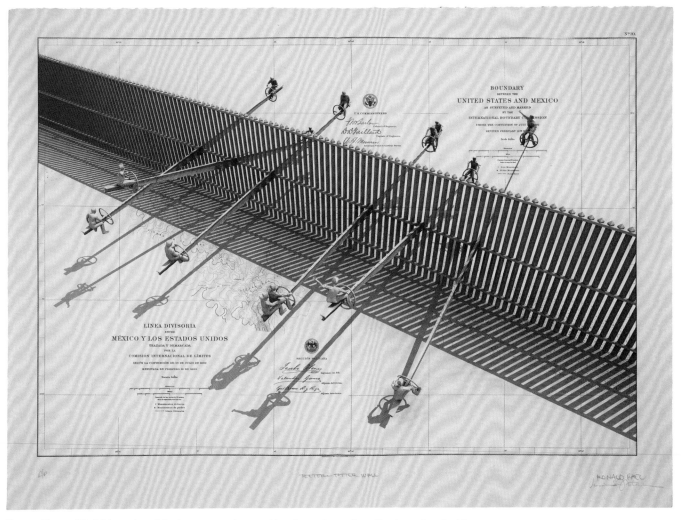

Teeter-Totter Wall/Muro de subibaja copper-plate etching from the project Borderwall as Architecture.
Etching by Rael San Fratello, 2014. Collection of Cooper Hewitt, Smithsonian Design Museum, New York.

Aerial view of teeter-totters installed at the US-Mexico border, with Mexico at left and the United States at right.

Papers, Please

Designer
Lucas Pope (Japan, United States)

Year 2013

Papers, Please digital game was inspired by the numerous immigration document checks Lucas Pope experienced while traveling internationally. Turning a gaming convention on its head, players take on the persona not of an international spy but of a low-level border agent tasked with catching spies, smugglers, and people looking for work or fleeing their home countries without the proper papers. As immigration inspectors for the fictional communist state of Arstotzka, players are asked to control the flow of people crossing the border after a war. Given the power to decide who can enter and who will be turned away or arrested, players experience the complexity of border regimes and negotiate a variety of moral dilemmas.

Pope created the dystopian thriller alone, keeping a public log of his progress over nine months as he alternated between programming the game, making the art, and composing the music. Its design—stark Soviet-style graphics, a highly limited palette, and a plodding, rhythmic anthem of synthesized horns and drumming—has contributed to its immense popularity.

In 2016 a revelatory working paper by the United Nations Educational, Scientific and Cultural Organization (UNESCO) and Gandhi Institute of Education for Peace and Sustainable Development described how digital gaming can build empathy and intergroup awareness—crucial components in conflict resolution and peace education—and game developers are increasingly designing digital games that foster these qualities. The mundane tasks of the *Papers, Please* border agent provide the necessary tools to build empathy in players, Pope has noted, while also confronting the stark realities of immigration inspection.

The *Papers, Please* title screen, animating the game's logo.

How can design support humane forms of peace and security?

stotzka   1982.11.23
istry of Admission
icial Bulletin

pector,

come to your new position at
stin Border Checkpoint.

mp passport ENTRY VISA and
urn documents to entrant.

ry is restricted to
totzkan citizens only.

y all foreigners.

y to Arstotzka.

M.O.A

1/4

Instruction bulletin for the first day on the job as a border agent tasked with controlling the flow of people trying to enter Arstotzka, which just ended a six-year war.

The Truth of Arstotzka reports on events in the game's universe.

A traveler's document is correlated with information from Arstotzka's Ministry of Admissions, assisting the player in deciding who is permitted to enter the country and who is turned away or arrested.

Members of the group Tech Girls for Change work on their safety app Women Fight Back
in Dharavi, India, one of the world's largest informal settlements, 2016.

How can design support humane forms of peace and security?

The Business of Peace

Jason Miklian and Kristian Hoelscher

Even as the world faces conflict and pandemics, and chronic violence pervades the daily lives of billions, an unlikely new partner in building peace has emerged: the private sector. Businesses of all types are becoming peacebuilders, encouraged to do so by their shareholders, the public, and even their own employees.

Nowhere is this promise more visible than in the technology sector. Digital technologies are proliferating as proposed solutions to complex social and political challenges, generating enormous excitement. Peace practitioners hope that these technologies can provide new service delivery or communications efficiencies and circumvent political barriers to enable a global leap forward in reducing poverty and suffering. Technology-based solutions are emerging in all corners of the globe, including everything from violence mapping and social activism in Kenya, to hot-spot policing and anonymous crime-reporting applications across Latin America, and blockchain-based development aid in the Democratic Republic of the Congo.

Of course, technology can have a dark side. Military generals used Facebook to promote and recruit for genocide in Myanmar. Twitter remains an effective dissemination machine for propagandist politicians. Artificial intelligence systems disadvantage minorities, reflecting the biases of their largely white and male designers. And technologies are increasingly securitizing our public spaces, further entrenching the global surveillance state. Pessimists believe that the very concepts of technology and peace are incompatible.

Jason Miklian is a senior researcher in business and peacebuilding at the University of Oslo. **Kristian Hoelscher** is a senior researcher at the Peace Research Institute Oslo.

Peace-Positive Business

- $35 trillion in global investment is now earmarked to be peace and sustainable development positive, particularly through United Nations Sustainable Development Goal 16: Peace, Justice, and Strong Institutions.

- Tens of thousands of companies are signatories to various peace initiatives globally, including twelve thousand signatories to the UN Global Compact.

- Business actions for human rights and peacebuilding have multiplied by over 300 percent since 2016 alone, including philanthropy in conflict communities, conflict-sensitive business practices, and even direct mediation.

The gap between technology's promises and its pitfalls shows that we're right to be skeptical of technology as a cure-all for societal ills. But what if we could harness its good while reducing the likelihood that it will harm? After all, any digital product is at heart a tool, not a destiny—what matters is how we use it. The answer is simple, yet it diverges fundamentally from the way most technologies are designed: What if we valued social impact just as much as scalability and profit?

Currently, most firms developing new technologies—even those specifically created for peace and development—rarely spend valuable design-phase time studying the sociocultural contexts of where and how their products will be deployed. Behemoths like Meta, the company formerly known as Facebook, and Twitter thought little about unintended consequences when they were fledgling startups. Myopic

Gender Classifier	Darker Male	Darker Female	Lighter Male	Lighter Female	Largest Gap
Microsoft	94.0%	79.2%	100%	98.3%	20.8%
FACE++	99.3%	65.5%	99.2%	94.0%	33.8%
IBM	88.0%	65.3%	99.7%	92.9%	34.4%

Gender Shades, a 2017 project by the Algorithmic Justice League, exposed algorithmic bias in facial-recognition software. Faces with darker skin tones and women's faces were less likely to be correctly identified.

"tech-as-panacea" ideologies and the for-profit nature of innovation often consider the global poor as either the product or a promising new market.

This isn't just some esoteric problem in Palo Alto. The next global innovation wave, driven by Silicon Valley but cascading to technology hubs worldwide, could create a societal shift unlike anything humankind has previously experienced. But while the technological capacity may exist to design products that measurably help to build peace, most technology firms still define *peace* in light of their own understanding of what is best for their company—not their users' ideas. Caught between regulators in democratic countries who see them as a threat to democratic speech and dictatorial regimes who use their products to control their subjects, companies like Meta struggle to make themselves compatible with helping the world's most vulnerable.

The consequences are more dire than just another failed app. Outcomes may be much more detrimental: the tracking and imprisonment of human rights defenders, promotional outlets that legitimize subversive propaganda, data mining for corrupt gain. The world's most vulnerable often bear the heaviest burden of such failures, as they are most likely to be the victims of them and least likely to have the resources or ability to escape from technological nets.

Thankfully, the fix may be simple. Start-up companies should ask themselves one question—*How could a nefarious individual use this product maliciously?*—and then ask it again and again, paying attention to issues of power, equity, and justice and to the consequences of failure and enlisting the help of peace and development experts until all conceivable societal loopholes are closed. It's not a foreign concept. Nearly all technology firms do this for hacking and breaching risks—so why not do it for broader social concerns as well? It won't completely prevent unintended consequences, but it will take us far beyond today's models.

What then does socially responsible for-profit technology look like? For most people, it wouldn't look

Digital technology must make positive contributions to society to be considered socially responsible, such as:

- creating civic space (instead of shrinking it)
- promoting equity (instead of exploiting inequality)
- improving access to government and government accountability (instead of limiting them)
- bolstering human rights and democracy (instead of undermining them)
- battling misinformation (instead of amplifying it)
- bringing communities together (instead of compartmentalizing them)
- documenting and highlighting misdeeds (instead of burying them)
- working with the poor as a partner (instead of exploiting them as a product)

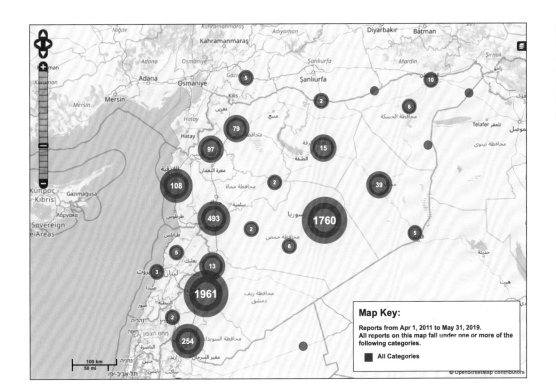

Syria Tracker, a project Initiated in 2011 by Humanitarian Tracker, combines artificial intelligence with crowdsourced information on topics from disease to human rights violations, accessed via an interactive map.

that much different. But for the most vulnerable, it would be a game changer, in ways proven to build peace. It would be good business, too: integrating moral principles into the design stage reduces the risk of hand-wringing later—over whether to work with authoritarians to "access a market," for example—and extinguishes in advance the reputational damage that would have come with such a partnership.

We can help start-ups integrate socially responsible principles into the digital architecture of their products and, more importantly, help innovation communities understand more clearly why the design stage is key for ethical, peace-positive products. Doing so will shape the collective technological future, as the next wave of start-ups engages with the world. A more peaceful world depends on it.

PeaceTech Lab's Open Situation Room Exchange (OSRx) data hub provides critical insight into economic, social, and political conditions on the ground in conflict zones, incorporating digitally available information into customized dashboards for more than 150 countries.

The private sector can contribute to digital peacebuilding through:

- digital communications or mediation tools that support violence prevention and early warning of conflict

- products that combat misinformation from governments or communities

- planning or logistics applications that improve efficiency and effectiveness of delivering development aid and in crisis-response contexts

- platforms that facilitate coordination between civil society and vulnerable communities

- monitoring and communications services that facilitate natural disaster warnings and post-disaster coordination

- tools allowing top-down and bottom-up monitoring of government accountability

- services that facilitate secure and anonymous messaging

CONIFA ▶ p. 84

Regreening Africa
▶ p. 92

How can design address the root causes of conflict?

New World Summits

Jonas Staal

Is it possible that we—politicized citizens of countries fighting the so-called War on Terror—have more in common with those against whom this war is waged than with the criminal states that claim to act in our name? Could we imagine recomposing who or what constitutes Us in the infamous Us-versus-Them narrative that legitimizes this never-ending war? And could we conceptualize new spaces of assembly in which such a recomposition might take place?

These were some of the questions that drove the founding of the New World Summit, an artistic and political organization that began its work in 2012. The group consists of a changing roster of people from the fields of art, architecture, design, political theory, progressive diplomacy, and law, brought together with the aim of creating temporary alternative parliaments for stateless and blacklisted organizations. As of today six summits were held:

Berlin, Germany (2012), Leiden, Netherlands (2012), Kochi, India (2013), Brussels, Belgium (2014), Rojava, northern Syria (2015), Utrecht, Netherlands (2016).

We further initiated the New World Embassy project, which created temporary embassies for stateless and blacklisted organizations in Utrecht (2014) and Oslo (2016). The New World Summit also ran its own school for art and activism, the New World Academy, in

Utrecht in collaboration with BAK, basis voor actuele kunst (2013–16). Last, but not least, the New World Summit created a semipermanent parliament in the Van Abbemuseum in Eindhoven, Netherlands, titled Museum as Parliament (2018–) and a permanent public parliament for the autonomous government of Rojava in northern Syria (2018).

Throughout the various chapters and iterations of the New World Summit, New World Academy, and New World Embassy, around fifty stateless and blacklisted organizations participated in assemblies as political representatives, as ambassadors, or as teachers. These included:

Government of West Papua
Aboriginal Provisional Government
National Democratic Front
    of the Philippines
World Uyghur Congress
Tamil Eelam
Popular Front for the Liberation
    of Palestine
Congress of Nationalities for a Federal Iran
Baluchistan People's Party
Southern Azerbaijan Alliance
Kurdistan National Congress
Republic of Somaliland
National Movement for the
    Liberation Movement of Azawad
Ogaden National Liberation Front
Oromo Liberation Front
Basque Bildu and Sortu coalitions
Popular Unity Candidacy
We Are Here refugee collective

Jonas Staal is a visual artist whose work deals with the relation between art, propaganda, and democracy. He is the founder of the artistic and political organization New World Summit (2012–ongoing).

How can design address the root causes of conflict?

The summits were often planned and programmed in direct dialogue with these organizations, as well as with partners in the fields of progressive diplomacy and law, such as the Unrepresented Nations and Peoples Organization, which represents about forty groups, and the Progress Lawyers Network.

In ten years, the New World Summit has amassed a body of work with a foundation in both art and politics. Here I want to explore three questions: What in the work is artistic? What are its political components? How do the two intersect? I will do this by elaborating on two different terms: *assemblist imaginary* and *organizational morphology*.

Assemblist Imaginaries

The conceptualization of the New World Summit would not have been possible without my membership in Artists in Occupy Amsterdam, a group of about thirty artists and cultural workers. In fall 2011, during the occupation of the Beursplein, we ran a collective tent in which we held lectures and workshops with the goal of exploring and practicing art in the context of a new political movement. Judith Butler has written powerfully about the way popular assembly generates new social morphologies and architectures in the form of general assemblies, alternative media platforms, and centers of care.[1] From my experience in Amsterdam and following Butler's work, I started to articulate the notion of "assemblism" in my own artistic practice, focused on the role of art and culture in contributing to the morphologies of popular power.[2]

It was necessary that the prefigurations of an alternative political horizon that had manifested physically in city squares be translated into new durational infrastructures. We had to move beyond the protest, beyond the model of a counterpower, to enforce a new cultural and political hegemony, to ensure the possibility of egalitarian life forms through alternative emancipatory institutions.[3] Could the spaces of culture—contemporary art spaces, the museum, the theater—be sites where such insurgent institutionalities are composed and tested, turning the cultural infrastructure into not merely a mirror of the world but an incubator for new practices of world making?[4] As our parliaments increasing become dark

New World Embassy – Rojava, City Hall, Oslo, 2016. Produced by KORO Public Art Norway and the Oslo Architecture Triennale.

theaters of war and ultranationalism, could we in turn transform our theaters into parliaments?

These were the questions that drove the first two-day iteration of the New World Summit, held in 2012 in the Sophiensæle theater in Berlin, a venue where the Polish-born German Marxist philosopher, economist, and revolutionary Rosa Luxemburg (1871–1919) once gave speeches. The goal was to invite to this first alternative parliament, commissioned by the 7th Berlin Biennale, all the organizations then on international blacklists, no matter their political or ideological backgrounds.[5] The summit was organized in a circular structure, doubling the semicircle of a traditional parliament. Unlike the latter, where the speaker faces the public, in our assembly part of the public was in front of the speaker and part was behind, making visible how spatial and performative dynamics impact the reception of political discourse. When a political representative sits next to you or in front of you, and stands up to speak, the spatial performativity indicates that they are speaking on *behalf* of you. When such an individual stands up across the room and speaks to you, the spatial performativity suggests that the person is trying to *convince* you, to bring you to their side. Our alternative parliament was aimed at resisting representational exclusion in the War on Terror, but it also sought to explore the morphology and performativity of the concept of the parliament.

The backdrop of the circular structure in Berlin consisted of the flags of all the groups on international lists of terrorist organizations, ordered by color. Together they formed a deeply politicized color scheme, each banner a canvas specific to a history and a struggle. During the summit, seven representatives of blacklisted organizations spoke on behalf of their legal and political struggles. To be blacklisted means that one is not allowed to travel, one's passport is revoked, and all bank assets frozen; one is essentially declared *stateless*. This is deeply perverse, considering that many blacklisted organizations are already stateless, and it creates a double negation: the stateless are declared stateless. Here we touch on the propagandistic dimension of the War on Terror and its use of existential censorship to create an abstract enemy, the terrorist Them—rogue actors whose hatred of democracy and the "West" is so fundamental that they are essentially no longer to be considered human. This narrative enables the parallel legal realities of the War on Terror, from blacklisting to interrogation at so-called black sites to extrajudicial drone killings.[6] But even the War on Terror has its gray zones. Governments often maintain diplomatic channels with blacklisted organizations, meaning that some of their representatives—negotiators—must be permitted to travel internationally; in some cases, these representatives are also the

organization's lawyers. And organizations blacklisted in one country are not necessarily blacklisted in another. We created the New World Summit and its various assemblies by building on these gray zones and legal contradictions.

The organizations that accepted our invitation in no way corresponded to the image of Them constructed through the War on Terror. The assembled Basque, Kurdish, Azawadian, and Filipino representatives in Berlin embodied decades-long liberatory and anticolonial struggle. Rather than espousing the "hatred of democracy" attributed to the figure of the terrorist, they conceived of democracy in radically egalitarian ways. In advocating these principles, such organizations pose a threat to the dominant model of capitalist democracy that the War on Terror propagates through its imperialist, state-building endeavors.[7] One contribution in particular profoundly influenced the development of our organization. Fadile Yildirim was present at the summit representing the Kurdish Women's Movement, which emerged from the Marxist-Leninist Kurdistan Workers' Party (PKK), founded in 1978—an organization that waged armed struggle for decades to create an independent Kurdish nation-state in their historical lands. The Kurdish Women's Movement initiated an internal critique of the male-dominated PKK, arguing that the very idea of the nation-state was structured on a patriarchal, capitalist, and nationalist mentality. The PKK's leader, Abdullah Öcalan, began restructuring the party and its aims in response to this critique from the 1990s onward, replacing the ideal of an independent Kurdish state with a model of *stateless democracy*—a liberation of democracy from the construct of the state.[8] It was through our contact with Yildirim that we began to understand the potential of our own organization as a *stateless parliament* for stateless democracies.

In 2012 the New World Summit was still very much a "project," in the way artists make projects, exploring specific themes then moving on. This process risked becoming exploitive, as struggles are not to be thematized: one must engage them through lifelong commitment and friendship. At the first assembly, a clear expectation became manifest; the representatives present began planning the next summit with us. It was clear that this meeting of alternate political imaginaries, of conflicting democracies that challenged the dominance of the Us-versus-Them dichotomy, was beginning to author itself. This meant that we needed to shift toward organization: a structural engagement demanded an *organizational art* rather than an assemblist art.[9] Here we began to move from the field of assemblist imaginary into that of organizational morphology.

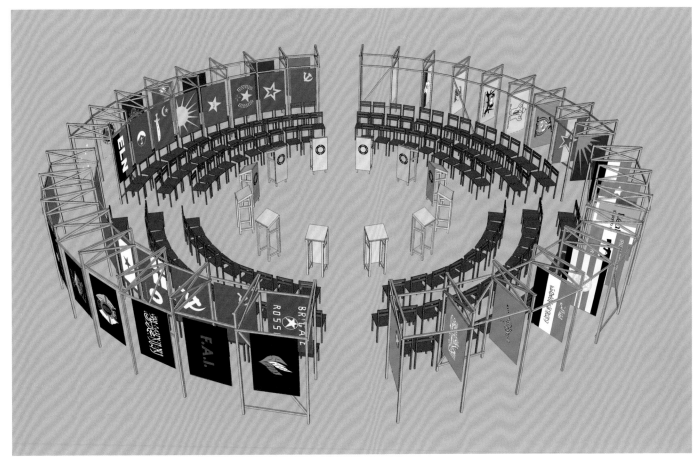

Study sketch of New World Summit – Berlin, 2012.
Drawing by Paul Kuipers and Jonas Staal.

Organizational Morphologies

As Sven Lütticken has argued, to enable the emancipatory dimensions of performance, we need to address preformations: the preexisting infrastructures, narratives, and imaginaries that structure the conditions of performance.[10] A lot of the work of the New World Summit was invested in the preformation of the parliament and the way its morphologies—its architecture, visual, and design components—might shape the assembly or collective. The 4th New World Summit, held at the Royal Flemish Theatre in Brussels in 2014 and titled Stateless States, involved about twenty representatives of stateless and blacklisted organizations and aimed to performatively narrate history according to resistance movements: a mapping of the world not as it is given, structured on colonial lines of division, but rather as a world in struggle, in transformation. It was necessary to recompose the preformed parliament and the preformed world map in response to the insurgent histories and forms of popular power represented by the organizations we worked with.

The oval parliament in Brussels shared some of the spatial performativity of the circular summit in Berlin, with political representatives sitting between groups of the public. But in Brussels the flags were replaced by maps, each of which we developed with the political organization in question to depict its claim to self-determination. In some cases, as in the unrecognized states of Somaliland or Baluchistan, these took relatively traditional forms, with a clearly delineated territorial boundary and a national flag. Others depicted more complex propositions, like the National Democratic Front of the Philippines, which essentially governs a parallel state through its guerrilla army and therefore simply used the conventional territorial depiction of the Philippines but with a different flag. The Kurdish Women's Movement went even further, refusing to depict a claim to territory. Instead it proposed an ideological map in which its political project of stateless democracy was elaborated (p. 80). Some maps illustrated the historical travels of a people, others its principles or political practice. In this way the traditional understanding of the map was subverted, as the concept was harnessed to represent various dimensions of struggle—ideological as well as territorial. As our conception of the world shifted, so did the tools and forms we used to depict it.

An important morphological component—the bench—was introduced at the Brussels summit. In previous assemblies, chairs and stools had been used

New World Summit – Berlin, Sophiensæle theater, 2012.
Produced by the Berlin Biennale.

to seat the representatives and the public, but it became clear to me that these components could not be regarded as neutral. A chair can only be empty or full, and when it is empty it still consumes our attention: who is absent? The chair is hyper-individuated; it leaves no room for negotiation about its use, like a liberal sovereign. The bench, on the other hand—which has its own utopian history[11]—is full whether one person sits on it or ten. Its fullness is also negotiable; users can choose to limit their own "private" space by making room for an additional person. With benches there is ongoing democratic deliberation about the way we use and share space, whereas in the case of the chair the division of space preexists the gathering.

This might seem like a minor component of the event, but thinking through the relationship between preformation and performance sheds light on the way visual morphologies shape the possibility of collectivity and shared narratives. It is not just what we say but where and with whom we say it, and through which geometries and spatial configurations. Ideology has a form, and form in turn contributes to particular ideological narratives.[12] For the same reason, lighting at the summit was divided equally between the speaker and the public, enabling the possibility that roles and agencies might shift between representative and the

represented. And there are also the mathematics of egalitarianism to take into account. How many bodies can share a space before the people on the outer edges start to feel that they are not part of a crowd but are instead looking at one? In our experience—having tested various geometries, from circle to oval to triangle—the limit for a sense of inclusion is around 250. Beyond that, those on the fringes begin to perceive the assembly unfolding before them almost as a mediation, a projection, and not an event—a *present*—to which they are contributing.

While the circular and oval shapes of the Berlin and Brussels summits most immediately generate a sense of communality, they are also the most exclusive. For those who are part of a circle from the beginning, the sense of shared embodiment is heightened to the extreme, but those arriving at a circle that is already formed experience a sense of exclusion, a wall of bodies rather than a parliament of bodies.[13] At the three-day 6th New World Summit, held in 2016 in the main hall of Utrecht University, we attempted to challenge the circular morphology dominant in various of our earlier projects. The Union of Utrecht, generally regarded as a historical milestone in the formation of the Dutch state, was signed in this hall in 1579. Titled Stateless Democracy, our summit gathered around twenty blacklisted, stateless,

How can design address the root causes of conflict?

and undocumented organizations to revisit the formation of the modern nation-state. What other life forms might have been possible, and what remain possible today? We asked these questions in a parliament structured by intersecting triangles stretched over the long hall, creating a fragmented and open-ended assembly that lacked the sense of immediate unification that our circular and oval spaces generated. Over the three days, the area operated much more like a collective public space, a mutable *space in the making* for *people in the making*. Paradoxically, the spatial organizations we associate most directly with collectivity are not necessarily those that enable genuinely collective processes.

Parliament as a Public Space

In the New World Summit, organizational morphology relates as much to the visual forms of the parliament as to those that emerge through the organizational dynamics of the assembly itself. The alternative parliaments we create are not the end form but an intermediate one, between redefining preformations and enabling transformative collective performance. This has manifested most clearly in a project undertaken in Rojava, an autonomous region in northern Syria. (The name Rojava, meaning "west," refers to western Kurdistan.) Our

dialogue with the Kurdish revolutionary movement continued throughout the various chapters of the New World Summit, leading to an invitation to my team to visit the region in late 2014, two years after it declared itself independent from Bashar al-Assad's regime in Syria.

During these and subsequent visits, the region was under attack by the Islamic State and, from 2018 onward, by Turkey, under Recep Tayyip Erdoğan. Nonetheless, the autonomous government had been able to develop its model of stateless democracy to an impressive extent. Local communes are the foundation of self-governance, and while municipal, cantonal, and transcantonal coordination structures were introduced, the communes hold the largest stake in executive power. The commune concept essentially reversed the conventional paradigm of institutional agency: the smaller the political component, the more executive power it has. The decades-long struggle waged by the women's movement clearly influenced Rojavan models of governance: each organization was co-chaired by a woman and a man, and quotas of 40 percent were instituted to ensure women's participation in all areas of public life. Women have their own armed forces—the Women's Protection Units (YPJ)—as well as their own universities, including the Star Academy, which taught jineology, or the "science of women."[14]

Amina Osse, co-chair of the Committee of Foreign Affairs of Rojava, proposed the development of a new

New World Summit – Brussels, Royal Flemish Theatre, 2014.
Produced by the Royal Flemish Theatre (KVS).

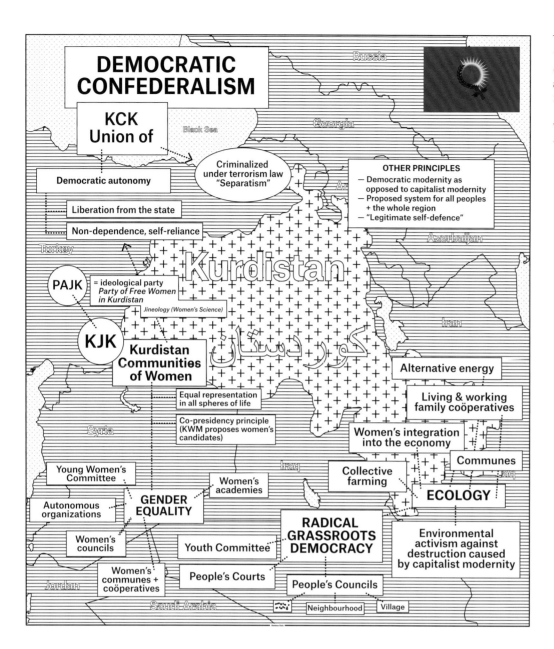

The values of democratic confederalism are laid over a map of the territory of Kurdistan in a document made for New World Summit – Brussels, 2014. Diagram by Dilar Dirik of the Kurdish Women's Movement, Remco van Bladel, and Jonas Staal.

parliament for the region. Most of the new revolutionary institutions operated in the modernist buildings of the former Assad regime, but Osse aimed to translate the revolutionary ideology of her movement in a new revolutionary architecture. This new parliament, though permanent, would always be stateless, she said, as Rojava rejected the model of the state altogether. And, Osse insisted, it would be a public parliament, not a separate space for elite representatives but a space of collective self-representation. From 2015 to 2018 we worked to create the public dome and surrounding park that would become known locally as the People's Parliament of Rojava. Combining the morphologies of the Berlin and the Utrecht parliaments, its circular central space is surrounded by a fragmented dome, on whose pillars the trilingual principles of the political project of stateless democracy are painted, ranging from democratic confederalism to gender equality to communal economy. The rooftop, formed by fragments of local flags depicting stars and suns, is a hybrid

"ideological planetarium." The parliament, inaugurated in April 2018, is a sculpture—a monument depicting the symbols and principles that shaped a new political paradigm—but it is simultaneously a concrete space of day-to-day assembly: a space between artistic imagination and political practice.

From Fadile Yildirim to Amina Osse, the New World Summit came full circle—but not a closed circle. Just like the fragmented dome of the Rojavan parliament, it is a circle with various break lines and disruptions, and one that aims not to institute a world in the singular but rather a world of many worlds.[15] Our morphologies do not presume to be final, but are dialogical, shaped between the imaginaries of art and of revolutionary politics. They are coordinates of a possible world, as real as we imagine it to be and as real as we are prepared collectively to act it into being.

1   For example, Butler discusses the assembly as "assemblage" and also speaks of the "theatrical" dimension of the assembly and the "morphology" of its social forms. Judith Butler, *Notes towards a Performative Theory of Assembly* (Cambridge, MA: Harvard University Press, 2015), 68, 85, 87.

2   For more on this concept, see Jonas Staal, "Assemblism," *e-flux journal*, no. 80 (March 2017). Whereas the term *morphology* has significance today in domains as varied as linguistics, biology, and mathematics, Johann Wolfgang von Goethe is considered to have defined the term in relation to the study of plants, explaining it as "the science of form [*Gestalt*], formation [*Bildung*], and transformation [*Umbildung*] of organic bodies." See Johannes Grave, "Ideal and History: Johann Wolfgang Goethe's Collection of Prints and Drawings," *Artibus et Historiae* 27, no. 53 (January 2006): 183.

3   "Life forms" is here to be read as "forms of life," meaning egalitarian political, economic, and cultural models of collective living, and in the broader sense of recognizing our stake in interdependent ecologies that include other-than-human actors, other "life forms."

4   The notion of world making follows the work of Upton Sinclair. Addressing artists in revolution, he expressed the wish that their "creative gift shall not be content to make art works, but shall at the same time make a world; shall make new souls, moved by a new ideal of fellowship, a new impulse of love, and faith—and not merely hope, but determination." Sinclair, *Mammonart* (San Diego: Simon Publications, 2003), 386.

5   At the 7th Berlin Biennale, curated by Artur Żmijewski and Joanna Warsza, various other (conflicting) artist organizations also came into being, ranging from Yael Bartana's—until then fictional—Jewish Renaissance Movement to the neocolonial gentrification organization Institute for Human Activities, founded by Renzo Martens.

6   For an extensive mapping of the parallel legal realities of the War on Terror, see Trevor Paglen, *Blank Spots on the Map: The Dark Geography of the Pentagon's Secret World* (London: New American Library, 2010).

7   Suthaharan Nadarajah, "From Jaffna to Geneva: National Liberation amid Globalizing Liberal Order," lecture delivered at the 4th New World Summit, Brussels, September 20, 2014; https://vimeo.com/121240853.

8   Abdullah Öcalan, *The Political Thought of Abdullah Öcalan: Kurdistan, Women's Revolution and Democratic Confederalism* (London: Pluto, 2017). For more on this subject, see Dilar Dirik, Renée In der Maur, and Jonas Staal, eds., *New World Academy Reader #5: Stateless Democracy* (Utrecht: BAK, basis voor actuele kunst, 2015).

9   Developing "organizational art" in practice led to the first Artist Organisations International, which I created together with curator Joanna Warsza and dramaturge Florian Malzacher, gathering twenty organizations formed and led by artists at HAU Hebbel am Ufer, Berlin, January 9–11, 2015. See www.artistorganisationsinternational.org.

10   Sven Lütticken, "Performing Preformations: Elements for a Historical Formalism," *e-flux journal*, no. 110 (June 2020).

11   See Francis Cape, *We Sit Together: Utopian Benches from the Shakers to the Separatists of Zoar* (New York: Princeton Architectural Press, 2013).

12   See Jonas Staal, "IDEOLOGY = FORM," *e-flux journal,* no. 69 (January 2016).

13   This is a reference to Paul B. Preciado's project The Parliament of Bodies, initiated at documenta 14, Athens, 2017.

14   See Gönül Kaya, "Why Jineology? Re-Constructing the Sciences Towards a Communal and Free Life," *New World Academy Reader #5*, 83–95.

15   This is a reference to the famous slogan of the Zapatistas. See *Zapatista Encuentro: Documents from the First Intercontinental Encounter for Humanity and against Neoliberalism* (New York: Seven Stories, 1998), 29–30.

New World Summit – Rojava

Designers
Democratic Self-Administration of Rojava (West Kurdistan), Studio Jonas Staal (Netherlands)

Concept
Sheruan Hassan, Amina Osse, Democratic Union Party (Rojava/West Kurdistan); Jonas Staal, Studio Jonas Staal (Netherlands)

Project Team
Younes Bouadi, Renée In der Maur (Studio Jonas Staal coordinators); Zana Muhammad (local project coordinator); Paul Kuipers (architect); Remco van Bladel (graphic designer); Hussein Adam, Dejle Hamo (urban planners); Tamer Kandal, Newzad Mohammed, Ibrahim Sado, Zozan Hassan (construction and development coordinators); Ruben Hamelink, Michiel Landeweerd, Rojava Film Commune (filmmakers); Ernie Buts (photographer); Saeed Seevan (translator); Cihad Hammy (subtitler); Suzie Hermán (delegation host)

Location Dêrik, Canton Cizîrê, Rojava

Years 2014–18

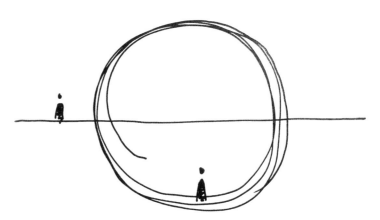

Visual study of the new public parliament for Rojava. Drawing by Jonas Staal, 2015. Collection Migros Museum, Zurich.

The artistic-political organization New World Summit, founded by the Rotterdam-based artist Jonas Staal, develops parliaments with and for stateless people, autonomist groups, and blacklisted political organizations. Six summits have been held so far. The fifth, New World Summit – Rojava, included the design and construction of a new public parliament building for Rojava (a self-governing region in northern Syria) as well as an international summit in 2015 that brought together representatives from the region with members of other stateless and progressive political groups.

In 2012, during the civil war in Syria, Kurdish revolutionaries and Assyrian, Arab, and other peoples of the region declared the autonomy of Rojava, or West Kurdistan, and founded the Democratic Self-Administration of Rojava. This alliance (now known as the Autonomous Administration of North and East Syria) practices "stateless democracy," a system based on self-governance, gender equality, a communal economy, secularism, and cultural diversity—values that inspired the design of the parliament building. Its circular form emphasizes collective self-representation, pillars reinforce the key concepts of Rojava's social contract in three languages, and hand-painted flags of various social and political groups hang above the assembly space. The structure embodies the foundational values of the new democracy both symbolically and spatially while providing a physical form in which its ideals may be brought to life. The Rojava project reimagines the world by embracing a democratic paradigm that allows power and resources to be shared, inviting artists, designers, and other citizens to contribute their creativity in making this new world a reality, in the same way Rojava has made its new stateless democracy a reality for its people.

Amina Osse (center) of the Rojavan Committee of Foreign Affairs and the co-mayors of Dêrik inaugurate the new public parliament for Rojava, 2018. Design by the Democratic Self-Administration of Rojava and Studio Jonas Staal.

Aerial view of the public parliament in Dêrik, Rojava, 2018. Design by the Democratic Self-Administration of Rojava and Studio Jonas Staal.

CONIFA

Organizers
Per-Anders Blind (founder and president, Sweden), Francesco Zema (global director for No Limits Initiatives, Italy), Loïck Blouet (cultural director, France), Alejandra Calderon (Spain and United States), Confederation of Independent Football Associations

Teams*
Africa: Barawa, Barotseland, Biafra, Chagos Islands, Kabylia, Matabeleland, Somaliland, Western Sahara, Yoruba, Zanzibar; Asia: Arameans Suryoye, East Turkistan, Karen, Kurdistan, Lezghian, Panjab, Rohingya, Ryukyu, Tamil Eelam, Tibet, United Koreans in Japan, Western Papua; Europe: Abkhazia, Artsakh, Chameria, Cornwall, County of Nice, Délvidék, Donetsk People's Republic, Elba Island, Ellan Vannin, Felvidék, Franconia, Greenland, Jersey, Kárpátalja, Lazistan, Luhansk People's Republic, Monaco, Northern Cyprus, Occitania, Padania, Raetia, Romani People, Sápmi, Sardinia, Skåneland, South Ossetia, Székely Land, Two Sicilies, Western Armenia, Yorkshire; North America: Cascadia, Québec, Asociación Nationale de Balompié Mexicano, Kuskatan; Oceania: Australian First Nations Mariya, Hawai'i, Kiribati, Tuvalu; South America: Mapuche, Rapa Nui (✳ Dynamic list continues to evolve and includes current and former teams.)

Years 2013–present

Football kept Per-Anders Blind alive as he faced daily bullying and abuse growing up in Sweden, where he was targeted for being Sámi, a group Indigenous to the European Arctic region. In 2013—combining his business acumen with his lifelong affinity for sports and his identification with minorities—he formed the Confederation of Independent Football Associations (CONIFA), an alternative global football federation for minority groups, stateless people, and states unaffiliated with FIFA, soccer's existing global governing body.

The second-largest soccer organization in the world, CONIFA, with around sixty teams, represents more than 675 million people. Every two years, six Continental Championship tournaments lead to a World Football Cup the following year. The member teams represent a range of affiliations, from bioregions such as Cascadia which spans the US and Canada border, to autonomous regions such as Kurdistan in Iraq, and self-declared independent states like Abkhazia within Georgia.

Dedicated to inclusion, CONIFA has since introduced tournaments for women, those with mixed abilities, and youth, along with other supporting programs. The games are festive events, attracting enthusiastic local and diaspora fans who wave flags and sing team anthems. Players display badges laden with symbolic imagery on their jerseys. While the transnational nonprofit organization remains politically neutral, the league provides opportunities for participants to elevate their causes and represent themselves and their people on an international stage, building bridges through friendship, culture, and sport. Each player essentially acts as an ambassador for their people.

CONIFA Team Logos (from left to right), Australian First Nations Mariya (Australia), Sahrawi Football Federation (Western Sahara), Tibetan National Sports Association (Tibet), Rapa Nui (Easter Island), Cascadia Association Football Federation (United States, Canada), and FA Sápmi (Lapland region).

How can design address the root causes of conflict?

Members of the Tamil Eelam and Darfur United (former CONIFA team) teams at the first CONIFA World Football Cup, Östersund, Sweden, 2014. Darfur United's chant was "Humanity united."

A fan of the Football Federation of Abkhazia shows her pride at the CONIFA World Football Cup in the self-governing state of Abkhazia (Georgia), 2016.

Women's team of the US-based Karen Football Association, which was formed to provide a platform for the struggles of the Karen ethnic group in Myanmar, play in San Diego, California, 2020.

A New Climate Change Council

Michael Adlerstein

The United Nations Security Council, one of the six principal organs of the UN, is charged with maintaining international peace. The only UN body with the authority to issue binding resolutions on member states, it has earned a reputation as "the most important room in the world." The Security Council's membership, its negotiation process, its voting structure, and its physical spaces were conceived immediately after World War II and were designed specifically to prevent the outbreak of another, similar global conflict. Now, in a very different world—with a transformed political landscape, a globalized economy, and ever-evolving forms of conflict—there have been calls to reshape the Security Council for the twenty-first century. As consideration is given to the creation of a peace-guarding body designed to meet our current challenges, it may be instructive to look back at the origins of the Security Council model.

Talking Peace

After centuries of continuous and costly conflict between countries, colonies, city-states, and tribes beginning in ancient times, the twentieth century

saw the development of new military technology and the capability of waging unprecedentedly devastating warfare. In 1914 a war between a few European countries expanded to include most of the world, killing many millions of soldiers and civilians. After the Treaty of Versailles was signed, bringing World War I to an end, the participants decided that a sanctuary for discussion was needed, a forum for mitigating future conflict. The League of Nations was founded in 1920. Its purpose was to avoid another world war.

Unfortunately, within twenty years the League failed, and the atrocities of World War II surpassed those of World War I. History informs us that what led the world back to war was the League's failure to allow peace-seeking nations to focus their discussions on peace. Its democratic voting method—all member nations had an equal vote—encouraged the creation of multiple competing factions on strategic issues and thus made it difficult to arrive at a majority decision, even on the contentious matter of war. Winston Churchill, prime minister of the United Kingdom, and Franklin D. Roosevelt, president of the United States, envisioned a new institution that might better manage the myriad complexities of global diplomacy and, most importantly, avoid future wars. Out of the ashes of the League of Nations, the United Nations was born on October 24, 1945.

With insight gained from past failure, the designers of the United Nations inserted a nondemocratic structure into the mix. Critical issues—such as natural disasters, food and economic development,

Michael Adlerstein is a preservation architect at Columbia University's Graduate School of Architecture and a fellow of the American Institute of Architects. As Assistant Secretary-General of the United Nations, he successfully managed its eight-year renovation before stepping down in 2017.

How can design address the root causes of conflict?

children's and women's rights, control of the oceans and poles—and all other topics that did not threaten imminent multi-state violence, would be decided upon by the General Assembly, made up of all member states, and its principal organs. Matters of war and military intervention, however, were to be discussed within a much smaller subset of nations: the Security Council.

The Security Council would ultimately consist of fifteen countries, five of which are permanent members. The permanent members—China, France, the Russian Federation, the United Kingdom, and the United States—have one vote each, plus the authority to veto any Security Council resolution. The remaining ten members, elected on a regional basis to serve a term of two years, have one vote each but no veto authority. All members serve in turn as the president of the council on a one-month rotation. When a conflict is brought to the Security Council, the disputing parties must state their case and defend their interests in a controlled exchange of formal statements. It is a rigid process, and once it is entered upon neither party can exit or initiate armed conflict without the consent of the group. The avoidance of armed conflict is the sole purpose of the Security Council, and it is the key to the negotiating process.

Designing an Architecture for Peace

The UN Headquarters complex in New York originally consisted of three main structures: the General Assembly, the Secretariat, and the Conference buildings. It was designed to serve its member state delegations, the organization's administrative staff, numerous journalists, and a million visitors each year. Completed in 1952, the complex sits on seventeen acres of land considered international territory and exempt from local laws.

More than fifty years later, after decades of growth, underfunded maintenance, and heavy use, the UN Headquarters needed a major upgrade. To counter aging and potentially unsafe infrastructure, an ambitious eight-year renovation program, the Capital Master Plan (CMP), commenced in 2007. I was asked by Secretary-General Ban Ki-moon to lead that program.

The General Assembly building—the world's parliament—is the spiritual and architectural hub of the UN complex and occupies the center of the site. It contains a variety of small, medium, and large conference rooms and is dominated by the General Assembly Hall. Although a team of a dozen architects from all over the world cooperated on the UN's master plan, Oscar Niemeyer (1907–2012) of Brazil is given primary credit for the design of the General Assembly building, which

View from the East River of the original United Nations Headquarters complex in New York (left to right): Secretariat, Conference, and General Assembly buildings, c. 1950s.

has the graceful curves and simplicity of the 1940s modern movement that Niemeyer later brought to Brasília. The CMP fully restored the elegant midcentury features of the General Assembly Hall's rooms. The art and the original desks and seating were restored, though the podium looks unchanged, and all the rooms were upgraded with state-of-the-art heating, air conditioning, electronics, and communications and security systems. The entire compound was also structurally reinforced to protect its occupants from an explosive blast.

The tall, very photogenic high-rise building facing east–west on First Avenue near Forty-Second Street is the Secretariat building, which provides the majority of the office space for the secretary-general's staff. It is the elegant landmark of the UN. The Swiss-born, France-based architect Charles-Édouard Jeanneret (1887–1965), known as Le Corbusier, is given credit for its design. It was one of the earliest all-glass curtain-wall buildings in the United States and an architectural landmark that generated thousands of copies. Its beautiful glass and aluminum exteriors were fully restored. Upon the completion of the CMP, the leadership of the various UN departments and agencies, which had been previously spread all over midtown Manhattan, was returned to totally redesigned modern open-office floors in the Secretariat building, and the secretary-general's office moved back into restored spaces on the top floors.

The Conference building, its large glass walls facing the East River, is the least visible from First Avenue. It houses the Security Council Chamber, the Economic and Social Council Chamber, and the Trusteeship Council Chamber, along with the Delegates Lounge, often referred to as the "fourth chamber," as lengthy negotiations often extend into the evenings there. With a collection of conference rooms of various sizes supporting the various council chambers, this building is the main workplace for UN member states, and multiple General Assembly committees meet there every day. In 1948 the UN offered several member states the role of designing and decorating some of the interiors: Norway selected the Security Council Chamber, Denmark the Trusteeship Council Chamber, Sweden the Economic and Social Council Chamber, and Germany the Security Council Lounge. Expanding the negotiating facilities, a fourth floor was added to the building in the 1970s to accommodate the Delegates Dining Room.

Observing the Architecture of Negotiation

For most visitors, the Security Council Chamber *is* the Security Council. The large space designed by Norwegian architect Arnstein Arneberg (1882–1961) features a mural by Norwegian artist Per Krohg (1889–1965), beautiful

The United Nations Headquarters telephone switchboard was emblematic of the complex's outdated infrastructure, which was in desperate need of upgrading.

wall coverings, and the famous horseshoe-shaped table. The Security Council spaces encompass the Chamber plus a suite of rooms connected to it. Over the years, ambassadors and staff have created traditions and functions for each of the rooms, and in planning the renovations we interviewed past and present users of these spaces to establish which elements were fixed and, conversely, where we had flexibility for functional improvements. We thoroughly documented every surface and material in order to redesign the rooms to meet modern codes of lighting, heating, air conditioning, acoustics, accessibility, fire safety, and security, as well as the many new technological requirements of our electronic age.

Strategic dispute resolution within a government is a complicated task. Resolving disputes *between* governments, where the delegations represent distinctly different cultures and circumstances, is even more complex. In the Security Council, negotiation is the only path to resolution. The disputing parties begin with positioning statements that lay out their hopes and fears. What follows is a delicate and nuanced process of trust building that requires patience and a focus on incremental progress. The process may take months or years, with the world watching and holding to account the party that breaks trust and resorts to violence. Since the five permanent members of the Security Council retain veto power, to ensure that your plan gets approved it is necessary to convince all parties to vote yes. Trial and error has shown that a highly structured negotiation process is required to achieve this level of consensus. Although this process is not explicitly documented in UN policies, it is thoroughly understood by the users and managers of the Chamber.

I was asked to execute a full restoration of the Chamber but to change its appearance as little as possible and, most emphatically, not to alter the character-defining features for which it is known and respected worldwide. After documenting the space, we removed artworks, tables, chairs, and other distinctive elements for restoration. We brought the mural to our art conservator, who removed seven decades of nicotine and other airborne ills. The original tables and seats were restored, reupholstered, and cleaned. Even the leather desk blotters are the same (our recommendation to build in electronic tablets was rejected). Voting is still done manually, literally by raising a hand.

The Security Council negotiation process is separated into four rooms: the Chamber, the Consultation Room, the Staff Lounge, and the Caucus Room. Each has evolved over time, and there were modest changes in the CMP restoration, but their location, decoration, and functionality have generally remained unchanged. The Chamber is the core and most essential room of the suite. It is large, seating several hundred people. The entire space focuses on the horseshoe-shaped table at which the twenty or so participants sit in blue chairs with armrests, along with their approximately eighty advisors, also on blue chairs but without armrests. Hundreds of red chairs are organized auditorium-style on three sides of the horseshoe, for ambassadors from neighboring countries, global advisors, scholars, geographers, historians, and other guests and political leaders. There are also red chairs toward the back of the room for members of the press, who are admitted when deemed appropriate, and for visitors to the UN when there are no meetings scheduled. Overlooking the Chamber on the floor above, on the north and south sides of the room, are glass-walled booths reserved for interpreters. Every seat in the room has an earphone through which attendees may hear the proceedings translated into their chosen language. UN interpreters are highly skilled translators who have studied the language of diplomacy and understand its subtleties. They translate the proceedings into the six official languages of the UN; two extra booths are staffed for

The cloth wall covering in the renovated Security Council Chamber features hearts symbolizing compassion, grain for feeding the hungry, and anchors for stability. The original Norwegian mill remade the fabric exactly matching the original, 2015.

translation into additional languages as needed. Only the twenty or so key participants seated at the table in the blue chairs have microphones and are invited to speak. The members of the council are seated alphabetically. Every person speaking in the Chamber during a session is recorded by audio and video, and the recordings and transcriptions are published and archived.

During the initial construction of the Security Council Chamber, the iconic horseshoe-shaped table was mocked up to determine its exact shape prior to cabinet fabrication, c. 1950s.

These are the official records; the general understanding is that "if it isn't recorded, it wasn't said."

When a session is scheduled, which can happen at all hours on any day, all fifteen Security Council member states are represented in their assigned seats. The Council president and the secretary-general, or their representatives, are seated at the head of the horseshoe-shaped table, the two disputing parties are seated opposite the head, at the two ends of the horseshoe, and the fifteen members are seated alphabetically, with their four advisors behind them on blue chairs. Other invited participants are in their red chairs. If it is a closed meeting, as most are, no press or other guests are invited; the meeting is documented by cameras, and recordings are sometimes made partially or fully available later. Conflicts, new or old, that are accepted for a Security Council hearing are eventually discussed in a publicly announced session, which might be closed. The disputing member states make opening statements, which are followed by comments by the participating member states. These opening statements, each about five to fifteen minutes long, are mainly for domestic consumption: the head of state or spokesperson is speaking to their domestic audience and establishing their national political position (which may lead into a second or third round of formal

statements). Following the open sessions and held the same day or night or weeks later, are closed sessions, often in the Consultation Room.

This room, adjacent to the Security Council Chamber, is totally different in character. It is a relatively small space with a smaller horseshoe-shaped table and with seating for very few advisors and no observers or press. It is not a normal UN meeting room; it is almost never open to the public or the press, nor are any recordings made of the proceedings. Everything said in the Consultation Room is confidential, and no video or audio recording is allowed. Discussions continue freely, and, except where there are leaks, what is said is not binding except between the participants. If an agreement is reached, the parties might decide to announce it publicly, or they might agree to hold the announcement. This room is designed for the resolution of global crises without public oversight. Negotiations can go on for hours or years, but they generally do lead to some sort of understanding.

Achieving this kind of closure can require significant time, and the discussions may be quite informal. The Staff Lounge plays a significant role in the less formal aspects of global negotiation, as a space in which ambassadors and their representatives may arrange to meet at any hour. Staffers can meet

The Security Council Chamber before renovation, 2010. In the sunken area at the center of the deliberation table, précis writers recorded meetings in real time.

How can design address the root causes of conflict?

there in quiet, out of the hearing of others, to test the waters, to seek common ground on issues where the head of the delegation might not want to appear flexible. The Staff Lounge also hosts a wide variety of social events. Food and drink, which are discouraged in the Chamber and the Consultation Room for cleanliness, are allowed there. The Lounge hosts breakfast and lunch meetings, holiday celebrations, and other parties and social events. These offer opportunities for informal negotiation. While it will never be known exactly how many Security Council issues have been resolved by informal discussion in the Lounge (for obvious reasons), it is certainly a fruitful and productive venue.

The last room in the Security Council suite is the Caucus Room. This is the smallest of the four rooms and the least documented. It is only a few hundred feet square, and the furniture is very sparse: a small conference table seating about eight, plus several single chairs lining the side walls. It has almost no decoration. Its purpose is to host one-on-one meetings between disputing heads of state or ambassadors, sometimes without the secretary-general or anyone else in attendance. It is a room in which to seal a deal worked out in the other three rooms or to find the least bad solution between the two parties.

A New Climate Change Chamber

In the twenty-first century, the world's nations are facing an unprecedented new set of challenges. Of all the emerging threats to peace, those generated by climate change may be the most formidable. Urgent global crises are multiplying at a dizzying pace, among them an increasing number of refugees, rising sea levels, diminished biodiversity, and species extinction. Their impact is such that they have begun to challenge the effectiveness of the Security Council. It is evident that problems this complex may not be resolvable among a select group of fifteen member states; the Security Council was not designed to manage such borderless, civilization-threatening issues. Currently, these new threats are discussed by all member countries at convenings of the UN Framework Convention on Climate Change. The search for common, constructive, and sustainable solutions—a project requiring ever greater levels of cooperation and coordination—might diminish our eagerness for warfare and conquest. In working to reduce our environmental impact and ensure our future existence on Earth, perhaps we will come to see all the planet's people as partners. If so, a new Climate Change Chamber could replace the Security Council as the "most important room in the world."

The Security Council Chamber on testing day post-renovation, 2015. The digital tablets were ultimately vetoed and replaced with more traditional ceiling-mounted projection screens.

Regreening Africa

Designers
Muhammad Nabi Ahmad, Benard Onkwareh, Tor-Gunnar Vagen, Leigh Winowiecki with Susan Chomba, Mieke Bourne, World Agroforestry (Kenya)

Collaborators
CARE International, Catholic Relief Services, Oxfam, World Vision (international), Sahel Eco (Mali)

Locations
Ethiopia, Ghana, Kenya, Mali, Niger, Rwanda, Senegal, Somalia

Years 2017–22

The Regreening Africa mobile app helps farmers and extension agents collect data on key indicators of land restoration using easily identifiable icons. Clockwise from top left: Community, Fodder, Tree planting, Tree produces leafy vegetables, Containerized seedling production, Tree coppicing (new shoot regeneration).

More than 80 percent of people living in sub-Saharan Africa are dependent on land for their livelihood, yet almost half of the land, particularly in the drylands, is environmentally degraded. Soil erosion, deforestation, and biodiversity loss have reduced the land's capacity to protect against drought or storms and to deliver the soil nutrients necessary for growing food and fodder. This massive loss of productive land increases competition for dwindling resources, which in turn leads to migration and conflict.

To meet this urgent challenge, World Agroforestry initiated its ambitious Regreening Africa project, which aims to reverse land degradation across eight African countries in five years. One element of this project is a mobile phone app designed to harness the knowledge and experience of local farmers and augment it through scientific methods. Acting as citizen-scientists, farmers use the app to record their regreening and restoration efforts. The collected data is analyzed to optimize land-restoration options. Designed for universal use, the app features simple icons that allow farmers speaking more than forty-five different languages to participate. It is divided into modules that inform the user about tree-planting methods, nursery establishment, low-cost replicable land-restoration methods, and farmer trainings.

Restoring degraded soil using locally appropriate and affordable methods is key to improving livelihoods, food security, and climate resilience in this part of Africa. The app fills a critical gap by providing evidence on where restoration is happening, how it is happening, and for whom—a level of detail that would be difficult to attain through any other method. It also puts a powerful analytic and data-gathering tool into the hands of local stakeholders, who are vital contributors to effective land-restoration efforts.

The Regreening Africa mobile app modules allow for the tracking of tree planting, farmer-managed natural regeneration practices, tree nursery geolocation, and farmer trainings.

The Regreening Africa mobile app.

Tracking land-restoration efforts by monitoring and collecting data on a tree's diameter, Ghana, 2021.

Astropolitics: Depletion of Terrestrial Resources and the Cosmic Future of Capitalism

Designer
Bureau d'Études (France)

Collaborator
Ewen Chardronnet (space culture advisor, France)

Initial Presentation
La lune: Zone imaginaire à défendre (The Moon: Imaginary Zone to Defend), exhibition organized by Planète Laboratoire, Festival Hors Pistes, Centre Pompidou, Paris, 2019

Locations Earth and Moon

Years 2018–19

Revealing hidden relationships and providing context for disparate elements within the larger whole, the design group Bureau d'Études creates critical cartography that maps contemporary political, social, and economic systems. These mural-sized visual analyses of transnational capitalism are based on extensive research.

In 2019 the studio exposed the potential for conflict over resource extraction on the Moon with the Astropolitics map, first displayed in Paris as part of the Planète Laboratoire collective's critique of past and future Moon annexation. The map visualizes specialized information often buried in technical journals, international treaties, or legislation, such as the 2015 Commercial Space Launch Competitiveness Act, which allows US citizens and industries to engage in commercial exploration for and recovery of space resources. India, Russia, and China are making similar plans. This stands in contrast to the 1967 Outer Space Treaty, which established the use of space for peaceful purposes and the common interest of all. The map depicts this potential exploitation, locating existing and possible future satellite systems, areas of environmental and social crisis linked to mining, lunar bases, and machines required for observation and extraction, along with lunar mining resources—minerals and elements required for fuel cells and energy generation.

As tools for liberation, the designers provide free versions of their maps to share their learning about these intertwined technological-industrial-economic systems. The visualization of an imperiled future is key to the creation of a counternarrative—reimagining the Earth, the Moon, and other celestial bodies as live, interlinked sites of experimentation with new political and economic systems that will benefit us all.

How can design address the root causes of conflict?

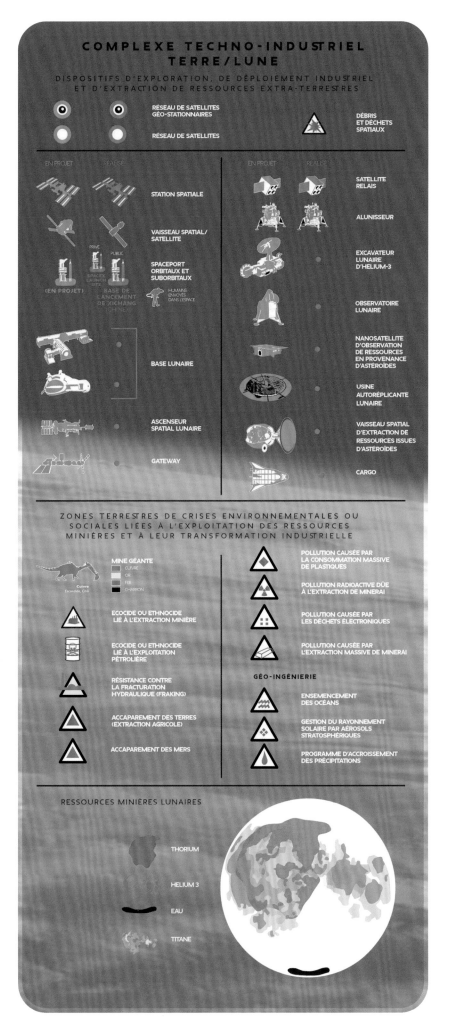

Techno-Industrial Complex Earth/Moon

Plans for the Exploration, Mining, and Industrial Deployment of Extraterrestrial Resources

Geostationary Satellite Network	Space Waste and Debris
Satellite Network	

Planned	Completed		Planned	Completed
Space Station			Relay Satellite	
Spaceship/Satellite			Lunar Lander	
Orbital and Suborbital Spaceport (In Planning Stage)			Lunar Miner of Helium-3	
Private SpaceX Launch Site				
Public Xichang Launch Center (China)			Lunar Observatory	
Humans Launched Into Space			Asteroid-Prospecting Nanosatellite	
Lunar Base				
			Self-Replicating Lunar Factory	
Lunar Space Elevator			Asteroid-Mining Spaceship	
Gateway				
			Cargo	

Terrestrial Zones of Environmental or Social Crises Linked to the Exploitation of Mineral Resources and to Their Industrial Transformation

Mega Mines Copper Gold Iron Coal	Pollution Caused by Massive Plastics Consumption
Ecocide or Ethnocide Linked to Ore Exploitation	Radioactive Pollution Caused by Mining Ores
Ecocide or Ethnocide Linked to Oil Exploitation	Pollution Caused by Massive Extraction of Ore
Protests Against Hydraulic Fracturing (Fracking)	Pollution Caused by Electronic Waste
	Geo-Engineering
Land Appropriation (Agricultural Extraction)	Ocean Seeding
	Management of Solar Radiation through Stratospheric Aerosols
Sea Appropriation	Program to Increase Rainfall

Lunar Mining Resources

Thorium
Helium-3
Water
Titanium

The map's key explains its icons and identifies planned (green) and completed (orange) projects of exploration and mining and the industrial deployment of extraterrestrial resources.

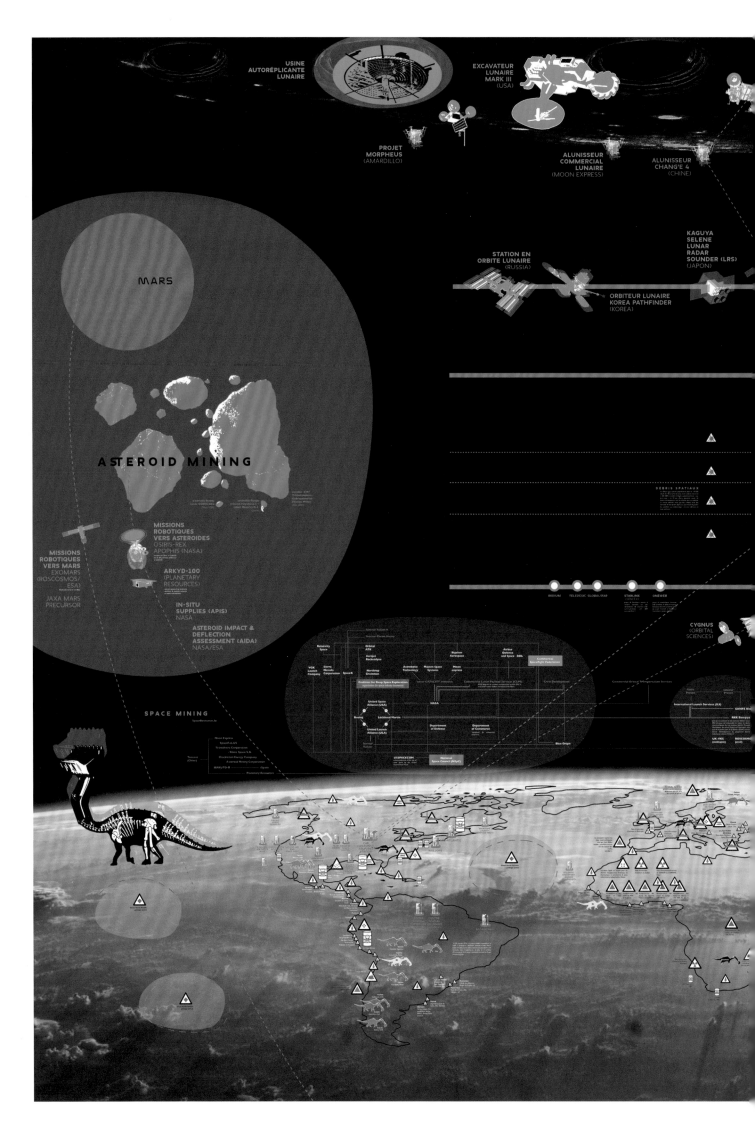

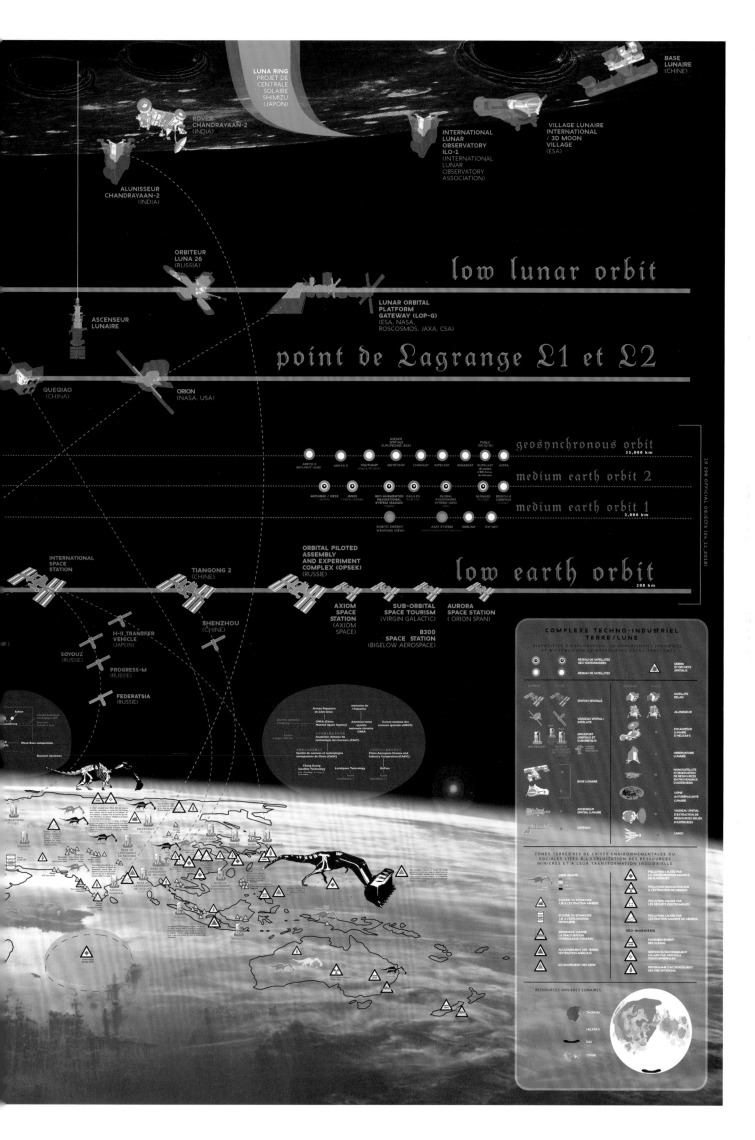

Rare Earthenware

Designers
Kate Davies, Liam Young, Unknown Fields (Australia, United Kingdom)

Collaborators
London Sculpture Workshop (ceramics), Toby Smith (film, photography) (United Kingdom); Christina Varvia (animation assistance) (Greece)

Commissioning Organization
Victoria and Albert Museum (United Kingdom)

Location Baotou, Inner Mongolia, China

Years 2014–15

The nomadic design studio Unknown Fields explores and exposes remote landscapes—from the iconic and ignored to the excavated and irradiated—that are part of the extended global systems supporting contemporary cities. One expedition traced the materials used in high-end electronics and green technology back through a complex global supply chain to their origins in Baotou, Inner Mongolia. Along with creating a film documenting the journey, the team collaborated with a ceramicist to produce three vases, forming them of mud dug from a Baotou tailings lake—a toxic mixture of acids, heavy metals, carcinogens, and radioactive material. The size of the Rare Earthenware vases corresponds to the amount of toxic waste created in the production of three high-tech products: a smartphone, a lightweight laptop, and a smart-car battery cell.

The shift to a low-carbon future will require significant mineral and metal resources, including highly sought after rare-earth metals. China produces more than 95 percent of these metals, two-thirds of which come from Baotou, one of the most polluted regions on the planet. As with conflict minerals, the extraction and distribution of rare-earth metals can lead to violence or aggravate existing conflicts along supply chains. Their mining and processing can also be highly toxic— impacting soil, water, and human health—inflaming regional tensions. Echoing the iconic forms of Ming dynasty porcelain, the tall, tapered Rare Earthenware vessels are physical embodiments of the global network that displaces earth and disperses extracted elements around the globe. As such, they illuminate those hidden systems for all to see.

← Unknown Fields collaborates with the London Sculpture Workshop to fashion vases made from mud collected at a radioactive tailings lake, 2015. The vases' shapes evoke prized Ming dynasty porcelain.

→ Rare Earthenware ceramic vessels sized in relation to the amount of toxic waste created in the production of a smartphone (smallest), a smart-car battery cell, and a lightweight laptop (largest).

The "unmaking" of certain high-tech products led to the making of the Rare Earthenware vases, which were carefully crafted from the items' toxic byproducts. Unknown Fields, with photographer Toby Smith, documented this reversed tracking from container ships and ports to the banks of a barely liquid radioactive lake in Inner Mongolia.

↑ Shipping containers at a port in China, one link in the global supply chain for everyday electronics.

→ A worker assembles electronics at a factory in Shenzhen, China. Shenzhen produces 90 percent of the world's electronics, almost all of which contain rare-earth metals.

Workers monitor molten iron at a Baogang Steel Company blast furnace, Baotou, China.

Coal is transported from a surface mine to power the furnaces of a nearby rare-earth metal refinery, Baotou, China.

A toxic lake of mine and refinery tailings stretches over 3.8 square miles (6 square kilometers) at the Baogang rare-earth metal refinery, Baotou, China.

Unknown Fields collects radioactive mud from the tailings lake at the outflow from the Baogang Iron and Steel Corporation's rare-earth metal refinery, Baotou, China.

Hate Speech Lexicons

Design and Research
PeaceTech Lab (United States)

Collaborators
Local Youth Corner Cameroon (Cameroon Lexicon);
Action des Jeunes pour le Développement Communautaire
et la Paix, Terre de Paix (Democratic Republic of
the Congo Lexicon); Centre for the Advancement of
Rights and Democracy (CARD), Destiny Ethiopia Project
(Ethiopia Lexicon); Center for Advancement of Rights
and Democracy, Destiny Ethiopia Project (Ethiopia
Lexicon); Albany Associates, Better World, Iraqi
Alfourdus Organization, Iraqi Network for Social
Media, United States Institute of Peace, Youth Without
Borders (Iraq Lexicons); DAI, local Mombasa organiza-
tions, Wasafiri Consulting (Kenya Lexicon); Develop-
ment Transformations, Elbiro Media Foundation (Libya
Lexicon); Centre for Information Technology and
Development (Nigeria Lexicon); Media Monitoring
Africa (South Africa Lexicon); local NGOs not listed
due to safety concerns (South Sudan Lexicons);
Andariya, Sudanese Development Initiative, Regional
Center for Training and Development of Civil Society
(Sudan Lexicon); Development Transformations, Peace
Track Initiative, Mohammad Al-Shami (Yemen Lexicon)

Locations
Cameroon, Democratic Republic of the Congo, Ethiopia,
Iraq, Kenya, Libya, Nigeria, South Africa, South Sudan,
Sudan, Yemen

Years 2009–present

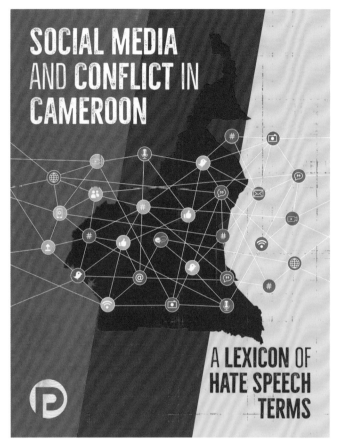

Social Media and Conflict in Cameroon: A Lexicon of Hate Speech Terms 2018. Researched, designed, and published by PeaceTech Lab.

! *Please note that the sample posts as well as the world clouds not only contain offensive and inflammatory terms, but also obscene terms.*

Each lexicon bears a warning to the reader.

In 2009 a group within the United States Institute of Peace's Centers of Innovation—the future PeaceTech Lab team—assembled Iraqi journalists, academics, and government officials to discuss media incitement to violence in Iraq, identifying the problem of inflammatory language in reporting. There was no consensus as to what constituted such language, making it difficult to regulate or even to consistently identify. One outcome of the meeting was an early example of a "hate speech lexicon." Made in collaboration with members of the Iraqi media, it contained definitions of incendiary terms, contextual examples, and a framework for conducting conflict-sensitive coverage of the Iraqi elections.

Since then, as social media has become perva-sive, PeaceTech Lab has pioneered a process for identifying hate speech and has published a growing portfolio of lexicons that can be used in various countries by civil society organizations, social media and technol-ogy companies, and other interested individuals and organizations to identify, track, combat, and remove hate speech. Machine learning helps the team monitor online language use, detect hate-filled terms and phrases, and analyze the narratives underpinning them. The lexicons are validated through a "ground-truth" process of dialogue with local actors. The Cameroon Lexicon, for example, rooted in in-depth interviews with Cameroonians, provides background on offensive words and phrases while offering alternatives. One term, *rats*, when applied to a protesting group, dehumanizes its members (equating them to pests to be exterminated) and dismisses its grievances and right to protest; a suggested alternative term is *demonstrators*. A United States Lexicon has been planned and is awaiting funding.

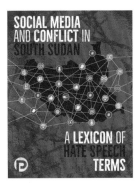

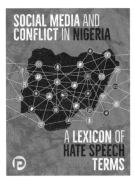

Hate Speech Lexicons. Clockwise from top left: Democratic Republic of the Congo (2019), Iraq (2019), Yemen (2019), Libya (2019), South Africa (2019), Sudan (2020), Nigeria (2018), Kenya (2018), Ethiopia (2020), South Sudan (2016).

Terms are listed in the lexicon by "frequency of use" and "potency" (how likely they are to lead to harm or trigger violence).

Stalled!

Designers
Joel Sanders, Seb Choe, Caitlin Baiada, Marco Li,
Matthew Liu, Lee Onbargi, Catherine Shih, Edward Wang,
JSA/MIXdesign (United States)

Collaborators
Quemuel Arroyo (accessibility), Antonia Caba
(public health), Terry Kogan (law), Susan Stryker
(gender and sexuality), with students from Yale
School of Architecture and Yale School of Public
Health (United States)

Location United States

Years 2015–present

In response to the headline-grabbing bathroom wars of 2015, an architect joined forces with a trans historian and activist to form Stalled!—an ongoing multi-pronged design and research initiative with dozens of collaborators from the humanities, law, medicine, design, and public health. Together they raise awareness of an urgent social justice issue: the need for safe, sustainable, and inclusive public restrooms.

Public restrooms have been at the center of a number of important societal shifts in the United States: separate "ladies' rooms" were created for working women in the 1880s, "whites only" public restrooms were a critical issue during the civil rights movement, AIDS transmission was erroneously linked to public lavatories in the 1980s, and access to restrooms was expanded in 1990 with the passage of the Americans with Disabilities Act. The latest debate coalescing

around the restroom is the question of access and choice for people who identify as transgender, a challenge that Stalled! believes can be addressed through design innovation. Using a high-volume, mixed-used public airport facility as a case study, the group reconceived conventional sex-segregated restrooms as a semi-open public square, with separate activity zones dedicated to grooming, washing, and eliminating.

In 2018 the group expanded its mission to include considerations of physical health and mental well-being in its prototypes and design of safe, accessible, socially equitable public spaces. Designing for "non-compliant bodies"—people of different ages, genders, races, cultures, religions, and abilities—Stalled! applies its inclusive methodology to a range of gathering spaces, including university campuses, hospitals, clinics, workplaces, and museums.

Activists protest North Carolina's 2016 Public Facilities Privacy and Security Act, or HB2, which restricted the use of gender-segregated bathrooms to users with the corresponding sex listed on their birth certificates, Chapel Hill, NC, 2016.

Protestors demonstrate to pressure the United States Congress to pass the Americans with Disabilities Act, Wheels of Justice March, Washington, DC, 1990.

How can design address the root causes of conflict?

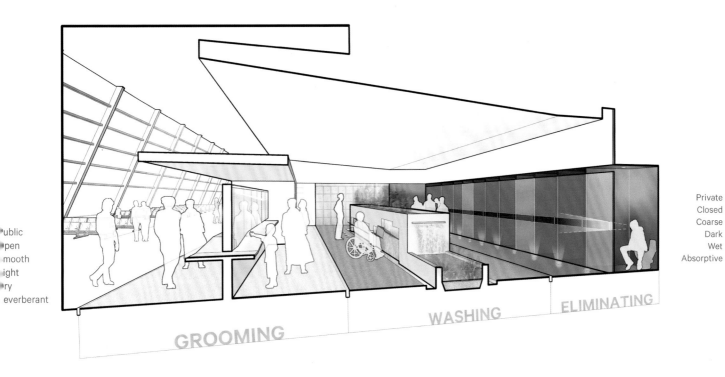

Public
Open
Smooth
Light
Dry
Reverberant

Private
Closed
Coarse
Dark
Wet
Absorptive

GROOMING   WASHING   ELIMINATING

Stalled! prototype airport restroom with three zones of use and a multisensory
gradient shift from private to public. Drawing by JSA/MIXdesign, 2018.

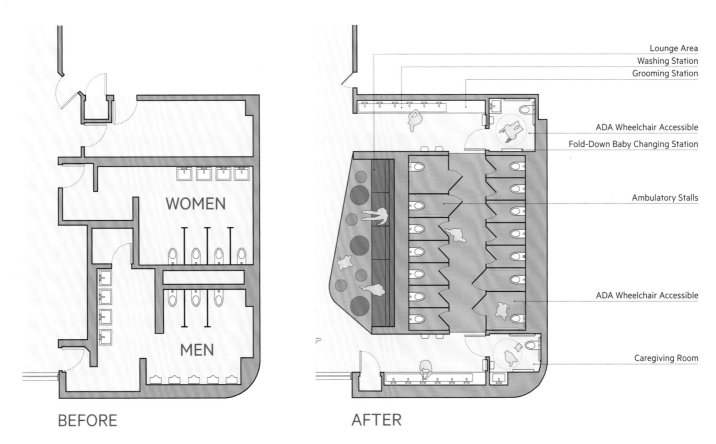

WOMEN

MEN

BEFORE

Lounge Area
Washing Station
Grooming Station

ADA Wheelchair Accessible
Fold-Down Baby Changing Station

Ambulatory Stalls

ADA Wheelchair Accessible

Caregiving Room

AFTER

Before and after plans visualize the difference between the layout of a traditional public restroom
and a Stalled! prototype restroom at Gallaudet University, Washington, DC. Drawing by JSA/MIXdesign, 2018.

Peace Pavilion

Design Team
Mujib Ahmed, Lalita Tharani, Shoukath KP, Muneeb KP,
Naufan Naseer, Collaborative Architecture (India)

Collaborators
Arup (structural, building services, sustainability,
museum consultant), Landscape India (landscape
architecture), Suranjana Satewalker (museum consultant), Kapil Suralekar Associates (lighting)
(India); Shibu Raman (urban design) (United Kingdom)

Client Government of India

Location New Delhi, India

Year 2017

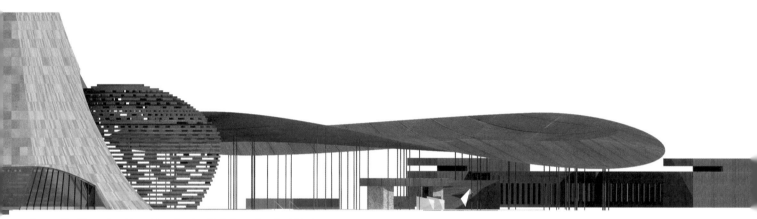

Peace Pavilion elevation. Drawing by Collaborative Architecture, 2017.

In response to a call for designs for a national war museum, a team of Mumbai-based architects proposed a "peace museum," aiming to shift India's discourse on war and nationalism. Noting that the country's history is as much about peace as about aggression, the design reflects the ancient Indian principle that war is the last resort and must be fought only in pursuit of universal peace. This ideal of nonviolence—expressed in the karmic teaching of *ahimsa* (causing no harm to other living beings) and in Gandhi's vision for India—is integral to the museum's content and programming.

Proposing a new type of open space for India's capital city, the team designed an approachable architecture and site. Visitors first encounter a large, low circular canopy, the Peace Pavilion, which is centered in a public plaza. Like a tree canopy, the welcoming structure is designed to provide shelter from the elements and from the daily chaos and scrutiny many encounter in urban India. The pavilion opens into a perforated, light-filtering dome at the museum's entrance, inspired by India's ancient stupas, the stone-covered burial mounds that convey the Buddha's message of enlightenment and nonviolence. The building itself, a series of segmented volumes, is less imposing and amenable to the asymmetrical site. The surrounding park offers respite from the dense urban fabric and is accessible and open to residents twenty-four hours a day. This ambitious design aims to emphasize the role of nonviolence in the country's history, while creating democratic spaces for its future.

The Peace Pavilion's tessellated dome echoes the Sanchi Stupa, a venerated Buddhist structure and symbol of nonviolence. Rendering by Collaborative Architecture, 2017.

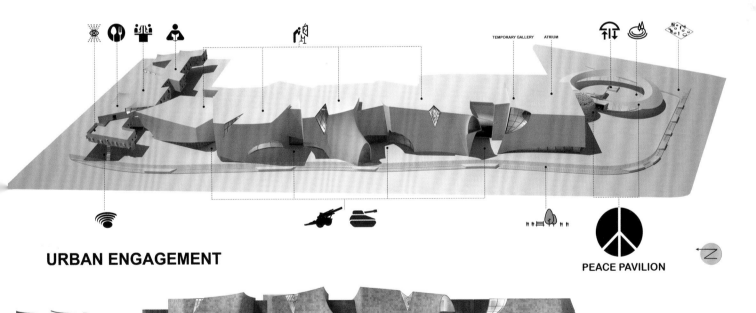

URBAN ENGAGEMENT

FRONT ELEVATION

Diagram (above) identifying the urban engagements for the museum and site; and front elevation (below). Drawing by Collaborative Architecture, 2017.

House
of Peace

Designers
Junya Ishigami, Wataru Shinji, Tei Shuma,
Taeko Abe, Takashi Matsuda, Eiko Tomura,
Junya Ishigami + Associates (Japan)

Collaborators
Svendborg Architects (Denmark)

Structural Engineers
Jun Sato Structural Engineers (Japan)

Environmental Engineers
Transsolar KlimaEngineering (Germany)

Client HOPE Foundation (Denmark)

Location Copenhagen, Denmark

Years 2014–present

With a singular dream to create a lasting monument to peace, four friends envisioned an architecture that would actively symbolize peace: a quiet, welcoming place for personal reflection, with neither political nor religious ties. The only content would be the visitors' own thoughts.

After review of four invited submissions, the newly formed House of Peace Foundation (HOPE) selected the evocative Cloud proposal, by Japanese architect Junya Ishigami. The design explores the ambiguity of space and the relationship between the natural phenomena of light, air, wind, and water and the built environment. The concept, a pure white cloud floating on water, gives visitors an opportunity to surrender to their senses and free their minds from escalating available information and engagement. Located in a harbor north of Copenhagen, the ocean serves as the structure's floor and a vaulted concrete cloud as its roof. Visitors enter by an underground passage, after which they can explore the House of Peace on small boats or by walking a platform. Around them the space gently rocks with rippling waves; reflected light is constantly changing, and the scents of the ocean fill the air warmed by the sun.

With the first House of Peace built in Denmark, the goal is to build similar iconic landmarks in the global East, West, and South. A building, a sculpture, and a symbol, the interactive site serves as metaphor for peaceful coexistence, an open invitation to people from all over the world to share their hopes for peace, and a reminder of the important role each individual has in promoting it.

The proposed House of Peace, Denmark, in the shape of a cloud, appears to float on the water. Exterior rendering by Junya Ishigami + Associates, 2014.

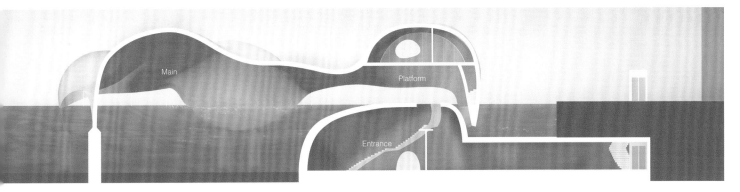

Visitors enter the floating landmark through an underground tunnel. Section elevation by Junya Ishigami + Associates, 2014.

Ever-changing natural light reflects off the surface of the water and the building's undulating concrete form. Rendering by Junya Ishigami + Associates, 2014.

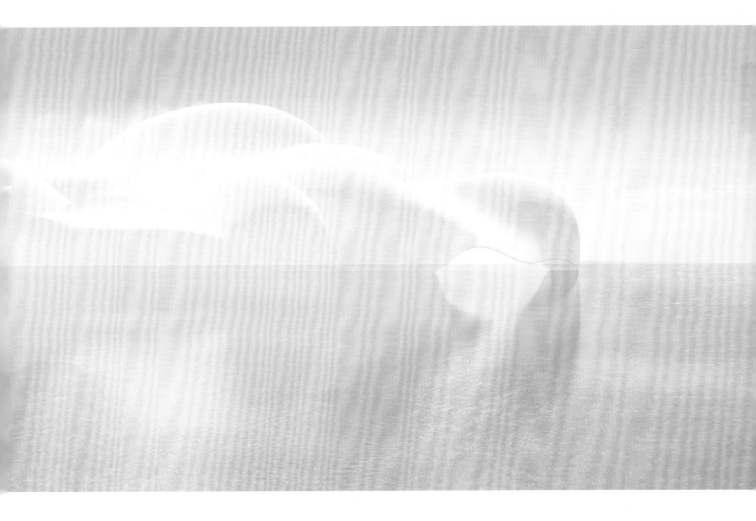

Universal Declaration of Human Rights Posters

Designers
Daniel Chang, Cindy Chen, Benny Chu, Heather East,
Ani Gevorgian, Christopher Kosek, Sharon Levy,
Bennett McCall, Brooke Reidt, Brian Scott, Matt Wood
(students), Martha Rich, Esther Pearl Watson (faculty),
Department of Illustration and Designmatters,
ArtCenter College of Design (United States)

Collaborator
United Nations Department of Public Information

Year 2008

A transdisciplinary studio at California's ArtCenter College of Design partnered with the United Nations Department of Public Information to design a series of posters communicating the ideals expressed in the Universal Declaration of Human Rights. Created in 1948, the groundbreaking document proclaimed for the first time that every person in the world has essential rights and freedoms, which are to be protected: these include the right to life, asylum, liberty, free speech, privacy, health, and housing. The global agreement is as relevant today as when it was first drafted.

With the support of a United Nations liaison and a human rights academic and guided by two illustration professors, multidisciplinary student teams combining specialties in illustration, fine arts, graphic design, product design, fashion, and photography studied the themes raised by the Declaration and together selected one or more of its thirty articles to visually interpret in poster form. They also designed postcards with text that illuminated their personal relationships to the posters' visual messages. For example, graphic designer Cindy Chen chose to make a poster about homelessness after witnessing it firsthand in her own community. Her poster "This Is My Home" is based on Article 25 of the Declaration, which states, "Everyone has the right to a standard of living adequate for the health and well-being of himself and of his family, including food, clothing, housing, and medical care." A selection of posters was displayed at United Nations Educational, Scientific and Cultural Organization (UNESCO) headquarters in Paris before traveling to venues throughout the United States.

"Sweat Shop Labor." Poster based on the Declaration's Article 23: "Everyone has the right to work ... to equal pay..." Design by Cindy Chen, 2008.

"Your Thoughts Are Illegal." Poster based on the Declaration's Article 18: "Everyone has the right to freedom of thought, conscience, and religion." Design by Christopher Kosek, 2008.

"This Is My Home." Poster based on the Declaration's Article 25: "Everyone has the right to a standard of living adequate for health and well-being." Design by Cindy Chen, 2008.

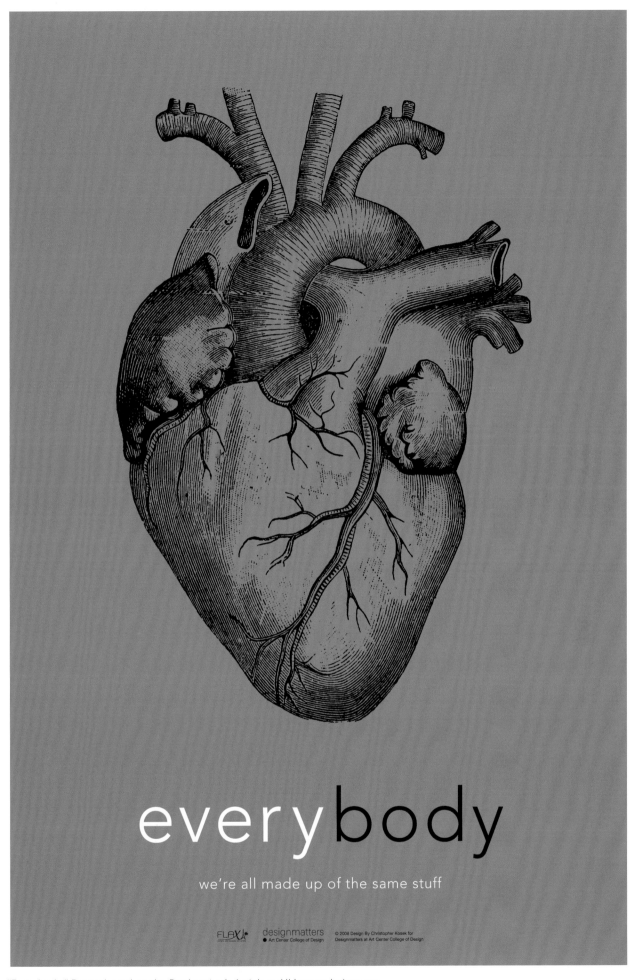

everybody

we're all made up of the same stuff

"Everybody." Poster based on the Declaration's Article 1: All human beings are born free and equal in dignity and rights. Design by Christopher Kosek, 2008.

Positive Peace Index

Designer
Institute for Economics
and Peace (Australia)

Index Locations
163 countries worldwide

Years 2014–present

2022 POSITIVE PEACE INDEX

A SNAPSHOT OF THE GLOBAL LEVELS OF POSITIVE PEACE

THE STATE OF POSITIVE PEACE

Very high	High	Medium	Low	Not included
1	2.53	3.18	3.66	5

2022 Positive Peace Index.

Countering the vast amount of research devoted to conflict and war, the Institute for Economics and Peace (IEP) instead systematically explores the drivers and determinants of peace. It has designed a set of tools to quantify peacefulness around the world, including an annual Positive Peace Index, which provides a snapshot of the level of positive peace—the attitudes, institutions, and social structures that create and sustain peaceful societies—in more than 160 countries. The Index identifies eight socioeconomic factors, such as the free flow of information, a well-functioning government, and equitable distribution of resources, that are key not only to sustaining peace, but also in building resilient societies that can absorb, adapt, and recover from shocks, such as global warming or economic downturns. Mutually reinforcing, these "pillars of positive peace"

interact in a dynamic system; thus changes in even one of the pillars can impact the entire system.

The concept of positive peace provides opportunities to understand and address the many complex challenges facing communities, nations, and the planet as a whole. Practical application of the concept has taken place from Mexico City, Mexico, to Karamoja, Uganda, in IEP workshops. With a broader goal of community building, the City of Atlanta's urban agricultural program, AgLanta, applied the positive peace framework to create clear methods to settle conflicts in its shared gardens. With a mission to inform, educate, and inspire, IEP commits its data-driven research to "shifting the world's focus to peace as a positive, achievable, and tangible measure of human well-being and progress."

A Positive Peace workshop supports communities in proposing and evaluating projects to build peace locally, Rupa Sub County, Moroto, Uganda, 2018.

The IEP's mult-idimensional con-cept of positive peace comprises eight "pillars of positive peace" that work together in a system, not simply as simple singular components.

Changes in the Pillars of Positive Peace, 2009–2020

Seven of the eight Pillars have improved since 2009. *Low Levels of Corruption* deteriorated by around 1.8 per cent over the period.

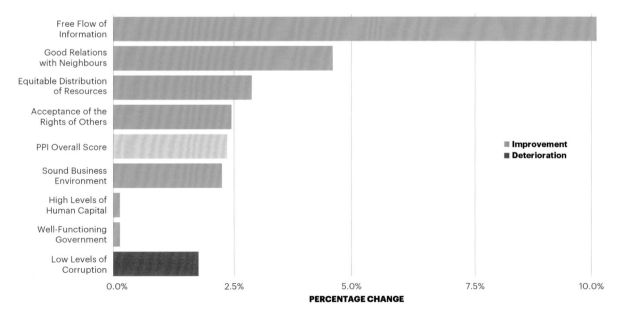

Extinction Symbol ▶ p. 138

How can design engage creative confrontation?

Beautiful Trouble Toolbox

Nadine Bloch and Andrew Boyd

The blending of art and protest is nothing new: tactical pranks go back at least as far as the Trojan Horse. Fools, clowns, and carnivals have always played a subversive role, while art, culture, and creative protest have for centuries served as fuel and foundation for successful social movements.

Contemporary global campaigns, such as Black Lives Matter (advocating for racial equity and justice) and Extinction Rebellion (reckoning with the climate emergency), are taking protest to another level. Creativity and possibilities for reframing social action are amplified by internet connection and fed by the urgency of multiple existence-level crises. From memes and virtual sit-ins to media pranks and viral campaigns, the need to mobilize and the will to do so have increased exponentially.

The Beautiful Trouble toolbox is a direct response to these social movements, and one that is designed to evolve in tandem with their needs. Assembled collaboratively in 2011 by more than seventy artists and activists, the toolbox lays out the core tactics, principles, and theoretical concepts that drive creative activism, providing analytical tools by which change makers can learn from their own successes and failures.

Creative activism offers no one-size-fits-all solution, and neither does the Beautiful Trouble toolbox. It's less a cookbook than a pattern language—a network of patterns that call upon one another, each providing a timeless solution to a recurring design problem, according to architect Christopher Alexander, originator of the concept.[1] Rather than dictating a strict course of action, the Beautiful Trouble toolbox offers a matrix of flexible, interlinked tools that practitioners can pick and choose among and apply in unique ways, varying with each situation they may face.

Millions around the world have awoken not only to the need to take action against deepening inequality and ecological devastation, but also to our own creative power to do so. The Beautiful Trouble toolbox can help. Please use it.

Nadine Bloch is the training director of Beautiful Trouble, working as an activist artist and strategic nonviolent organizer. **Andrew Boyd** founded Beautiful Trouble in 2011 after a career of working on creative campaigns for social change.

1   See Christopher Alexander, *A Pattern Language: Towns, Buildings, Construction* (Oxford, UK: Oxford University Press, 1977).

How can design engage creative confrontation?

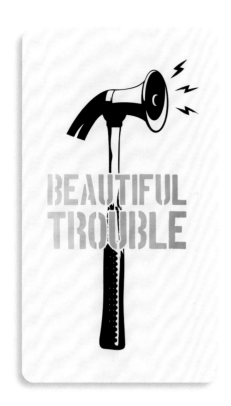

BARAZA

A large community gathering to discuss important matters, share information, & hold leaders to account.

People everywhere have organized baraza-like gatherings under various names: "town halls" in New England, "indignados" in Madrid, "diwaniyat" in much of the Arab world. It is fundamental to the human way of being, filling a need to come together, belong, & work toward a better community. What is the baraza of your culture? How can you harness it to improve things?

METHODOLOGY

SPECTRUM OF ALLIES

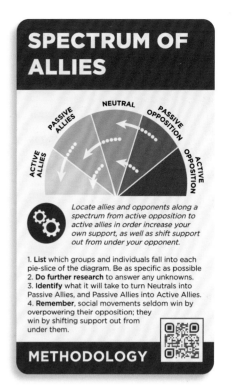

Locate allies and opponents along a spectrum from active opposition to active allies in order increase your own support, as well as shift support out from under your opponent.

1. **List** which groups and individuals fall into each pie-slice of the diagram. Be as specific as possible
2. **Do further research** to answer any unknowns.
3. **Identify** what it will take to turn Neutrals into Passive Allies, and Passive Allies into Active Allies.
4. **Remember**, social movements seldom win by overpowering their opposition; they win by shifting support out from under them.

METHODOLOGY

Methodologies
Strategic frameworks and hands-on exercises to help you assess your situation and plan your campaign. The Spectrum of Allies exercise helped civil rights activists in the United States expand their struggle for universal voting rights to sympathetic white citizens in the North.

Principles
Hard-won insights that can guide or inform creative action design.

MAINTAIN NONVIOLENT DISCIPLINE

Time and again, unarmed masses of people have triumphed over armed-to-the-teeth forces using humble techniques like strikes, occupations, boycotts, and sit-ins. But only because people have remained nonviolent.

PRINCIPLE

MAKE THE INVISIBLE VISIBLE

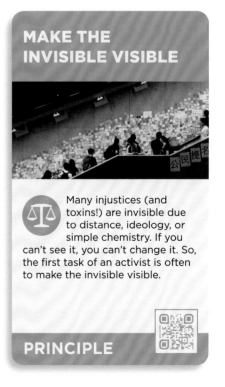

Many injustices (and toxins!) are invisible due to distance, ideology, or simple chemistry. If you can't see it, you can't change it. So, the first task of an activist is often to make the invisible visible.

PRINCIPLE

← **2020** National Nurses United lined up pairs of white shoes in front of the White House to memorialize eighty-eight nurses who had died of Covid-19.

SCHOOLS OF STRUGGLE

Latin America

Students occupied over 200 schools in São Paulo to protest the governor's plan to close schools, forcing him to reverse course, and igniting a wave of student resistance across the country.

STORY

GEZI PARK IFTAR

Middle East

When Turkish authorities tried to break the unity between secular and religious anti-capitalist protesters, Observant Muslims responded by inviting everyone to a public feast during the Ramadan Iftar.

STORY

Stories
Accounts of memorable actions and campaigns—analyzing what worked (or didn't) and why. Useful for illustrating how principles, tactics, theories, and methodologies can be successfully applied in practice.

Theories
Big-picture concepts and ideas that help us understand how the world works and how we might go about changing it.

↓ **2013** Bold Nebraska, a citizen group, put the theory of prefigurative politics into action, erecting a solar- and wind-powered barn on the proposed path of the Keystone XL oil pipeline to both block its construction and model an alternative vision of the future.

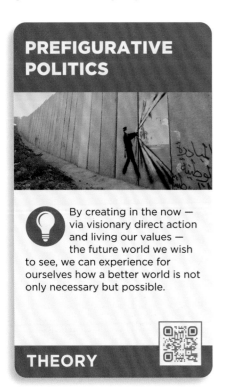

PREFIGURATIVE POLITICS

By creating in the now — via visionary direct action and living our values — the future world we wish to see, we can experience for ourselves how a better world is not only necessary but possible.

THEORY

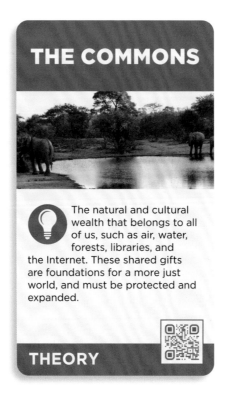

THE COMMONS

The natural and cultural wealth that belongs to all of us, such as air, water, forests, libraries, and the Internet. These shared gifts are foundations for a more just world, and must be protected and expanded.

THEORY

How can design engage creative confrontation?

GUERRILLA PROJECTION

With a clever image, a high-powered projector, and a little moxie, you can literally shine a spotlight on your opposition.

TACTIC

HUMAN BANNER

A political rally arranged into a huge work of human aerial art, composing a single iconic photo that captures what's at stake.

TACTIC

↑ **2020** George Floyd, a forty-six-year-old African American man, died in Minneapolis on May 25, 2020, after being pinned to the ground with a white police officer's knee on his neck for nine minutes and twenty-nine seconds. Black Lives Matter activists projected a portrait of Floyd onto a statue of Robert E. Lee in downtown Richmond, Virginia.

Tactics
Forms of creative action that result in a flash mob, blockade, or guerrilla projection.

Debates
Eternal questions (such as, change the world or change yourself?) that must be constantly wrestled with.

BE THE CHANGE YOU WANT TO SEE

YOU MUST BE THE CHANGE YOU WISH TO SEE IN THE WORLD.

Mahatma Gandhi

Our tactics and process should embody our values and goals.

If we want to bring about a more just and peaceful world, we have to model peace and justice in our activism. How can we say we want social justice if we're using manipulative (or even violent) means to advance our goals? "The master's tools," Audre Lorde admonishes, "will never dismantle the master's house."

DEBATE 2: SIDE A

BY ANY MEANS NECESSARY

We declare our right on this earth to be a man, to be a human being, to be respected as a human being, to be given the rights of a human being in this society, on this earth, in this day, which we intend to bring into existence **by any means necessary.**

- Malcolm X

Overcoming conditions of oppression, exploitation, and ecological crisis requires acting in ways that are not always consistent with our values.

According to Saul Alinsky, "The man [sic] of action views the issue of means and ends in pragmatic and strategic terms... He asks of ends only whether they are achievable and worth the cost; of means, only whether they will work." And so should we. If a controversial tactic has the potential to end a grave injustice, we can't afford not to use it.

DEBATE 2: SIDE B

Black Lives Matter Harlem Street Mural

Team
Harlem Park to Park; VALINC PR; LeRone Wilson
(mural artist curator); Got to Stop LLC; Thomas Heath,
Omo Misha McGlown, Guy Stanley Philoche, Joyous Pierce,
Dianne Smith, Jason Wallace, and LeRone Wilson
(northbound mural artists); more than three hundred
Harlem community members (southbound mural artists),
(United States)

Collaborators Rockwell Group (letter and stencil
design), Advantage Reprographics (stencil painting),
United Scenic Artists Local USA 829 (letter and stencil application), City of New York Department of
Transportation (pavement-marking plan) (United States)

Location Adam Clayton Powell Jr. Boulevard between
125th and 127th Streets, Harlem, New York

Year 2020

Protests exploded around the world after the murder of George Floyd in Minneapolis in May 2020. After the mayor of Washington, DC, renamed a street Black Lives Matter Way and had it painted with the phrase, dozens of street murals were created in small towns and large cities across the United States.

The Black Lives Matter Harlem Street Mural—one of eight painted in New York's five boroughs—runs along both sides of Adam Clayton Powell Jr. Boulevard in Harlem, the historic capital of African American culture. A team of Harlem-based social entrepreneurs and creatives joined forces, commissioning eight artists to each design and paint two each of the twenty-one-foot-high letters for the northbound mural. The southbound side spelled out the same words, "Black Lives Matter," in red, black, and green, the colors of the Black Liberation flag. More than three hundred community members, representing more than twenty-five youth, social, and cultural groups, community organizations, and merchants, came together over a two-day period to complete the project, which was as much a historic event as a work of public art.

Some of the city-backed murals received criticism for not directly addressing policing reform, while others provided a platform to reframe the conversation about public space by identifying the need for safe spaces for people of color to gather, create, and thrive. The Harlem project was designed with an aim to "heal and prosper the community, nation, and world," embodying a future we want to live in.

Volunteers paint the word *BLACK* on the community-designed southbound mural, Harlem, 2020.

How can design engage creative confrontation?

A volunteer works on the letter *K*, designed by artist Omo Misha McGlown, Harlem, 2020.

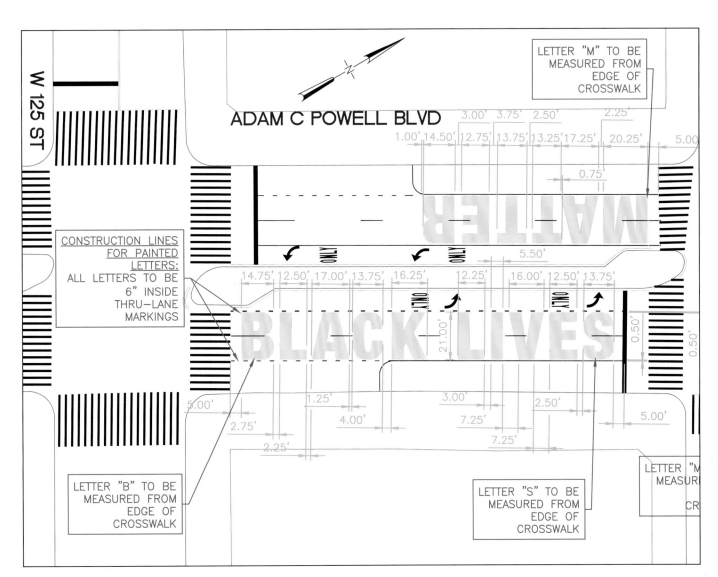

City of New York Department of Transportation's temporary pavement-marking plan for Adam Clayton Powell Boulevard, for safely locating the mural on the street. Drawing by S. Shapiro and S. Farber-Kaiser, 2020.

Aerial view of the Black Lives Matter mural in Harlem, 2020. Bottom (northbound): created by LeRone Wilson (BL), Jason Wallace (AC), Omo Misha McGlown (KL), Guy Stanley Philoche (IV), not included (ES), Thomas Heath (MA), Dianne Smith (TT), and Joyous Pierce (ER). Top (southbound): created by community members.

Art the
Arms Fair

Organizers
Octavia Austin, Emily Graham, Roxy Minter, Katy
Oliver, Sally Oliver, Jonathan Rebours, Art the Arms
Fair Collective (United Kingdom)

Collaborators
Campaign Against Arms Trade (United Kingdom)

Location London, United Kingdom

Years 2016–present

Many in the United Kingdom are not aware that every two years London is host to one of the world's largest arms fairs, Defense and Security Equipment International. Official delegations from around the world, including countries with poor human rights records, trade and purchase weaponry, from tanks and bombs to warships and combat aircraft. Aiming to expose the international arms trade and expand the discourse on its role in contemporary society—Britain is a top arms exporter, along with the United States, Russia, France, Germany, and China—a group of like-minded individuals organized a parallel two-week event: Art the Arms Fair. Through visual art exhibitions, lectures, and workshops along with poetry, comedy, and music events, the fair provides a way for artists and the wider public to voice their opposition to the war industry while also envisioning alternatives.

Free to the public, the diverse offerings are accessible for people who are not comfortable engaging in confrontational protests. Artists from any discipline may submit work in an open call, and established artists, such as the Guerrilla Girls and Anish Kapoor, have also contributed. Through art sales and donations, the all-volunteer effort raises significant funds for a partner organization, Campaign Against Arms Trade.

A model for creative confrontation, the fair encourages regular citizens to question their own complicity in the sale of implements of war. One participating artist, the Iraqi British architect Mayassah Alsader, explained her choice to participate: "I decided to join and call for peace. It is my duty as a human being in the first place and as an artist second."

Tristan Oliver, *Pattern Tank* (2019). The photograph was on display at Art the Arms Fair, London, 2019.

War Boutique, *Striking Suit* (2017), on display at Art the Arms Fair, London, 2019.

Shepard Fairey, *End Gun Violence Together* (2019; left), *Peace Guard II* (2016; center), and *Rise Above* (2015; right), on display at Art the Arms Fair, London, 2019.

Advertisement for Art the Arms Fair, London, 2021: "The World's Biggest Bomb Sale Is Coming to London."

Objects, People, and Peace

Caroline O'Connell

Our world and our lived experiences are shaped by objects. We rely upon, construct, sort, alter, cherish, fight over, and share them. We imbue objects with meaning, consciously and unconsciously, and thus they reveal much about the individuals and communities who made and use them. In considering any human-made or human-altered thing, we see not only the physical object but also the culture that created it. Objects are not neutral, just as people are not without perspectives. They are, rather, proxies for belief systems and their legacies.[1] Objects bind us to one another. As curator and scholar Glenn Adamson writes, "Every object represents a potential social connection. By better understanding the tangible things in our lives, we better understand our fellow humans."[2] The study of objects, often referred to as material culture, is an inquiry into things made in the past but also an examination of how they function in the present, and it may be a method by which we can conceptualize a better future. Here I will consider a few design projects, some featured elsewhere in this book, and make a short case for the potency of objects and for the study of materiality in service of supporting, waging, and sustaining peace.

Form, Expectations, and Dialogue

Size, shape, color, and content—the formal qualities of things—are entry points for observation. These physical characteristics help us analyze and attempt to

understand them.[3] But when there is a gulf between the assumptions we have made based on initial impressions and the physical traits of an object, our comprehension is upended, and questions arise. This is the case with Maps (Bullet Rug Series, pp. 130–131) by the art collective DETEXT, begun in 2013, in which rug-sized textiles incorporate bullet casings threaded onto the weft yarns and woven into the fabric. These shimmering pieces belie our common associations with domestic textiles, forcing us to reconcile evocations of comfort, warmth, and decoration with the sinister relics of war. Each casing bears a manufacturer's code and country of origin, a reminder of the geographical breadth of the international arms trade. Woven together en masse, the casings suggest uneasy links between consumerism, weaponry, and geopolitical power, creating space for awareness and ongoing dialogue, critical components of peaceful endeavors.

Sensory Engagement and Empathy

All objects connote, but those that invoke senses beyond the visual can elicit distinct affective responses. Food, for example, is experienced at the intersection of multiple senses and has a privileged status in personal and public consciousness; it is at once quotidian and extraordinary. The act of nourishing, from growing and obtaining food to preparing and eventually consuming it, extends from deeply ingrained individual and familial practices to local, regional, and broader cultural customs. Thus, the proverbial act of "breaking bread together" offers opportunities for mutual experiences, some of which may be rooted in nostalgia and ease and others which may be thrilling and new.

This premise was at the forefront in Conflict Kitchen (pp. 164–165), a takeout restaurant in Pittsburgh,

---

Caroline O'Connell's work explores the intersections between design and material culture. She is Curatorial Assistant at Cooper Hewitt, Smithsonian Design Museum where she contributed to the *Designing Peace* exhibition and publication.

How can design engage creative confrontation?

The AIDS Memorial Quilt on the National Mall, Washington, DC, 1987.
At the time, it featured 1,920 panels; today it comprises around fifty thousand.

Pennsylvania. Between 2010 and 2017, Conflict Kitchen had seven iterations, each focused on a different nation that was then in conflict with the United States. Complete with themed menus, aesthetics, and attendant programming, the project used the food of each nation as both a material and a process through which to build empathy. By creating a safe, accessible space for dialogue, learning, and shared sensory engagement, Conflict Kitchen moved beyond reductive narratives of conflict and division and into the realms of curiosity, education, and culture. This is a crucial step in establishing peace.

Process as Example

The physical act of making is at the heart of material thinking. The processes by which people create are critical to understanding the impact of objects. In the realm of textiles, where method keenly delineates form and type, process helps elucidate the profoundly

symbolic relationship that textiles have with the human body. As artist and textile historian Karen Nickell explains, "Cloth relates to humanity in its mortality and transience—both cloth and our body can be cut, [be] stitched, age, decay."[4] Robust textile traditions are braided into cultures across the globe and they have been incorporated into healing and reconciliation work in numerous contexts.[5] Patchwork quilting, for example, lends itself to communal making, since the form is modular; various makers can contribute individual portions, and aesthetic variation across the patchwork squares is not uncommon. The technique has long been connected with collective and often women-powered groups such as quilting circles, bees, and associations.

In Northern Ireland, artist- and community-led initiatives during the decades-long period of sectarian violence known as The Troubles included collaborative textile making in service of collective mourning, remembrance, and expression.[6] In 1970, against this volatile backdrop, the peacebuilding group Women

Women Together's Northern Ireland Peace Quilt (1994; left) and Northern Ireland Reconciliation Quilt (1995; right). Documented in the Conflict Textiles digital archive, Ulster University, Northern Ireland.

Together was established to unite women across the religious spectrum and offer a safe space for dialogue and coordinated initiatives in opposition to the violence perpetrated both by the government and by paramilitary groups. The three patchwork quilts Women Together created in the 1990s, two of which are pictured here, are symbolic of the organization's broader ambitions and are tangible examples of its achievements. In a process led by Pat Campbell, a longtime member, the quilts were composed of squares sent in by more than fifty individuals and organizations. Once the quilts were completed, Women Together further activated these textiles by traveling with them and displaying them at peace walks and conferences.[7] The quilts, like the work of Women Together, were ambitious and volunteer driven. They marshaled the form, texture, and process of the patchwork tradition in service of a united and defiant stance for peace.

Memories and Futures

The physical presence of an object may be less powerful than the ways in which that thing manifests in public consciousness. Past and present are often intertwined in objects, codified in items ranging from heirlooms to elements of urban infrastructure. In addition to exploring the formal properties and processes that created an object, we must also investigate the cultural, economic, and social stories of its makers and those for whom such things were made. This can also tell us a great deal about those for whom an object is not intended—and even about those whose exclusion is embodied in an object's form.

Seeking to create an inclusive and relevant dialogue about public monuments, the organizers of Paper Monuments (pp. 148–149), a public art project begun in 2017, solicited the opinions of New Orleans residents. Organized amid the furor surrounding the removal of Confederate statues in the city, the project mobilized a collective brainstorming effort that resulted in hugely varied public proposals. By encouraging those who would be living and interacting with the monuments to share their thoughts, the project democratized the historically elite decision-making process around public commemoration to ensure it was aligned with the values of everyday stakeholders.

As the project's title wryly suggests, paper is a material counterpoint to the heavy stone and metal used to build most monuments, but the immaterial aspects of the proposals carry equal and possibly more weight. People like *things*, but ideas are powerful, though fragile. We must acknowledge both to understand how objects impact the present and might support a more equitable future.

1 Here I am indebted to foundational work of Jules David Prown, whose articulation of material culture methodology serves as a building block for this analysis. See Prown, "Mind in Matter: An Introduction to Material Culture Theory and Method," *Winterthur Portfolio* 17, no. 1 (Spring 1982): 1–19, and "In Pursuit of Culture: The Formal Language of Objects," *American Art* 9, no. 2 (1994), 2–3.

2 Glenn Adamson, *Fewer, Better Things: The Hidden Wisdom of Objects* (New York: Bloomsbury, 2018), 8.

3 Formal analysis is a starting point for studying an object but it must be done carefully.

Each observer's personal and cultural biases impact how they may describe the physicality of an object.

4 Karen Nickell, "Troubles Textiles: Textile Responses to the Conflict in Northern Ireland," *Cloth and Culture* 13, no. 3 (2015), 236.

5 See Rozsika Parker, *The Subversive Stitch: Embroidery and the Making of the Feminine* (New York: Bloomsbury, 2018), and Julia Bryan-Wilson, *Fray: Art and Textile Politics* (Chicago: University of Chicago Press, 2017).

6 The Troubles were marked by extreme violence and a culture of silence that made acknowledgment and healing very difficult. Women Together was founded by Ruth Agnew, a Protestant, and Monica Patterson, a Catholic. The group worked to support their communities, promote dialogue across the religious spectrum, and give voice to the families and victims of sectarian violence.

7 Women Together had initially planned to make only one quilt, but they received so many squares that they decided to make three. See Karen Nickell, "Embroidery in the Expanded Field: Textile Narratives in Irish Art Post-1968" (PhD thesis, University of Ulster, 2014), 194.

A statue of the Confederate general Robert E. Lee is removed from its pedestal on St. Charles Avenue, New Orleans, Louisiana, May 19, 2017.

Maps (Bullet Rug Series)

Designer
DETEXT (Spain, United States)

Locations Casings Gathered
Colombia, Guatemala, Lebanon, Mexico,
Spain, United States

Years 2013–present

Manstopper bullet rug woven with .45 caliber bullet casings, 2016.

Raúl Martínez, founding member of the art collective DETEXT, hand-weaves rugs that incorporate thousands of used bullet casings. His Maps series, which echoes the Italian artist Alighiero e Boetti's embroidered Mappe tapestries, features rugs made in different sizes, following the proportions of the flag of the country in which the bullet casings were gathered.

Building on DETEXT's previous work employing discarded material (including spam email) to bring hidden narratives to light, Martínez's weavings offer evidence of international arms-trafficking routes, backdoor diplomacy, and secret military interventions. Each bullet casing is marked with a manufacturer's code and its country of origin. His first rug, woven with 9mm bullet casings gathered in Guatemala—stamped made in the United States, Russia, and Israel—identifies the main suppliers of

weapons in that country's civil war. In this way Martínez uses textiles, which have long conveyed histories and religious traditions, to expose intricate stories of covert operations and profiteering from violence.

Growing up in Spain, where access to guns is restricted, Martínez was fascinated by the United States' reverence for guns. So far he has sourced fifty thousand bullet casings in the US to make seven rugs, including one incorporating .40 caliber bullet casings. It is the caliber preferred by law enforcement, and the caliber that killed Michael Brown in Ferguson, Missouri, as well as many other victims of police shootings. The bullet was designed by and for US law enforcement agencies for enhanced "stopping power"—the power to kill faster and more efficiently—a chilling fact Martínez hopes his work will prompt viewers to consider.

How can design engage creative confrontation?

DETEXT's Raúl Martínez weaves a bullet rug, New York, 2015.

Maps #3 bullet rug woven with 9mm bullet casings sourced in Guatemala City, 2013–14.

Universality through Visual Symbols

Lee Davis

The decades following World War II were years of growing international cooperation, telecommunication, trade, and air travel, but they were also an era of heightened conflict, nuclear proliferation, political division, racial inequity, and environmental degradation. With increasing globalization, new channels and methods of communication were necessary if cross-cultural communication, international cooperation, mutual understanding, and peace were to be achieved.

In the summer of 1968, American anthropologist Margaret Mead (1901–1978) and Austrian-American graphic designer Rudolf Modley (1906–1976) called for a system of universally understood pictographic symbols, or "glyphs," with the goal of facilitating worldwide communication. The need for such glyphs was so urgent, they argued, that without them "hungry, frightened, confused people will continue to . . . contribute to the situation and hostility in which many human communities live today."[1] Universal, unambiguous symbols, they believed, would immediately provoke "visual thinking" and help overcome the current "chaos" of communication in international travel, trade, health and safety, scientific research, and intercultural relations.

This rather utopian idea might have been dismissed as fantastical had its principal author not been Mead, a renowned cultural anthropologist and international peace advocate. Together Mead and Modley founded a nonprofit, Glyphs Inc., and endeavored for over a decade, until 1976, to build it into an international, coordinated movement to promote and develop a

universal system of graphic symbols. They were allied in the belief that communication was at the heart of the problem in national and ideological conflicts (the Cold War, the Vietnam War, environmental degradation) and in cross-cultural relations (international trade, travel, cross-disciplinary scientific research).

Mead's growing fascination with signs and symbols was evident as early as the 1930s and 1940s, during and after World War II. Her writings on cross-cultural communication and visual anthropology—most notably her 1947 article "The Application of Anthropological Techniques to Cross-National Communication"—laid the philosophical groundwork for Glyphs Inc. two decades later.[2] She is credited with coining the term *semiotics* in 1962 to denote the study of "patterned communication in all modalities."[3] In 1964 she called upon the United Nations Committee for the International Cooperation Year to create a system of universally recognized graphic symbols. Mead pointed to the tremendous "social and economic fragmentation" and the lamentable "state of communication" of the world and the urgency to save humankind from nuclear annihilation.[4] What was needed, she believed, was a "new, shared culture," a common ground that would align and synchronize humankind in order to achieve worldwide intelligibility.[5] She proposed the development of a new, universal second language alongside an international system of visual communication to be learned by every child: "What is needed, internationally, is a set of glyphs which does not refer to any single phonological system or to any specific cultural system of images but will, instead, form a system of visual signs with universally recognized referents."[6]

Mead saw a critical role for anthropologists in ensuring that the design of glyphs acknowledged and incorporated diverse cultural references and styles.

Lee Davis is an author, designer, educator, and social entrepreneur. He is co-director of the Center for Social Design at Maryland Institute College of Art (MICA) and co-chair of the Winterhouse Institute.

How can design engage creative confrontation?

In her foundational 1969 article "Anthropology and Glyphs," she argued that there are no naturally universal symbols:

> It is important to insist that there are no universal symbols, although there are many widely distributed symbols which are based on widely distributed artifacts (like the arrow) and widely distributed forms of representation (like the sun). As long as anyone believes that human beings naturally "follow the arrow," treat red as a signal of danger, think a skull and crossbones means poison, or express negation by a head shake, we will be seriously prevented from accomplishing an urgent international enterprise.[7]

Mead realized that creating a universal visual language would require more than anthropologists. She envisioned a global interdisciplinary effort involving "the clearest minds in every field of the humanities, the sciences, the arts, engineering, and politics."[8] She found in Modley a unique and ardent design ally. Born and educated in Vienna, he spent his high school and university years working alongside Otto Neurath, the inventor of the International System of Typographic Picture Education (ISOTYPE), a method of pictorial statistics.[9] He emigrated to the United States and in 1934 established Pictorial Statistics, Inc., a consultancy dedicated to promoting and developing ISOTYPE-like pictographs for government and corporate use and for application in education and public information.

In a 1959 keynote speech to the Art Directors Club in New York, Modley called for the creation of a new science, the science of symbology: "We need symbols which can bring closer to us the newly revealed aspects of nature and the increasingly complex workings of our social and economic world."[10] Modley had strong opinions about the attributes of effective glyphs, writing in a memorandum to designers in 1965 that "good graphic symbols are simple and concise."[11] He argued for a uniformity of design, relying on image- or concept-related symbols, and he suggested a system of basic building blocks for glyphs. Like Mead he believed that universality could only be achieved if designers developed a deeper understanding of cultural context: "The designer will be faced by many . . . problems which require thorough acquaintance with the modes of work, the habits of thought, the religious, political, and cultural patterns before he can design a truly valid symbol."[12] He challenged standardization efforts that were culture or industry specific and argued that a symbol such as the crossed fork and knife, for example, was "unacceptable as a 'universal' symbol of food" because it failed to recognize cultural context.[13]

Modley, like Mead, also recognized that the process of creating glyphs would require disciplines and expertise beyond his own: "Designers alone are not able to solve these problems," he wrote. "The task requires

Proposals for a glyph indicating dangerous levels of radioactivity, submitted in response to *Glyphs for World Communication*, an international call for designs in twenty categories, 1966–67.

The competition called for glyphs visually communicating a range of concepts, including proposals for a glyph denoting "fire alarm," 1966–67.

COMMUNICATION AMONG ALL PEOPLE, EVERYWHERE

by Margaret Mead and Rudolf Modley

While preserving man's wealth of languages, we can achieve worldwide communication by adopting two languages and a system of signs that will be universally understood

Long before modern technology brought the peoples of the world within speaking distance of each other, prophets and philosophers had begun to think about the possibilities of universal languages that would remove the dangers symbolized by the story of the Tower of Babel. In the Western world, there have been serious attempts to invent new languages based on European grammatical forms. It was hoped that these languages would do what Latin once did for the tiny literate medieval European community and what diplomatic French did for the nineteenth-century political community. Esperanto was the language most vigorously pursued by idealistic enthusiasts. Interlingua, a written scientific language, is a current attempt to provide those of us whose languages are Indo-European with better forms of communication.

Since foresighted individuals first began thinking about these problems, however, the world has changed. While new technologies have made former dreams obsolete in detail, they are still relevant to the world's needs. Today we have to deal with new and demanding conditions. Anyone on this planet can travel to any part of it in 36 hours. But the people of the earth speak some 2,800 languages, and it would be impossible to provide enough interpreters at airports to aid these potential travelers. Even the simultaneous arrival at an airport of aircraft from a variety of countries, whose pilots speak only their own languages, occasionally causes difficulties at control towers.

These conditions present a challenge to the inventiveness of the modern world. To people who cannot travel, get on and off trains, ships, and airplanes, or find an inn because of language barriers, the new freedom of movement is meaningless.

The Instantaneous Message

A first requirement, then, for our technologically developed world is a set of clear, unambiguous signs that can be understood by the speakers of any language, and by the members of any culture, however primitive. These signs will enable mankind to use the great new freedom of worldwide travel. Without them, hungry, frightened, confused people will continue to clog the travel lanes, come to grief on the roads, return disenchanted to their small provincial worlds, and contribute to the isolation and hostility in which many human communities live today.

Such signs are necessary for all travelers—for the boy riding a bicycle as well as for the motorist in a large city. We call these signs glyphs.

Glyphs are the only universal graphic communications device that is in public use. They are beginning to appear on highways, in world's fairs, at hotels and inns, and on machines and appliances the world over.

Glyphs communicate visually. Their message provokes "visual thinking" instead of "verbal thinking." Visual thinking has a direct and immediate impact on the viewer: a picture of a horse is an image of a horse to all men. No further interpretation is required. Verbal thinking, on the other hand, requires a more complex process. The word *horse*, or *cheval* (French), or *Pferd* (German) has to be heard or read first, and only then (if he can speak or write the specific language) can the intended recipient of the message interpret the meaning.

The advantages of a glyph are thus twofold:

1. Glyphs don't require knowledge of a language, spoken or written. The message of a glyph is unambiguous, simple, and understandable to anybody who has once "learned it." An arrow pointing right means "turn right"; two moving legs mean "go."

2. Glyphs create a direct and immediate impact and thus permit immediate response. This applies as well to those who know a language as to those who do not. This immediacy of response saves thinking. What Alfred North Whitehead has said of mathematical notations applies also to glyphs: "By relieving the brain of

Glyphs—universal graphic symbols—should be immediately understandable. A symbol that shows an object's image fills this need, but such symbols (the telephone, for example) may become badly outdated. Concept-related symbols—the bent arrow (turn right), walking legs (go), and wavy line (water)—are clear and timeless. The question mark and plus sign are arbitrary symbols and give no clue to their meanings.

56

57

Spread from Mead and Modley's only jointly written article, "Communication among All People, Everywhere," *Natural History* 77, no. 7 (August–September 1968).

the combined efforts of psychologists, linguists, educators, anthropologists, sociologists, lawyers, engineers, designers, and many others. The need is so important that we cannot afford to take hasty and inadequate measures, but we should not delay in undertaking this essential task."[14]

Mead and Modley believed that the biggest obstacle to universal symbol development was the lack of global coordination. More organizations and agencies were realizing the need for graphic symbols and developing them on their own, without international coordination and cooperation. Mead and Modley advocated instead for an "intensive transnational and interdisciplinary effort" by the world's governments and scientific and business communities to develop a standardized and universal visual system.[15] Facilitating this global coordination was the principle mission of Glyphs Inc. According to Mead and Modley, the organization "does not design symbols but acts merely in an advisory capacity to others interested in the same objectives."[16] They identified three priorities: compiling a symbol archive and dictionary of graphic symbols organized according to a graphic classification system; assembling a transnational, interdisciplinary effort concerned with determining those symbols most urgently needed, specifying their graphic characteristics, and evaluating and testing them against a set of generally accepted norms and working hypotheses; and engaging in a worldwide education effort to promote, adopt, and teach glyphs as widely as the alphabet and numerals.

These efforts gained momentum in the late 1960s and early 1970s through Mead and Modley's writing and speaking engagements and Modley's participation in international standardization committees and commissions among governments and industry, principally in Europe and the United States. In 1966, Glyphs Inc. began publishing a quarterly newsletter documenting its output.

As their efforts shifted from ideas into practice, the magnitude of the undertaking became evident. Mead and Modley faced increased criticism and competition, and they struggled with funding shortages and limited capacity. The challenges of realization were especially evident in the organization's flagship undertaking, the planned exhibition *Glyphs for World Communication* in 1966–67. Mead and Modley called upon designers and design schools around the world to participate in a collaborative effort to develop a limited number of universally usable graphic symbols related to specific, predetermined applications in industry, travel, and trade. Proposals were received from twenty-seven designers from nine countries and were reviewed by a panel of design jurors representing eight countries. Although they were offered a gallery in the Time-Life building in New York, the exhibition was never realized and the submitted glyphs never published, due in part to insufficient funds. After reviewing the submissions, Modley noted, the jurors "felt that publication of the designs at this time would not contribute to the furtherance of universal graphic symbols. . . . Extensive preparatory study by experts in many disciplines must be undertaken before design work on glyph 'candidates' can be fruitfully started by designers."[17]

Modley died in 1976, and Glyphs Inc. quickly faded from Mead's list of priorities. Just before his death, Modley completed his *Handbook of Pictorial Symbols*, a mammoth undertaking compiling 3,250 pictorial symbols "representing every facet of human existence, from having a baby to committing suicide."[18] But the two had not achieved their collective vision of a viable system of universal graphic symbols. They acknowledged that this goal was a daunting one: it had taken thousands of years to develop the world's existing alphabets.

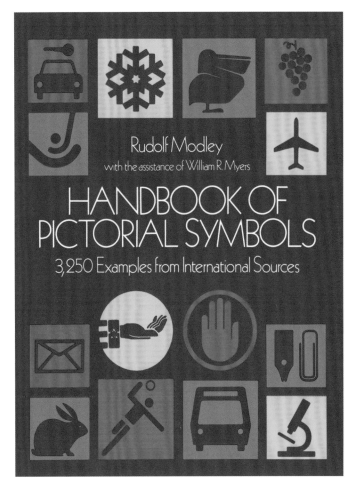

Rudolph Modley. *Handbook of Pictorial Symbols: 3,250 Examples from International Sources*. New York: Dover, 1976. Cover design by Kiffi Diamond.

1   Margaret Mead and Rudolf Modley, "Communication among All People, Everywhere," in *Natural History* 77, no. 7 (August–September 1968): 57. The author is indebted to the archivists and librarians at the Library of Congress (Margaret Mead papers and South Pacific Ethnographic Archives) and the Rockefeller Archive Center for their patience and professionalism in supporting this research.

2   Mead, "The Application of Anthropological Techniques to Cross-National Communication," *Transactions of the New York Academy of Sciences* 9, no. 4 (February 1947).

3   Mead, "Vicissitudes of the Study of the Total Communication Process," in Thomas Albert Sebeok, ed., *Approaches to Semiotics* (Boston: Mouton & Co., 1972): 277–88.

4   Mead, "The Future as the Basis for Establishing a Shared Culture," *Daedalus* 94, no. 1 (Winter 1965): 138.

5   Ibid., 141.

6   Ibid., 146–7.

7   Mead, "Anthropology and Glyphs," *Print* 23, no. 6 (November–December 1969), 53.

8   Mead, "Future as the Basis," 146.

9   Modley, "The Challenge of Symbology," in Elwood Whitney, ed., *Symbology: The Use of Symbols in Visual Communications* (New York: Art Directors Club, 1960), 19.

10 Ibid., 30.

11 Modley, "Guidelines on Designing Universally Usable Graphic Symbols (Glyphs)," memorandum, June 23, 1965.

12 Modley, "Challenge," 13.

13 Modley, "Guidelines," 6.

14 Modley, "Graphic Symbols for World-Wide Communication," in Gyorgy Kepes, ed., *Sign, Image, Symbol* (New York: George Braziller, 1966), 124–25.

15 Modley, "Prospects and Problems for Universally Usable Graphic Symbols (Glyphs)," *International Journal of Symbology* (December 1969): 45.

16 Modley, *Handbook of Pictorial Symbols: 3,250 Examples from International Sources* (New York: Dover Publications, 1976), x.

17 *Glyphs, Inc.*, quarterly newsletter, Summer 1968.

18 Modley, *Handbook*.

World Peace Symbol

Designer
Amijai Benderski

Location Montevideo, Uruguay

Years 2017–present

An emerging graphic designer in Uruguay was determined to create a symbol for peace that could be used freely by people all around the world, from friends sharing emojis to those in positions of authority. Existing signs and symbols associated with peace were imbued with problematic meanings and histories, potential barriers to universal acceptance. For example, the "peace" hand gesture, where index and middle fingers are held up to form a *V*, also signals victory, as famously used by Winston Churchill during the Second World War, and by Richard Nixon. It also stood for resistance, especially to the United States' involvement in the Vietnam War. The dove has been an icon of peace for thousands of years, but it is also a Christian religious symbol. The widely recognized circular peace sign—associated with counterculture and antiwar efforts—

was originally designed for a nuclear disarmament campaign by Gerald Holtom, who based the simple linework on the flag signals for the letters *N* and *D*.

The World Peace Symbol fuses Holtom's icon with a simplified globe, in a clear representation of our interconnected planet. Its lines of latitude and longitude connect to and radiate from the symbolic ideal of freedom and goodwill. Based on his previous work designing social posters, in which he demonstrated that graphic design can be a tool in promoting tolerance and human rights, Benderski invited designers and artists from fifteen countries—Argentina, Belgium, Canada, Chile, Dominican Republic, Ecuador, Greece, Ireland, Jamaica, Peru, Poland, Spain, United States, Uruguay, and Venezuela—to design a set of thirty-three posters using his hopeful mark.

Guidelines specify the relative proportions and colors of the World Peace Symbol.
White on blue is the default version. Design by Amijai Benderski.

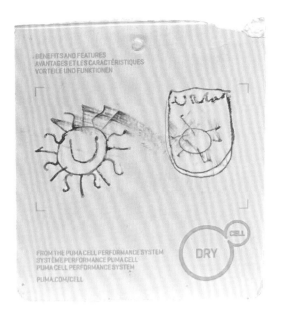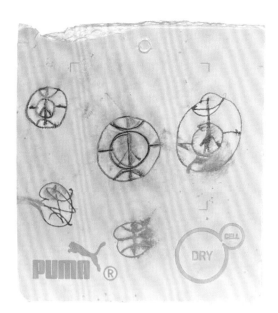

The initial sketches for the World Peace Symbol, on a piece of scrap paper (a discarded clothing label), combine symbols for the Earth and for peace. Drawings by Amijai Benderski, 2017.

"Embroidering Life." Poster inspired by the idea that "peace requires patient and permanent work and its beginning is at home, embroidering life." Design by Rosana Malaneschii, Montevideo, 2019.

The designer of this untitled poster noted that "hanging the world by a thread over a fiery abyss was a good way to describe our global situation." Design by Max Phillips, Dublin, 2019.

Extinction Symbol

Designer
ESP (United Kingdom)

Location Global

Years 2011–present

Demonstrators carry multicolored flags bearing the Extinction Symbol in a protest organized by Extinction Rebellion, Parliament Square, London, 2018.

The Extinction Symbol was created by the London-based artist ESP in 2011 to raise awareness of the need for transformative change in face of accelerating species extinction caused by humans. An unprecedented one million out of the eight million plant and animal species on Earth are currently threatened, and many face extinction within decades. The symbol is simple and easily replicable: a circle signifies the planet, and an hourglass form signals urgency—the fact that time is running out.

People are encouraged to share this "ecological symbol of peaceful resistance" via social media, but while creative use is encouraged, commercial and political exploitation of the work is prohibited in a stand against unchecked consumerism. Designed to be easily drawn and recognized, the logo has been used around the world: tattooed on activists, spray-painted on walls, taped to street signs, projected at a monumental scale, and formed by human figures in a meadow. It was adopted as the visual identity for the international Extinction Rebellion movement and has been featured on colorful banners and signs during direct actions demanding that governments do more to combat global warming and protect biodiversity.

Activists form an Extinction Symbol with their bodies at an event organized by Extinction Rebellion and Fridays for Futures in Central Park, New York, 2019.

The Extinction Symbol is deployed on large Extinction Rebellion banners, symbolizing the urgent need for climate action, London, 2018.

An Extinction Symbol is sculpted in sand at Mount Maunganui Beach, New Zealand, 2019.

Paper Monuments ► p. 148

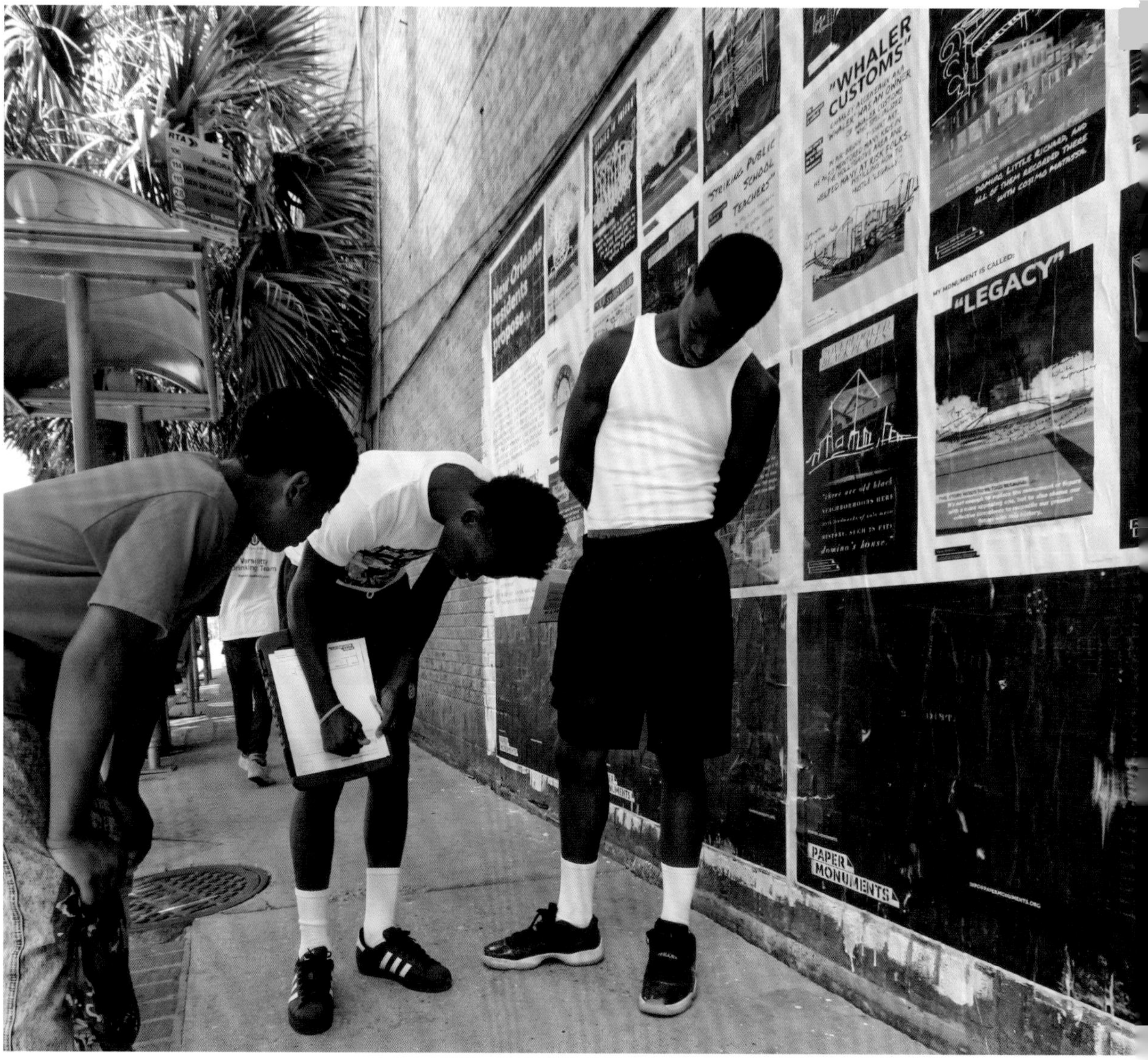

How can design embrace truth and dignity in a search for peace and justice?

The Murder of Halit Yozgat ▸ p. 146

Citizen-State, a Bottom-Up Reparation Model

Everisto Benyera

Colonialism has left a legacy for both the colonized and the colonizing.[1] Newly intertwined and umbilical relationships were forged, predominantly through dispositions, misrepresentations, and manufactured consent. The modern Western model of the state (or country) was the vehicle used to carry out and sustain this system, and it emerged along with colonialism during two events: the almost eight-hundred-year Reconquista of the Iberian Peninsula and North Africa, between c. 801 and c. 1492—a period of ethnic cleansing perpetrated by European Christian states—and the arrival of Christopher Columbus in the Americas in October 1492.

Besides having the same genealogy, the modern Western state and colonialism had the same purpose, and therefore they complemented and reinforced each other. The epistemicides and genocides of the Reconquista and the colonization of overseas territories in the Americas forced the world into five common systems: the international legal system, the global financial and monetary system, the world capitalist economy, a Euro–North American-centric world culture (especially in language), and a Euro–North American-centric moral order dominated by Christian thought. This overarching framework, used at the scale of the state, was codified with the signing of the Treaty of Westphalia on October 24, 1648.[2] These five systems remain as effectual today as when they were first imposed.

Law, morality, finance, language, and ideology were instrumentalized for colonial purposes. Cultures

Everisto Benyera is an associate professor of African politics in the Department of Political Sciences, University of South Africa, Pretoria.

Epistemicides is the systematic and deliberate destruction of existing knowledges. This is effectuated by deliberately giving legitimacy to one set of knowledge and making others invisible or even illegal.

The **Reconquista** was a period of brutal genocidal campaigns on the Iberian Peninsula (modern-day Spain and Portugal), during which the Castilian monarchy sought to create a homogenous national homeland for Christian Spaniards by converting or expelling Africans, Muslims, and Jews. The main perpetrators were Queen Isabella I (1451–1504) and King Ferdinand V (1452–1516) of Castile.

were permanently altered, languages and civilizations lost. How can compensation be made to populations and communities whose systems, institutions, and epistemologies were forcibly displaced? What reparation model would work in these circumstances? I propose reconstituting the model of the state away from the nation-state and toward a citizen-state.

The Global Legacy of Colonialism in Africa

Colonialism in Africa never ended; it simply mutated into something else. *Coloniality* is the continued asymmetrical relationship between the (former) colonizers and the (formerly) colonized. It exemplifies the effectiveness and resilience of the colonial infrastructure, whose apartheid system was formulated with built-in mechanisms for self-invention, resistance, and relevance. These included, for example, an education system that de-educated and

Colonialism operated through three main systems:

1 Violence was used to initiate, routinize, and maintain colonialism.

2 Extractivism took labor (in the form of slaves), natural resources, and epistemologies (human knowledge).

3 War was waged to deny the colonized their humanity.

un-educated its subjects, rendering them compliant and useful to the system. Coloniality has three main analytical concepts: coloniality of power, coloniality of being, and coloniality of knowledge. (Other analytical frames, such as coloniality of nature, coloniality of data, and coloniality of markets, are still being developed.) Operationally, it functions in the (formerly) colonized parts of the world in three ways: it either disciplines its people, absorbs them, or eliminates them. It renders global models of reparation a farce, because whatever happens at the reparation level will be nullified by coloniality.

The Challenges of Reparation

Three factors demonstrate the challenges faced by attempts at reparation: the capitalist world system; the Western model of the nation-state; and the breadth and depth of the atrocities and abuses suffered by the people of the Global South, including genocide, epistemicide, enslavement, apartheid, colonialism, and eugenics, among others. The nation-state is a problem for global reparation because it thrives on the will to power, a paradigm of war, a paradigm of difference, and survival of the fittest.

There are as many existing models of reparation as there are victims of human rights abuse. Since harms are suffered, first and foremost, at an individual level, in these models reparation tends to be responsive to the individual victims' worldviews and needs. However, there is one commonality: in all these models,

perpetrators must acknowledge the harm they caused. Once acknowledged, most harms will be half-solved, and will be less contested. The problem, however, is that in most cases atrocities were perpetrated by faceless agents of the state and of state institutions. With no one to take responsibility for slavery and colonialism, healing and reparation—let alone closure—will not be accomplished. Are there any alternatives to these models of reparation?

An Alternative Bottom-Up Reparation Model

The Global South was involved in developing the Global North; hence the citizens of the South must be included in the economies of the North as equal citizens and not as an invading, unwanted, and dispensable Other. Acknowledgement, followed by inclusivity, must be instituted as reparation not only for colonialism but for other crimes against humanity, such as the Euro-American slave trade (a better term than "Transatlantic slave trade," since the Atlantic Ocean never enslaved anyone), apartheid, genocide, and epistemicide. As an alternative reparation model, the Western model of the state must be rethought and then reconstituted—away from the nation-state and toward the *citizen-state*. This citizen-state will be characterized by the will to live (not to power), a paradigm of peace (not of war), a paradigm of inclusivity (not of difference), and the survival of all (not just of the fittest).

The reconstitution of the state is the most viable form of reparation available to both the perpetrators and the victims, who must be reconstituted as *survivors*.

As a concept, the legacy of colonialism is contestable, because for its victims colonialism never ended: it simply mutated, adapting to the many challenges it faced, including decolonization processes and Must Fall movements, among others. Rethinking and reconstituting the state away from the nation-state and toward the citizen-state is the best model of reparation for those who continue to suffer from the persistence and effectiveness of the colonial infrastructure.

1 Colonialism constituted not only the occupation of the land of the colonized. It was also, most importantly, a dispossession of the colonized peoples of their knowledges, institutions, networks, and ways of life, which were replaced with those of the colonizers.

2 The Treaty of Westphalia, signed in Westphalia, Germany, ended the brutal Thirty Years' War (1618–1648), which was fought predominantly between Catholics and Reformists over the control of Europe. The treaty established the principle of state sovereignty, wherein countries do not interfere in each other's internal affairs. Ironically, after swearing never again to interfere in this way, the same European countries met in 1884–85 in Berlin to partition Africa among themselves, inaugurating the colonization of the continent.

My Ancestors' Garden

Designer
Hood Design Studio (United States)

Collaborators
Pei Cobb Freed & Partners (United States)

Clients
International African American Museum,
City of Charleston (United States)

Location Charleston, South Carolina

Year 2022 (projected opening)

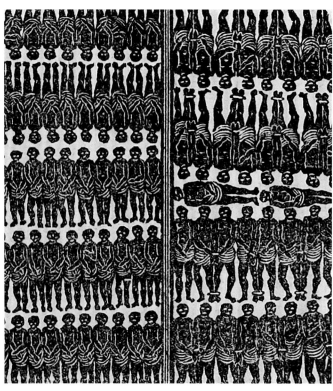

This diagram detail of the slave ship *Brookes*, depicting the inhumane conditions of the vessel loaded with 454 enslaved people, was used by abolitionists in the late eighteenth century in their fight against slavery.

Detail of the memorial at Gadsden's Wharf showing water filling in the outlines of bodies. Hood's design was informed by a diagram of the eighteenth-century slave ship *Brookes* (left).

My Ancestors' Garden memorializes the port of entry for nearly half of all the enslaved Africans brought to North America: Gadsden's Wharf, now the home of the International African American Museum in downtown Charleston, South Carolina. The museum's landscape design exposes what had been erased—the wharf's location had never been marked—revealing truths long obscured and unacknowledged. On this site, now considered sacred ground, thousands of enslaved people were warehoused and sold, and many died.

The landscape design strategy, developed by Walter Hood of Hood Design Studio in Oakland, California, takes its cues from "hush harbor" landscapes where Africans enslaved in the United States could meet freely and share stories and traditions from their homelands. Hood's final design, one of twenty-nine concepts developed with the local community, incorporates a sweetgrass field bounded by curving brick walls, forming a quiet and secure gathering space. A large, shallow tidal pool ebbs and flows, revealing, when low, the life-size outlines of bodies described in the well-known diagram of a packed slave ship. The museum's entrance is framed by mounds of Carolina low-country plantings and a stand of palm trees. To honor this hallowed place, the building is raised on pillars, creating unobstructed views out to the harbor, where ships bearing enslaved people once arrived, and an informal place of assembly where people may once again share stories and traditions.

How can design embrace truth and dignity in a search for peace and justice?

At the edge of Gadsden's Wharf in Charleston, South Carolina, the ebb and flow of water reveals and conceals hallowed ground in a memorial to African ancestors. Atlantic Passage renderings by Hood Design Studio, 2019.

The Murder
of Halit Yozgat

Project Team
Eyal Weizman (principal investigator), Christina
Varvia (project and research coordinator), Yamen
Albadin, Ortrun Bargholz, Franc Camps-Febrer,
Omar Ferwati, Stefanos Levidis, Nicholas Masterton,
Sarah Nankivell, Hana Rizvanolli, Simone Rowat,
Eeva Sarlin, Robert Trafford, Chris Cobb-Smith
(advisor), Lawrence Abu Hamdan (advisor), Forensic
Architecture (United Kingdom)

Collaborators
Ayşe Güleç, Natascha Sadr Haghighian, Fritz Laszlo
Weber, The People's Tribunal "Unraveling the NSU
Complex" (Germany); Cordula Hamschmidt, Christopher
Hupe, Haus der Kulturen der Welt (Germany); Khaled
Abdulwahed, Frank Bubenwer, Cem Kayan, Vanina Vignal
(filmmaking) (Germany, France); Dr. Salvador Navarro-
Martinez, Imperial College London (United Kingdom);

Armament Research Services (United States); Grant
Waters, Anderson Acoustics (United Kingdom); Başak
Ertür, Serdar Kazak, Norma Tiedemann (translation)
(United Kingdom, Germany); Mihai Meirosu, Nvision
Audio (United Kingdom); Sebastian Bodirsky (color
grading), Gozen Atila (Germany)

Commissioned by People's Tribunal "Unraveling the
NSU Complex," Initiative 6 April, Haus der Kulturen der
Welt, documenta 14 (Germany)

Official Inquiries Presented to Hessen Parliamentary
NSU-Inquiry, used in the Report of the German
Federal Parliamentary NSU-Inquiry, 2017 (Germany)

Original Incident Kassel, Germany, April 6, 2006

Investigation 2016–17

A composite of Forensic Architecture's physical and virtual
reconstructions of the internet café where Halit Yozgat was
murdered. Image by Forensic Architecture, 2017.

How can design embrace truth and dignity in a search for peace and justice?

The London-based research agency Forensic Architecture partners with activists, lawyers, international organizations, and media to investigate with and on behalf of those affected by conflict, police brutality, border regimes, and environmental violence. The team uses innovative spatial and architectural analysis methods, open-source investigation, digital modeling, and immersive technologies to gather and present evidence.

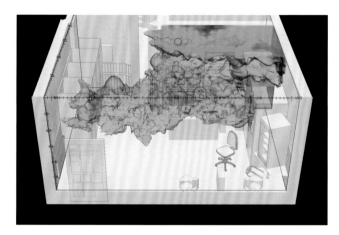

Fluid-dynamics simulation of gunpowder residue (ammonia) in the front room of the internet café where Halit Yozgat was murdered. Image by Forensic Architecture and Dr. Salvador Navarro-Martinez, 2017.

One such investigation sought to expose the institutional racism and structural violence embedded in Germany's security services. On April 6, 2006, twenty-one-year-old Halit Yozgat, the son of Turkish immigrants, was murdered in his family's internet café in Kassel, Germany. His was the ninth of ten racist murders committed in Germany between 2000 and 2007 by the neo-Nazi group National Socialist Underground (NSU). Andreas Temme, a German domestic intelligence agent, was in the café at the time but claimed not to have witnessed the murder.

Forensic Architecture constructed a full-scale physical model of the internet café and then reenacted and filmed nine minutes and twenty-six seconds of the incident based on a reenactment video Temme himself had previously made for the police. In addition, they analyzed witness reports and other data to pinpoint the relative positions of those present at the time of Yozgat's death—migrant community members, the state agent, and the racist murderers. The group's investigation was captured in a series of videos that analyze the events surrounding the murder. The project exposed Temme's testimony as untruthful, raising larger questions about the involvement of German state agencies with radical right-wing groups.

Paper
Monuments

Team
Suzanne-Juliette Mobley, Bryan C. Lee Jr. (co-directors); Nic Brierre Aziz, Chris Daemmrich, Colin Fredrickson, Shoshana Gordon, Brittany Lindsey, John Ludlam, Isabella Siegel, Katie Wills, Colloqate Design (United States)

Partners
American Library Association, Amistad Research Center, Antenna Gallery, Arts Council of New Orleans, Ashé Cultural Arts Center, A Studio in the Woods, Backatown Coffee Parlour, Crescent City Books, Community Book Center, Contemporary Arts Center of New Orleans, Habana Works, Historypin, Know NOLA Tours, Loyola University New Orleans Department of Design, Material Life, Midlo Center for New Orleans Studies at the University of New Orleans, Monument Lab, New Orleans Museum of Art, National Organization of Minority Architects Louisiana, Newcomb Art Museum at Tulane University, New Orleans African American Museum, New Orleans Public Libraries, New Orleans Recreation Department, New Orleans Redevelopment Authority, Octavia Books, Pagoda Cafe, Paper Machine, RIDE New Orleans, Studio Be, Tubby and Coo's Mid-City Book Shop, YEP Design Works (United States)

Location
New Orleans, Louisiana

Years 2017–20

Community volunteers help the Paper Monuments team paste posters on public-facing walls, New Orleans, 2018.

In 2017, after the city of New Orleans removed four Jim Crow–era Confederate statues, a collective of designers, artists, urbanists, and educators asked, "What's next?" Their two-year public art, history, and engagement project, Paper Monuments, invited residents to imagine new public monuments for the city. Not limited to a given site, they were encouraged to label and locate them where they seemed fit.

In a deeply democratic process, submissions—drawings accompanied by descriptions—were tracked by zip code, allowing participatory strategies to be adjusted as needed to ensure the project reflected the city's diverse population and reached as many people as possible. In the end, over a thousand proposals were submitted online and at public, private, and civic locations by participants aged three to seventy-eight years. Many of the proposals were what the group termed "truly monumental," asserting a vision for what the world should be, not venerating individuals on a pedestal but manifesting inclusion, empathy, and equity.

Expanding their focus, the team engaged artists and scholars to create a series of seventy-five posters relating contested or little-known histories of the city, which were then—via the Framing Histories initiative—pasted to walls or framed and mounted in public spaces in neighborhoods relevant to the stories they told. The themes expressed in the posters and public proposals were transformed by local artists into ten temporary, three-dimensional public artworks called Re:Present New Orleans. In another series, titled Imagined Monuments, the group created renderings of twenty representative public monument proposals, imagining their creators' visions brought to life within the city.

Paper Monuments Framing History posters, Canal Street, New Orleans, 2018.

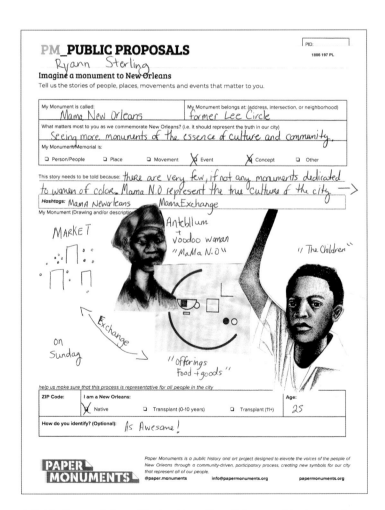

A Public Proposals form filled out by a New Orleans resident, one of over a thousand collected, suggests a monument dedicated the city's women of color, capturing "the essence of culture and community."

Artist Langston Allston installs his work *12 14 16 18*, one of ten ephemeral artworks in the Paper Monuments series Re:Present at the New Orleans African American Museum, 2019.

Women, War, and Peace

Binalakshmi Nepram
interviewed by Cynthia E. Smith

Cynthia E. Smith You are an Indigenous scholar, author, and civil rights activist, and you also advocate for disarmament and women-led peace. What led you to this work?

Binalakshmi Nepram I was born in a war zone in one of Asia's longest-running armed conflicts. It is still going on. On the day of my birth there was a military operation; my mother could have died because of lack of access to medicine. The older I grew the more I understood the violence, the more I became committed to finding ways to resolve it. Honestly, I was not aware that I was growing up in a war zone. We once had one hundred days of no school because of military operations and lockdowns called by armed and civil society organizations and I thought this was normal. The military coming into our house—I thought it was normal. The insurgents coming and asking for food and shelter—I thought it was normal. "Don't ask questions or you will be shot"—I thought that was normal. The culture of repression and silence was prevalent. When I came out of that war zone and started sharing my experience, I realized that I had grown up in an abnormal situation. What's going on there? It's not written. It's not recorded. It's not spoken of. It hurts when you realize the world is completely silent about it. You ask, why is the world silent? That made

Binalakshmi Nepram speaks at a side meeting during a session of the United Nations Commission on the Status of Women, New York, 2015.

Binalakshmi Nepram is the founder of Manipur Women Gun Survivors Network and Control Arms Foundation of India, convener for the Northeast India Women Initiative for Peace, and cofounder of the Global Alliance of Indigenous Peoples, Gender Justice and Peace.

How can design embrace truth and dignity in a search for peace and justice?

me speak about this issue, to work with survivors. Not just on a theoretical level, but to provide support to so many women, the survivors of this conflict.

Thank you for sharing your personal story. What is the history of Manipur? Why does it remain a war zone?

Manipur was an independent nation-state, which has a three-thousand-year recorded history. We have our own script [written form of a language] called Meitei Mayek. I speak Meiteilon, a Tibeto-Burman language that is different from Burmese and Tibetan but is a similar language genre. We have our own written constitution. We are an ancient Asiatic nation-state, in existence from the year 33 AD. And then this region of Asia came under British colonial rule. In 1891 we fought a war with Britain. We were defeated, and our leaders were executed. However, Britain let our sovereign rule as they took charge of defense and economy. Then in 1947 India's independence treaty with Britain stated that Manipur could choose whether it wanted to be part of India. We stated that we were never part of India and so we were going back to our independent status, pre–British rule. India imprisoned the Indigenous king of Manipur and forced him to sign a merger agreement. Manipur had its own Indigenous Constitution, its own council of ministers, and a chief minister, based on a modern democratic system of universal adult franchise.

The Armed Forces Special Powers Act has been in place since 1958. This law gives Indian armed forces personnel impunity, and the extraordinary power to detain us, to shoot us, to kill us. As a result, over 20,000 lives were lost due to the violence in Manipur alone. There are over 1,500 extrajudicial killings recorded, and this has been submitted to the Supreme Court of India, and there have been many cases of enforced disappearances. India refuses to recognize what it has done, but history cannot lie to us. These decades of violence have been hidden away from the rest of the world, as global journalists are not allowed into Manipur and many other parts of the Northeast region. Nor is the history of forty-five million Indigenous peoples recorded in the historical narrative of the world's largest democracy. If you visit India with an Indian visa, you are not allowed in our territories. There are three hundred thousand troops in the Northeast of India right now. India has colonized this region for the past six decades. It doesn't want the world to know this, and that's why news and information from this region are really cut off, not just from the rest of the world but from the rest of India, which doesn't know what its own government is doing to its own people.

You've described how in your home state of Manipur, forty-five million people have been left out of the global narrative. There are more than three hundred similar unknown and unreported conflicts in the world. Can you talk more about the harm caused by this underreporting in your efforts to build peace?

Conflict will happen as long as human beings exist. When India denies the existence of conflict in Manipur, it denies our history, our struggles, and efforts for humanitarian aid to reach us to help thousands impacted by seven decades of war. We maintain our neutrality while working for Indigenous people's rights and gender justice. We're not with the army, and we're not with the insurgents, we are not with any political party. We are a neutral, humanitarian, civilians' network working to help survivors of the violence, sandwiched between the guns of the state and the guns of non-state actors. We work with the casualties of conflict: women, young children, ethnic minorities, Indigenous peoples. Civilians are left on their own, without any humanitarian aid during a raging war. There is violence every day in our lives, but there is no help coming. Having experienced that and survived that, I felt it was so wrong. There is a huge humanitarian crisis that the world hasn't woken up to. With Manipur as a case study we hope the world will start pushing policy makers, thinkers, and those who work for peace to ask about the other unreported conflicts in the world.

This lack of visibility. Did it influence your early research into the proliferation of weapons, state violence, and insurgent groups on the border? How did mapping this activity inform your research?

My 2002 book *South Asia's Fractured Frontier* has become one of the key resources for understanding this conflict and the interactions between gunrunning and the trafficking of arms, drugs, women, and children.[1] I discovered in my research that killing is magnified when there is a heavy influx of weaponry and "technologies of killing." AK-47s can fire six hundred rounds in a minute. The Indian army carry sophisticated weapons; insurgents carry small arms such as M-16 and AK-47 rifles. I started researching these tools of violence and how they reached Manipur and Northeast India. To my amazement I discovered the presence of more than fifty-eight types of guns from thirteen countries. This is when I realized that America may have never heard of Manipur, but its M16s are flooding my region. China may say that it is not involved in the Manipur conflict, but its cheaply made 9 mm guns and hand grenades are easily available and used for

Binalakshmi Nepram discusses the mitigation of sexual violence in conflict zones with Indigenous Manipuri women at a village community meeting, Wokha, India, 2016.

committing acts of violence. I also realized that those benefiting from this conflict are not the warring parties, not even the government of India or the armed groups. It is arms manufacturers and gun dealers. It is important to note that that it is the permanent five members of the United Nations Security Council who manufacture 88 percent of world's weapons and it's these weapons that are found in conflict zones around the world.

I interviewed gunrunners, people who traffic AK-47s, asking why they are doing this. They said, "I have to feed my children. I don't want to do it." I have interviewed Indian military personnel as young as twenty-two years old patrolling the streets of Manipur. *Why are you a part of the killings?* "I have to feed my children too." I realized whether it is state or non-state, many young lives are put at the front line of battlefields and they come from very poor and marginalized families. Those who colonize, create wars and conflicts, and divide communities live in fortified bunkers, away from the conflict zone, while it is the poorest and most vulnerable living in our villages that bear the brunt. I realized the humanity of what's happening, and I realized that someone was playing us as puppets, one against the other and this must stop.

What do you see as the role of Indigenous people and women, in Manipur and elsewhere, in attaining peace, security, and disarmament? In your experience, what are the most helpful ways to amplify these hidden and forgotten stories?

We launched the Manipur Women Gun Survivors Network in 2007 to help women and families who are survivors of the conflict. We help to feed these families, get children to school, make occupational therapy accessible, and work with pro-bono lawyers to register these killings. Around the same time, we launched the Control Arms Foundation of India in New Delhi—India's first disarmament organization to impact policy makers. Our organizations are diverse, inclusive, and women-led because the narrative of war and conflict has always been a masculine one of power and guns on both sides of state or non-state. Currently, there have been seventeen peace talks in Manipur and Northeast India without a single woman involved. We realized that we had to bring a gender dimension, a humanitarian dimension, otherwise this war would go on endlessly.

I thought whatever was happening in Manipur was a local and regional concern. However, when I started traveling for work meeting women from Rwanda, from Peru, Mexico, Brazil, Argentina, Afghanistan, from Guatemala, Myanmar, Nepal, Sri Lanka, Kenya, Philippines, I learned about their conflicts. I saw the parallels with Mothers of the Plaza de Mayo in Argentina.

In Manipur we have a 116-year-old non-violent women's movement that formed to resist British colonial policies. Our work for peace is built on the courage of the many extraordinary Manipuri women who have walked before me: those who fought against colonialism using their bodies as a site of resistance, such as the Manipuri Meira Paibi or "Manipuri women with bamboo torches" movement.[2]

How can design embrace truth and dignity in a search for peace and justice?

After I started traveling, I met women from different war zones, such as women from the Congo, where I learned the Congolese people were made to fight each other because of coltan, a metallic ore that is refined and used in our cell phones. Biodiversity hotspots have been the sites of armed conflicts for decades, with Indigenous peoples making up 80 percent of these areas' populations. With the growth and perpetuation of corporatized democracies, there is no end in sight to the patterns of conflict and irreversible environmental damage.

As a visiting scholar at Columbia University in 2017, I discovered the strength of the collective world of indigeneity in a course on Indigenous people's rights and attended the United Nations Permanent Forum on Indigenous Issues. I met more strong, powerful Indigenous women from around the world whose stories and struggles were similar to ours.[3] We cried together when a woman told me how nuclear dumps poisoned the waters her children drank. We bonded as we shared the familiar stories of militarization, weaponization, and exploitation of Indigenous lands and resources. It made me realize that a lot of Indigenous territories around the world have become sites of military and nuclear testing. We saw the importance of working together because the stories are so similar, and so in 2019 we formed the Global Alliance of Indigenous Peoples, Gender Justice and Peace. In March 2021 we brought together women from seven sociocultural Indigenous zones around the world for the first time to talk about what's happening in our territories and find what I call "Indigenous ways of peace making and peacebuilding." The "non-peace" that we have in the world is due to the fact that modernity, the way in which modern nation-states have been created, has been implemented so violently. If we are to find that peace, we will have to take the hands and wisdom and knowledge of Indigenous peoples. And if we do not do that, we will only keep hurting one another. I'm invested in the concept of Indigenous peace, constitutions, and democracies. Treaty making that honors who we are together.

Today's world is interlinked, and we cannot stay in isolation and separation. It's about recognizing our histories and giving respect to each other's struggles; saying sorry for what has happened and then moving on by inclusive, diverse policy in our nation and community building—that's what we are asking for. But to this day, it has been denied to us. For peacebuilding to work, nation-states must have the courage to acknowledge their mistakes to their marginalized and Indigenous communities. Once that healing starts, the world will have much more peace.

Can you talk more about the work you do with the Manipur Women Gun Survivors Network and how this work supports sustainable livelihoods along with Indigenous culture and traditions?

It is the soul of our work. We work directly with women and family survivors of conflict—there are twenty thousand registered widows due to armed conflict. One mother we work closely with, whose two sons—ages seventeen and twenty-seven—were shot dead by Indian paramilitary in one day, told us she was just waiting to join her sons in death. I kept meeting with her regularly and told her "We feel your pain." Our team saw a loom in her house, so gave her a bit of silk cocoons to reel. She started reeling the silk cocoons, began selling the silk, and then weaving on her loom. She now runs the Weaving Enterprise, with five looms, and employs several women weavers. When I first met her, her cheeks were sunken, but now her cheeks are pink. The healing is what inspires us at Manipur Women Gun Survivors Network .

Our work for gender justice, peace, and disarmament consists of three basic steps. First, put food on the table. In a war zone, we cannot teach human rights or gender justice on an empty stomach. We always see how the family is doing. Are they eating healthy? Are the children going to school after a killing? Second, we ask what the surviving family member wants to do. We provide a little seed money, two thousand to three thousand Indian rupees, like eighty or a hundred dollars. We did not know what an NGO was when we began. Then we open bank accounts for them, because in Asia, particularly in Manipur and the Northeast Region women don't have anything to call their own. Third, we start the process of what I call collective healing, through addressing the wrongs done. We ask if they want to work with pro bono lawyers to find justice through litigation. We train the women to know what government programs and services they are entitled to as survivors of conflict. We use art as a way of expressing the trauma and violence they have gone through— painting, drawing, theater—where the women play out what happened in their lives. Indigenous festivals bring us together for collective healing from trauma caused by decades of war. Because we come from a culture of weaving, our team explored the idea of "weaving peace," using Indigenous textile weavings from Manipur to create a "culture of peace and resilience." We supported over a hundred women weavers in Manipur and set up Weaving Villages to help in economic strengthening and managed to raise the income level of women 30 to 100 percent. In my Indigenous culture, many homes have looms, a lot of women weave every day. I've seen homes where there have been deaths and killings, but the women and children learn to weave. And the fabric is so strong compared to the fragility of life. Hope is the strongest human emotion that carries us toward global peace.

In 2016 you edited *Where Are Our Women in Decision Making on UNSCR 1325?*[4], a book about the landmark United Nations Security Council Resolution on women and peace and security, which was adopted in 2000. Why is it important for women to take the lead?

The two-page resolution was the first gender resolution ever passed in the Security Council. This historic document on women and armed conflict spoke to us. I remember the joy I felt when I first laid my hands on it a decade after it was passed. It talks about how women are disproportionately affected in conflict areas. It's the men who mostly go to war, and the women are left to pick up the pieces of life. Women are not at the negotiation table, so even if the "men made peace with nations" it was not sustainable peace, as it excluded half the population. In Manipur and Northeast India, peace was negotiated with Indian government on one side and the rebels negotiating on the other. No one was taking women's voices into consideration. The UNSCR 1325 states that women be included in all forms of decision making—socio, economic, and political—in times of war and peace.

Why did seventeen peace accords in Manipur fail?

Because they excluded half the population. We have got to change how power is defined; we need a narrative of power that gives agency to every human, not just men. It's so important to have a gender perspective—to see where our voices are included and respected and where we have the agency to define what we want for the next ten or twenty years.

Knowledge is such a beautiful thing. It's like light. Once we discovered UNSCR 1325, our little team realized we had to share the knowledge. The UN has many challenges, but one thing it produces are good documents. We took this document, translated it into several Indigenous languages, and did a series of trainings across Manipur, Northeast India, and the Indo-Burma region letting women know they are not alone in the struggle and that there's a world body out there trying to mitigate violence in conflict zones. The book is a product of the trainings. It was the collective work of many people.

Are there systems we could put in place—at a local, national, or international level—that could support these efforts to bring women to the negotiating table?

We had the third Northeast India Indigenous Women Peace Congregation in 2020, which yielded several directives for the future. One resolution calls for rejecting any peace talk, whether in Manipur or around the world, that does not make women equal stakeholders in the negotiations. Another calls for the inclusion of voices from forgotten conflict zones. In Northeast India we have had more than four hundred thousand people living in more than three dozen displaced people's camps since 1990. A third directive is about including the voices of the 476 million Indigenous people living in ninety countries and territories with 80 percent of the world's biodiversity hotspots. This calls for equitable sharing of resources, which is important to peacebuilding work, because as long as greed exists, for-profit exploitation will continue. We also affirmed that peacebuilding cannot be a project where after two years you suddenly abandon everything and go away. That creates more misunderstanding. Generally peacebuilding is done on a project-by-project basis, but funders need to align, know what others are doing in different parts of the world, and have a more cohesive interaction to really transform peace.

"Peace is not a project, it is a way to fight back." Can you expand a little on this idea? How might peace be active?

Peace starts from within. With how we relate to ourselves and the world around us and how we nurture that and think of a larger collective rather than just "me, myself." Peacemaking has to be a process of continuous dialogue. Peace is hard work, every single day. It is a commitment for a lifetime.

What is your definition of peace?

For me, growing up in Manipur, peace is when our lives are not controlled by the barrel of a gun. Not put under surveillance and militarized. Peace is the freedom to be who we are and to live our life, without threats or exile for what we believe and what is enshrined in our constitutions or in the Universal Declaration of Human Rights or law of nature. Peace is the ability to go to school freely without fear or being locked down by humans or by a pandemic. Peace for the Indigenous peoples of Manipur and Northeast India is the removal of the former British colonial martial law called the Armed Forces Special Powers Act imposed on our people since 1958 by the government of India. Peace

Demanding justice for the twenty thousand women whose husbands and children were shot and killed by Indian armed forces and state security agencies in Manipur, Binalakshmi Nepram and others protest at the India Gate, Delhi, 2017.

is when we are able to get justice for the decades of violence done to our bodies, to our lives, to our territories, to our consciousness, to our histories. Peace is when nation-states apologize for the wrongs and the genocide committed against Black, Brown, and Indigenous communities, and set up truth and reconciliation measures. Peace is to take the first step towards collective healing within ourselves, in our communities, and in our nations.

How might we design for peace?

Designing peace is about hope. Hope that things will become better, less violent than they are now.

If we are to create a culture of peace, it has to start from a very young age, so our children will be able to take a stand when they become adults. Designing peace means reimagining and rewriting our histories, where cultures of Indigenous peoples and nations are woven equally in the narrative of the world. Where Indigenous peoples are not labeled "savages."

It is an inclusive process, listening to one another and respecting one another, then finding the collective courage to create that collective peace that every being and non-being in this world deserves.

1   Binalakshmi Nepram, *South Asia's Fractured Frontier: Armed Conflict, Narcotics, and Small Arms Proliferation in India's North East* (New Delhi: Mittal, 2002).

2   Manipuri women, especially mothers called *Meira Paibis*, have been at the forefront of a nonviolent peace and resistance movement since the late 1970s. Women's groups in Manipur have developed many powerful nonviolent actions designed to confront the insurgency that has engulfed the region in the last seven decades. See

Nepram, "The Meira Paibis: The Brave Mothers of Manipur at the Forefront of a Strong Nonviolent Resistance Movement," *Minds of the Movement* (blog), September 20, 2019, nonviolent-conflict.org/ blog_post/the-meira-paibis- the-brave-mothers-of-manipur- at-the-forefront-of-a- strong-nonviolent-resistance- movement.

3   The United Nations Permanent Forum on Indigenous Issues (UNPFII) is a high-level advisory body to the Economic and Social Council. The forum was established on July 28,

2000, with the mandate to deal with Indigenous issues related to economic and social development, culture, the environment, education, health, and human rights.

4   Binalakshmi Nepram, ed., *Where Are Our Women in Decision Making? Seminal Studies on United Nations Landmark Security Council Resolution 1325: Women, Peace & Security with Focus on Northeast India with Mentions of Bangladesh and Myanmar* (New Delhi: Control Arms Foundation of India, 2016).

"To Whom Does the Earth Belong?"

Julia Risler and Pablo Ares

This world map surveys the work of the 1.7 billion rural and farmer women around the world who, in addition to producing 70 percent of the food we eat, resist patriarchal violence and Western domination, and organize in their communities. The practices and knowledge that support the economies of care for these women, who in turn protect food sovereignty and public goods, are threatened by the agroindustrial food system's extractive projects and by the violence that results from it—genocides, deportations, and wars.

The landforms are based on the Gall-Peters projection, a map of the world created in 1855 by James Gall and revisited in 1974 by Arno Peters. This representation (here with its poles inverted) correctly illustrates the relationships in size among the areas of the Earth— unlike the more common Mercator projection, in which territories are enlarged as they approach the poles.[1] The Gall-Peters projection gained a special relevance in the 1970s, when national liberation movements challenged the Western domination of the world, and in our work it plays both a geographic and a symbolic role. The atypical projection and the placement of south at the top of the map upend conventional presentations of the Earth, thus providing a fitting basis for a visualization that identifies the presence of farmers, rural majorities, and biocultural diversity, and that labels extractive projects and armed conflicts while also highlighting the efforts of women in defending the land.[2] Bilingual, in Spanish and English, the map is available for free download for domestic or communal use.

Julia Risler is a cofounder of the Buenos Aires–based design and research duo Iconoclasistas, which deploys cartography and other graphic arts in service of social justice. **Pablo Ares** is a cofounder of Iconoclasistas. A self-taught graphic artist, he has made comics for Argentine magazines, and his animated films have been shown in international short film festivals.

1 The Mercator projection, developed in 1569 by the Flemish cartographer Gerardus Mercator and widely adopted for use in navigation, preserves the shapes of the Earth's landforms but not their relative sizes. Size distortion increases toward the poles, so land masses in the far south and far north appear much larger than territories near the equator. For example, in the Mercator projection Greenland appears to be the same size as Africa, while in reality it is similar in size to the Democratic Republic of the Congo, which is just one of Africa's more than sixty states and territories.

2 The term "biocultural" describes and acknowledges the co-evolution and interdependence of biology and human culture. Biocultural diversity is a measure of the diversity of all life in a region, including human languages and cultures as well as plants and animals and their habitats and ecosystems.

How can design embrace truth and dignity in a search for peace and justice?

"To Whom Does the Earth Belong?"   Julia Risler and Pablo Ares   157

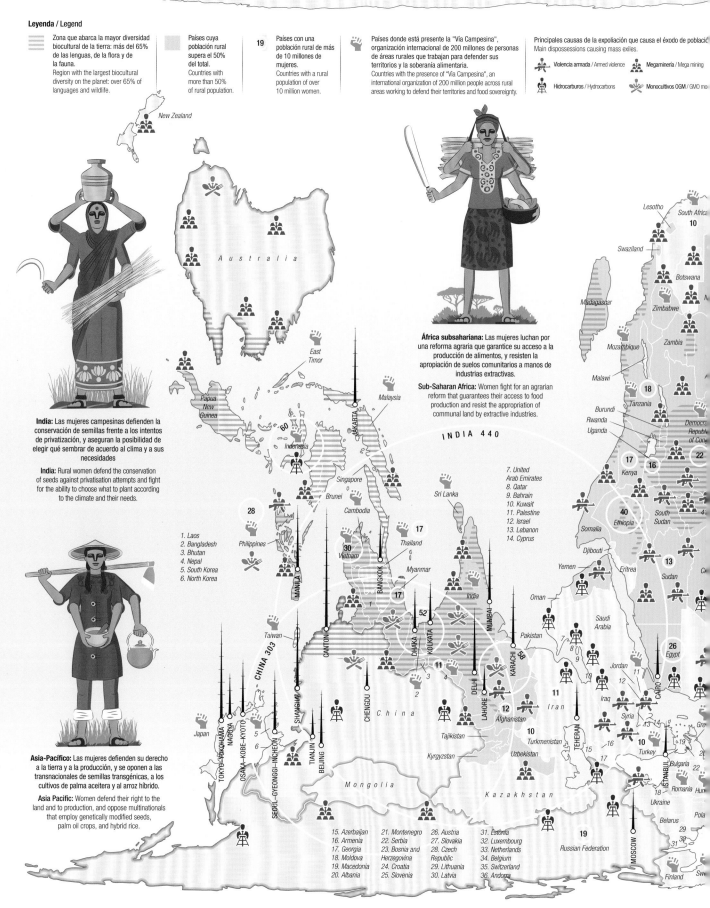

Leyenda / Legend

Zona que abarca la mayor diversidad biocultural de la tierra: más del 65% de las lenguas, de la flora y de la fauna.
Region with the largest biocultural diversity on the planet: over 65% of languages and wildlife.

Países cuya población rural supera el 50% del total.
Countries with more than 50% of rural population.

19 Países con una población rural de más de 10 millones de mujeres.
Countries with a rural population of over 10 million women.

Países donde está presente la "Vía Campesina", organización internacional de 200 millones de personas de áreas rurales que trabajan para defender sus territorios y la soberanía alimentaria.
Countries with the presence of "Vía Campesina", an international organization of 200 million people across rural areas working to defend their territories and food sovereignty.

Principales causas de la expoliación que causa el éxodo de población
Main dispossessions causing mass exiles.

Violencia armada / Armed violence
Megaminería / Mega mining
Hidrocarburos / Hydrocarbons
Monocultivos OGM / GMO mo

New Zealand

Australia

India: Las mujeres campesinas defienden la conservación de semillas frente a los intentos de privatización, y aseguran la posibilidad de elegir qué sembrar de acuerdo al clima y a sus necesidades
India: Rural women defend the conservation of seeds against privatisation attempts and fight for the ability to choose what to plant according to the climate and their needs.

Asia-Pacífico: Las mujeres defienden su derecho a la tierra y a la producción, y se oponen a las transnacionales de semillas transgénicas, a los cultivos de palma aceitera y al arroz híbrido.
Asia Pacific: Women defend their right to the land and to production, and oppose multinationals that employ genetically modified seeds, palm oil crops, and hybrid rice.

África subsahariana: Las mujeres luchan por una reforma agraria que garantice su acceso a la producción de alimentos, y resisten la apropiación de suelos comunitarios a manos de industrias extractivas.
Sub-Saharan Africa: Women fight for an agrarian reform that guarantees their access to food production and resist the appropriation of communal land by extractive industries.

East Timor

Papua New Guinea

Indonesia

Malaysia

Singapore

Brunei

Cambodia

Philippines

Vietnam

Thailand

Myanmar

Taiwan

Japan

INDIA 440

1. Laos
2. Bangladesh
3. Bhutan
4. Nepal
5. South Korea
6. North Korea

7. United Arab Emirates
8. Qatar
9. Bahrain
10. Kuwait
11. Palestine
12. Israel
13. Lebanon
14. Cyprus

28
30
17
17
52
58
11

Sri Lanka

India

Pakistan

Afghanistan

China

Mongolia

Kazakhstan

Tajikistan

Kyrgyzstan

Uzbekistan

Turkmenistan

Iran

Iraq

Syria

Jordan

Saudi Arabia

Oman

Yemen

TEHERAN

Turkey

Russian Federation

MOSCOW

Ukraine

Belarus

Finland

Bulgaria

Romania

19

CHINA 303

TOKYO-YOKOHAMA
NAGOYA
OSAKA-KOBE-KYOTO
SEOUL-GYEONGGI-INCHEON
SHANGHAI
TIANJIN
BEIJING
CHENGDU
CANTON
MANILA
JAKARTA
BANGKOK
DHAKA
KOLKATA
DELHI
LAHORE
MUMBAI
KARACHI
CAIRO
ISTANBUL

60

15. Azerbaijan
16. Armenia
17. Georgia
18. Moldova
19. Macedonia
20. Albania

21. Montenegro
22. Serbia
23. Bosnia and Herzegovina
24. Croatia
25. Slovenia

26. Austria
27. Slovakia
28. Czech Republic
29. Lithuania
30. Latvia

31. Estonia
32. Luxembourg
33. Netherlands
34. Belgium
35. Switzerland
36. Andorra

Lesotho
South Africa **10**
Swaziland
Botswana
Zimbabwe
Madagascar
Mozambique
Zambia
Malawi
Tanzania
Burundi
Rwanda
Uganda
Kenya
Democratic Republic of Cong
Somalia
South Sudan
Ethiopia **40**
Djibouti
Eritrea
Sudan
Egypt **26**

18
17
16
22
13
10

Megaciudades y crisis ambiental

En 2007, por primera vez en la historia, la población residente en ciudades es mayor a la población campesina. Aún así, en las zonas rurales viven unas 3.400 millones de personas que se dedican a producir alimentos y más de la mitad son mujeres. Ellas sostienen prácticas de reciprocidad, preservan las memorias y saberes ancestrales, trabajan y cultivan la tierra en equilibrio con los ciclos de la naturaleza; y aportan una solución a la crisis ecológica y a los desastres climáticos, cada vez más frecuentes en el mundo.

Megacities and environmental crisis

In 2007, for the first time ever, the population living in cities surpassed the one living in the countryside. However, some 3.4 billion people still live in rural areas and work in food production—more than half of them are women. They support reciprocity practices, preserve ancestral memories and know-how, work and cultivate the land in harmony with the cycles of nature, and provide a solution to the environmental crisis and the increasing climate-related disasters worldwide.

Trabajo rural y doméstico

Estas 1.700 millones de mujeres representan un 25% de la población mundial, y alimentan a un 70% de los habitantes del planeta. Las mujeres rurales, además del cuidado de sembradíos, la obtención de agua y leña y la cría de animales; realizan un trabajo invisible y no remunerado: el doméstico, el cual incluye el cuidado de los hijos y de personas enfermas, la limpieza del hogar y la elaboración de alimentos, todas labores consideradas como una extensión (obligada) de sus tareas de reproducción biológica.

Rural and domestic work

These 1.7 billion women represent 25% of th population and feed 70% of the world popula Aside from tending crops, gathering water an firewood, and raising animals, they perform ir work. They are not paid for their domestic wo which includes caring for children and the sic cleaning the home, and preparing food—all ac that are considered an (obligatory) extension o biological reproductive functions.

es donde se encuentran las casas centrales
as principales empresas armamentistas,
oleras, mineras, alimenticias, de semillas
sgénicas y agroquímicas.

ntries with headquarters of leading companies
e oil, mining, food, GMO seed, and
ochemical sectors.

20 — 15 — 10 — 5 ○ **Ciudades de más de 10 millones de habitantes.**
Cities with more than 10 million inhabitants.

lamérica: Las mujeres de movimientos rurales
de recuperación territorial, frenan la acción
ropiadora y privatizadora de las corporaciones
gronegocios y sus monocultivos de soja y maíz.

South America: Women of the rural movements
erritorial reappropriation resist to the expropriation
and privatisation attempts of large agribusiness
orporations and to soy and maize monocultures.

38. Equatorial Guinea
39. Benin
40. Togo
41. Central African Republic
42. Gambia
43. Senegal

Argentina
Uruguay
BUENOS AIRES
Chile
Paraguay
RIO DE JANEIRO
SÃO PAULO
Peru
Bolivia
LIMA
B r a z i l
15
44
Colombia
French Guiana
Suriname
Guyana
Venezuela
Grenada

Ivory Coast
hana
Liberia
Sierra Leone
Guinea
Guinea-Bissau
Burkina
42
43
Mali
Mauritania
Western Sahara
eria
Morocco
Spain
Portugal
France
United Kingdom
Ireland
LONDON
Iceland
Greenland (Denmark)

Mundo árabe: Las mujeres sostienen una
economía de cuidados en medio de enormes
conflictos armados, y supervisan en sus
comunidades la asistencia en salud,
alimentos, cobijo y educación.

Arab World: Women maintain a care economy
in the middle of massive armed conflicts and
supervise health, nutrition, shelter, and
educational assistance in their communities.

¿A QUIÉN PERTENECE LA TIERRA?
WHO OWNS THE LAND?

En un mundo donde los cuerpos y territorios creadores de vida,
son considerados objetos de conquista, expoliados en actos neocoloniales
y capitalistas, y amenazados por una violencia machista y patriarcal que se
manifiesta en múltiples dimensiones; las mujeres resisten y organizan sus
comunidades a través de economías del cuidado, protegiendo los bienes comunes
y la soberanía alimentaria.

In a world where bodies that give life and territories are considered objects of conquest,
plundered by neocolonial capitalist acts and threatened by multiple forms of sexist male
patriarchal violence, women resist and organise their communities through care
economies, protecting common goods and food sovereignty.

44. Ecuador
45. Panamá
46. Costa Rica
47. El Salvador
48. Guatemala
49. Honduras
50. Belize

46
45
47
48
Puerto Rico
Nicaragua
Haiti
50
Jamaica
49
Dominican Republic
Cuba
MÉXICO
Mexico
13
29
United States of America
LOS ANGELES
NEW YORK
C a n a d a
United States of America

Mesoamérica: Las mujeres se enfrentan a los
tratados de libre comercio, a la expansión de
conflictos armados y al maíz transgénico, y
protegen la diversidad de especies existentes.

Central America: Women stand against free
trade agreements, the spread of armed conflicts,
and genetically modified maize, and protect
the diversity of the living species.

---

ural y represión

limentario agroindustrial, basado en monocultivos
por trasnacionales, alimenta a un 30% de la
undial, y emplea en condiciones miserables a una
de los trabajadores rurales. Destruye el medio
mpobrece y expulsa a los pobladores originarios,
expande a través de la militarización
n, generando la pérdida de los derechos colectivos
enes naturales, y transformando lo común en
rivada.

Rural exodus and repression

The agro-industrial food system, based on monoculture
and dominated by multinational firms, feeds 30%
of the world population and employs—in appalling
conditions—a minuscule portion of rural workers.
It destroys the environment, impoverishes and drives
out native populations, and thrives through militarisation
and repression—thus causing the loss of collective rights
over natural assets and turning public goods
into private property.

Soberanía alimentaria y cultural

Las mujeres rurales, mediante prácticas de defensa de los
bienes comunes, de protección de la cultura popular y
solidaria, y de respeto hacia la naturaleza; aseguran la
agrodiversidad frente al avance del despojo neocolonial.
Custodian, además, las más de 7 mil lenguas vivas en todo el
mundo, cada una desarrollada durante siglos de costumbres y
portadoras de tradiciones y prácticas riquísimas, mayormente
desconocidas, lo que las convierte en guardianas de las
memorias de la tierra.

Food and cultural sovereignty

Through practices that defend public goods, protect
shared traditional culture, and respect nature, rural
women ensure agricultural diversity in the face of
neocolonial dispossession. They are also guardians
of the over 6000 languages spoken across the world,
which developed over the centuries, bear rich
traditions, and are mostly unknown. As a result,
these women are the keepers of the memories
of the Earth.

 Iconoclasistas 2017/2021

The Chronic

Designer and Publisher
Chimurenga (South Africa)

Distribution
Brazil, Egypt, Finland, France, Germany, Kenya,
Lesotho, Namibia, Netherlands, Nigeria, Rwanda,
Senegal, South Africa, Sweden, Tanzania, Uganda,
United Kingdom, United States, Zimbabwe (print),
online (digital)

Years 2011–present

Born out of an urgent need to write differently about the African world, the quarterly broadsheet *The Chronic* prints provocations instead of headlines. Reporting more than the news, it articulates the complexities, innovations, thoughts, and dreams that are a part of everyday life throughout the continent. Interviews, essays, and exposés are interwoven with critical cartographies, photography, original comics, and illustrated stories, histories, and geographies. Its accessible hand-drawn design offers evidence of the people telling and visualizing the stories while also honoring the reader's curiosity and imagination.

Each edition of *The Chronic* engages readers around the world with insightful and provocative stances on political, social, and cultural life across Africa, asking, "When will the new emerge—and if it is already here, how do we decipher it?" To engender new knowledge, fill historical gaps, and examine the complexity of xenophobic violence, *The Chronic*'s pilot issue, a fictional backdated newspaper, chronicled the attacks on African migrants in South Africa three years prior. Another issue harnessed the typically imperialistic tool of cartography, publishing critical maps made by Africans that visualize their own perceptions of life on the continent—from trade and power structures to the movement of people and ideas. And in another a series of illustrations depict a fictional conversation between James Baldwin and Terence Dixon.

The broadsheet is published by Chimurenga, a global platform for writing, art, and politics about Africa by Africans. Its motto, borrowed from Afrobeat pioneer Fela Kuti, is "Who no know go know," suggesting that if one does not yet have the knowledge, go forward and explore to find it—an ethos embodied in this creative broadsheet.

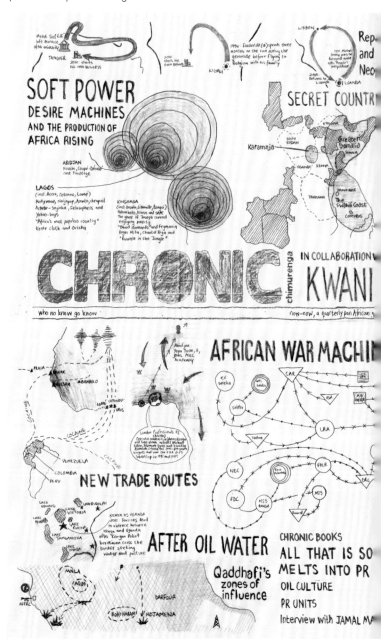

Cover of *The Chronic – New Cartographies*, 2015. Designed and published by Chimurenga in collaboration with Kwani?.

How can design embrace truth and dignity in a search for peace and justice?

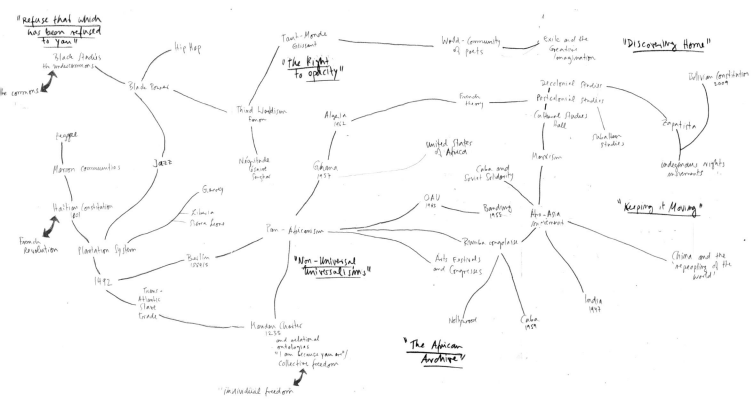

The diagram contains the following hand-written labels and phrases:

"Refuse that which has been refused to you"

Black Studies / the undercommons

the commons

Hip Hop

Black Power

Reggae

Jazz

Maroon communities

Haitian Constitution 1801

French Revolution

Plantation System

1492

Trans-Atlantic Slave Trade

Garvey

Liberia Sierra Leone

Berlin 1884/5

Third Worldism Fanon

Négritude Césaire Senghor

Pan-Africanism

Mandem Charter 1235 and relational ontologies "I am because you are" / collective freedom

"individual freedom"

Tout-Monde Glissant

"the Right to opacity"

Algeria 1962

Ghana 1957

"Non-Universal universalisms"

World-Community of poets

French theory

United States of Africa

OAU 1963

Arts Festivals and Congresses

Rumba congolaise

Nollywood

Cuba 1959

"The African Archive"

Exile and the Creative Imagination

"Discovering Home"

Decolonial Studies

Postcolonial Studies

Cultural Studies Hall

Subaltern Studies

Marxism

Cuba and Soviet Solidarity

Bandung 1955

Afro-Asia movement

India 1947

Bolivian Constitution 2009

Zapatista

indigenous rights movements

"Keeping it Moving"

China and the 'repeopling of the world'

ON CIRCULATIONS AND THE AFRICAN IMAGINATION OF A BORDERLESS WORLD

"On Circulations and the African Imagination of a Borderless World" map, extracted from *The Chronic – the African Imagination of a Borderless World*, 2018.

Cover of *The Chronic – the African Imagination of a Borderless World*, 2018. Designed and published by Chimurenga.

Extract from "Meeting the Man – a remake by Native Maqari," from *The Chronic – imagi-nation nwar*, 2021.

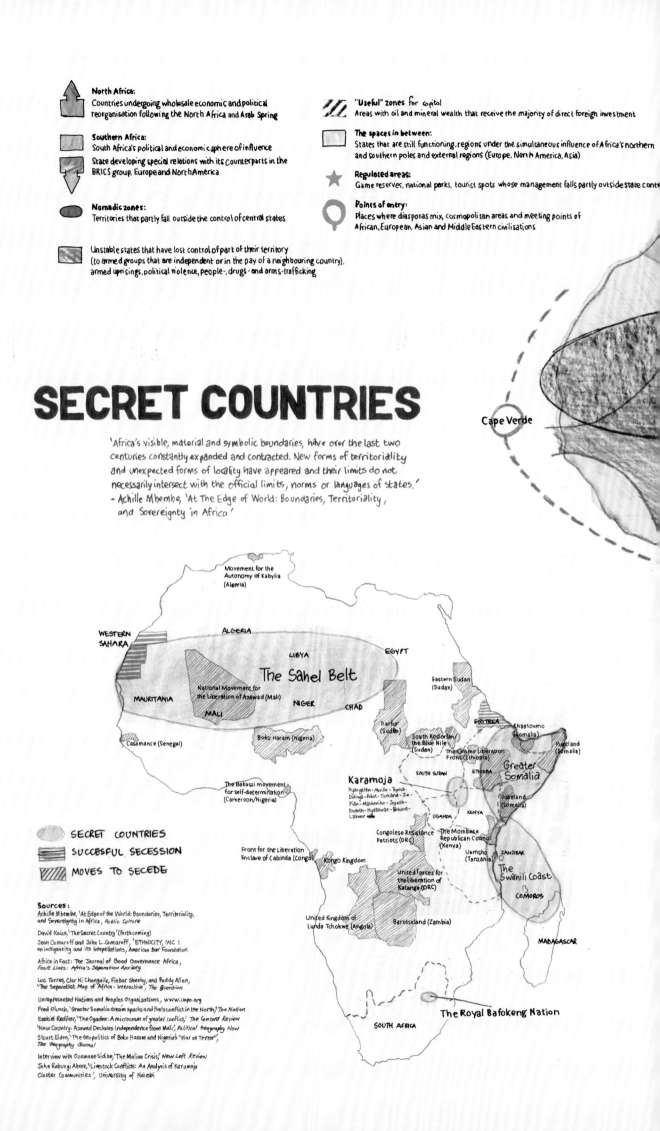

North Africa:
Countries undergoing wholesale economic and political reorganisation following the North Africa and Arab Spring

Southern Africa:
South Africa's political and economic sphere of influence

State developing special relations with its counterparts in the BRICS group, Europe and North America

Nomadic zones:
Territories that partly fall outside the control of central states

Unstable states that have lost control of part of their territory (to armed groups that are independent or in the pay of a neighbouring country), armed uprisings, political violence, people-, drugs- and arms-trafficking

"Useful" zones for capital
Areas with oil and mineral wealth that receive the majority of direct foreign investment

The spaces in between:
States that are still functioning, regions under the simultaneous influence of Africa's northern and southern poles and external regions (Europe, North America, Asia)

Regulated areas:
Game reserves, national parks, tourist spots whose management falls partly outside state cont...

Points of entry:
Places where diasporas mix, cosmopolitan areas and meeting points of African, European, Asian and Middle Eastern civilisations

SECRET COUNTRIES

'Africa's visible, material and symbolic boundaries, have over the last two centuries constantly expanded and contracted. New forms of territoriality and unexpected forms of locality have appeared and their limits do not necessarily intersect with the official limits, norms or languages of states.'
— Achille Mbembe, 'At The Edge of World: Boundaries, Territoriality, and Sovereignty in Africa'

Cape Verde

Movement for the Autonomy of Kabylia (Algeria)

WESTERN SAHARA

ALGERIA

LIBYA

EGYPT

The Sahel Belt

Eastern Sudan (Sudan)

MAURITANIA

National Movement for the Liberation of Azawad (Mali)

NIGER

CHAD

MALI

Darfur (Sudan)

ERITREA

Khaatoumo (Somalia)

South Kodorfan/ the Blue Nile (Sudan)

Puntland (Somalia)

Casamance (Senegal)

Boko Haram (Nigeria)

The Oromo Liberation Front (Ethiopia)

Greater Somalia

SOUTH SUDAN

ETHIOPA

The Bakassi movement for self-determination (Cameroon/Nigeria)

Karamoja

Nyangatom – Merille – Toposa – Didinga – Pokot – Turkana – Jie – Pian – Matheniko – Jepeth – Dodoth – Nyakkwae – Bokora – Labwor

Jubaland (Somalia)

UGANDA

KENYA

Congolese Resistance Patriots (DRC)

The Mombasa Republican Council (Kenya)

ZANZIBAR

Front for the Liberation Enclave of Cabinda (Congo)

Kongo Kingdom

Uamsho (Tanzania)

The Swahili Coast

United Forces for the liberation of Katanga (DRC)

COMOROS

United Kingdom of Lunda Tchokwe (Angola)

Barotseland (Zambia)

MADAGASCAR

SECRET COUNTRIES
SUCCESSFUL SECESSION
MOVES TO SECEDE

The Royal Bafokeng Nation

SOUTH AFRICA

Sources:
Achille Mbembe, 'At Edge of the World: Boundaries, Territoriality, and Sovereignty in Africa', *Public Culture*

David Kaiza, 'The Secret Country' (forthcoming)

Jean Comaroff and John L. Comaroff, 'ETHNICITY, INC: on indigeneity and its interpellations, American Bar Foundation

Africa in Fact: The Journal of Good Governance Africa, *Fault Lines: Africa's Separation Anxiety*

Luc Torres, Clar Ni Chongaile, Finbar Sheehy, and Paddy Allen, 'The Separatist Map of Africa: Interactive', *The Guardian*

Unrepresented Nations and Peoples Organizations, www.unpo.org
Fred Oluoch, 'Greater Somalia dream sparks and fuels conflict in the North,' *The Nation*
Ezekiel Rediker, 'The Ogaden: A microcosm of greater conflict,' *The Concord Review*
'New Country: Azawad Declares Independence from Mali', *Political Geography Now*
Stuart Elden, 'The Geopolitics of Boko Haram and Nigeria's 'War on Terror', *The Geography Journal*

Interview with Ousmane Sidibé, 'The Malian Crisis,' *New Left Review*
John Rabuogi Ahere, 'Livestock Conflicts: An Analysis of Karamoja Cluster Communities', University of Nairobi

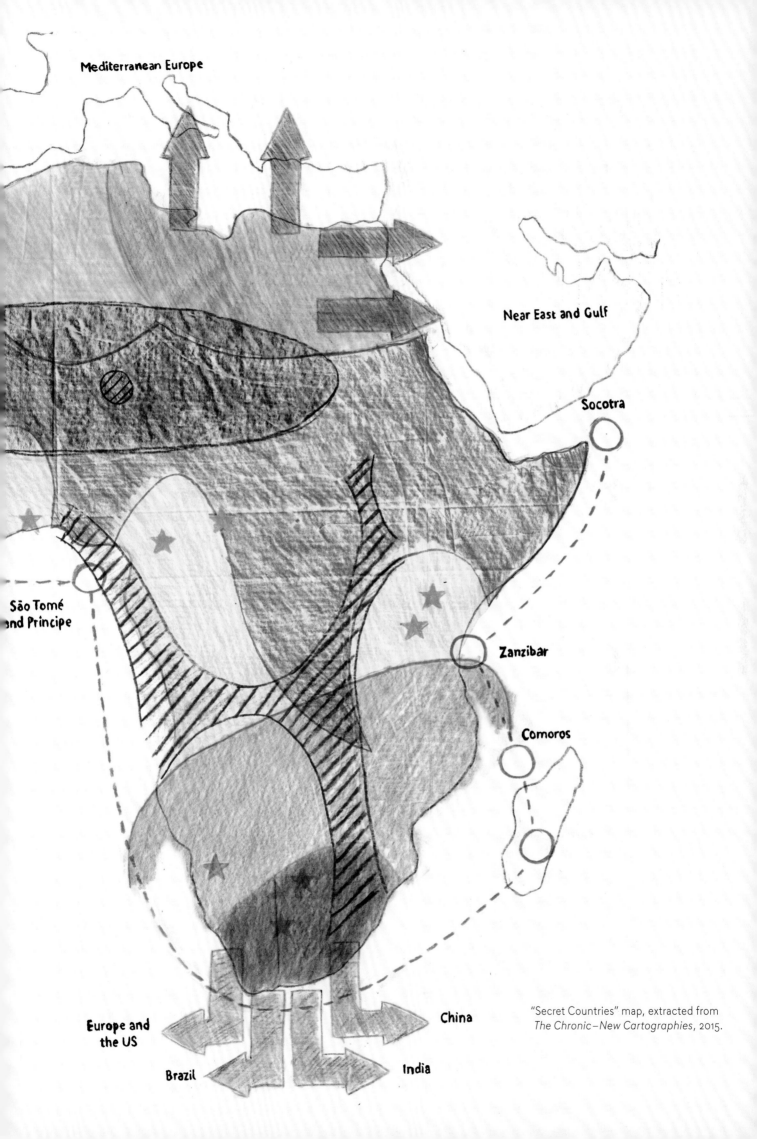

Mediterranean Europe

Near East and Gulf

Socotra

São Tomé
and Príncipe

Zanzibar

Comoros

China

Europe and
the US

Brazil

India

"Secret Countries" map, extracted from
The Chronic—New Cartographies, 2015.

Conflict Kitchen

Team
Jon Rubin and Dawn Weleski (lead artists), Brett Yasko
(graphic designer), Robert Sayre (culinary director)

Collaborators
Afghan, Black and African American, Cuban,
Haudenosaunee, Iranian, North Korean, Palestinian,
and Venezuelan communities in Pittsburgh and their
worldwide diasporas (stories, opinions, recipes,
and creative guidance)

Location Pittsburgh, Pennsylvania

Years 2010–17

Conflict Kitchen, a takeout restaurant in Pittsburgh, served cuisine from all nations with which the United States was in conflict between 2010 and 2017, from Afghanistan to North Korea. Open seven days a week, it rotated identities in relation to geopolitical events.

Each iteration of the restaurant was accompanied by publications, performances, discussions, and other events that expanded public engagement with the culture, politics, and issues at stake in the various regions. Interviews with people living in the focus country were printed on the back of food wrappers. Crowd-sourced speeches—ones people wished President Obama would deliver—were distributed during the Iran and Cuba projects, and they doubled as scripts for an Obama impersonator, who delivered remarks in front of the kitchen. An annotated North Korean cookbook and a book of interviews with

Palestinian children were published. In a program series called The Foreigner, customers were invited to eat lunch with a resident of the focus country, via an avatar—a local Pittsburgh resident who relayed questions between the parties in real time. Other events included simultaneous international public dinner parties and cooking demonstrations staged in more than ten time zones for those who could not visit the restaurant in person.

Research based on experiencing food and foodways around the world—the Conflict Kitchen team shopped, cooked, ate, and conversed with people at all locations—helped illuminate the economic and social relationships those networks uphold. The resulting multi-year creative exploration offered participants numerous ways to exchange knowledge, working to counter sometimes limited and biased understanding of the "other's" culture.

A Conflict Kitchen staff-member hands an Iranian kubideh kabob sandwich to a customer, 2010. The food wrapper is printed with interviews with people residing in Iran and the Iranian diaspora.

A Conflict Kitchen customer reads a food wrapper printed with interviews with North Korean defectors living in South Korea and the United States, 2013.

Clockwise from top left: Cuban, Iranian, Venezuelan, and Afghan iterations of Conflict Kitchen in the East Liberty neighborhood of Pittsburgh, 2010–12.

Designing the Kitchen

Merve Bedir

Mutfak مطبخ (Kitchen) Workshop was founded in 2015 in Gaziantep, Turkey, by women from Turkey and Syria. The Kitchen works on women's presence in, their collective production and appropriation of public space. The workshop promotes the idea of the kitchen as a cultural and common space, a space of proximities and collective decision making, and organizes gatherings around these notions of sharing. The participants conduct research and engage in cultural projects grounded in food, the kitchen, labor, and hospitality.

Merve Bedir is an architect and a member of the Matbakh-Mutfak women's collective kitchen and garden project in Gaziantep, Turkey. Her work focuses on looking for new socio-spatial relations through design.

The accompanying illustration imparts the essence of the Matbakh-Mufak women's collective kitchen.

> The kitchen is a space of gathering, a space of living together.
>
> The basis of collective belonging in the kitchen is "cityzenship" (living in the same city).
>
> The basis of learning to live together is the practice of the commons.
>
> Equality, justice, and freedom are shared aspirations and the basis of solidarity.
>
> The kitchen is a space of unconditional hospitality.
>
> The floor table in the kitchen guarantees seating at equal intervals.
>
> The basis of the floor table is equal participation—in sharing labor, food, and decision making.
>
> The kitchen is a space for producing ideas that promote life together in the city.

How can design embrace truth and dignity in a search for peace and justice?

The kitchen is a space of unconditional hospitality.

The kitchen is a space of gathering, a space of living together.

The collective belonging in the kitchen is 'cityzenship' (living in the same city).

Learning to live together is the practice of commoning.

UNCONDITIONAL HOSPITALITY

SOLIDARITY

SELF-ORGANISATION

LEARNING TOGETHER

The floor table in the kitchen is the guarantee of sitting in equal intervals.

The basis of the floor table is equal participation, labor, the food, and the decision making.

both in sharing the

Equality, justice, and freedom are shared aspirations and basis of solidarity.

JUSTICE

PARTICIPATION

EQUALITY

COLLECTIVE BELONGING

Recoding Post-War Syria ▶ p.186

Korea Remade ▶ p.192

How can design facilitate the transition from instability to peace?

Designing for Dignity

Designers
Jan Kristian Strømsnes and Manuela Aguirre Ulloa
(Norway)

Collaborators
Oslo School of Architecture and Design, Oslo
Emergency Hospital, Oslo Police District, Alex Asensi
Photography (Norway)

Location Oslo, Norway

Year 2012

A customized patient-information notebook was designed to help survivors retain information and make sense of advice while they are in shock and most vulnerable, 2012.

Right: A safety blanket provides comfort while securing evidence. Its pockets include antistress balls to help sexual crime survivors release tension, 2012.

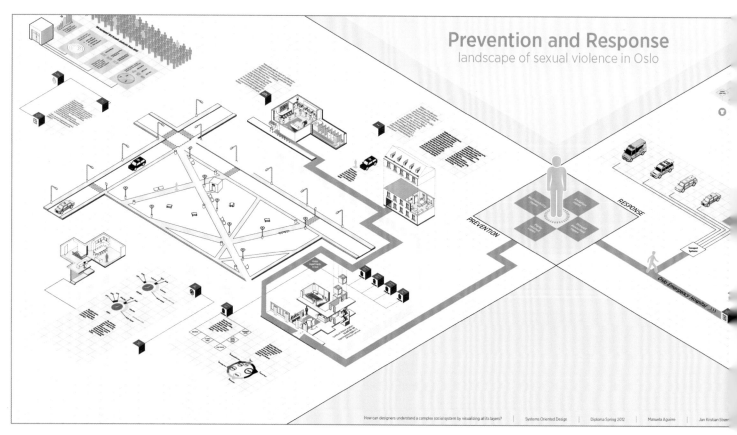

The GIGA-map visualizes interrelations within systems of prevention and response to help designers identify design interventions that improve the system for all stakeholders, by Jan Kristian Strømsnes and Manuela Aguirre Ulloa, 2012.

How can design facilitate the transition from instability to peace?

Responding to a notable increase in sexual assaults in their city, a student team reconceived Oslo's system of sexual violence prevention and response, tackling complex systems through interventions that spanned scales and disciplines, including product, information, interior, and service design. The team envisioned one that was less clinical, but more dignified for sexual assault survivors.

Through a systems-oriented design approach, the team examined the issue from multiple perspectives, gathering expertise, insight, and creativity from a wide range of stakeholders and institutions. The team created a GIGA-map, a design process tool that enables its users to organize and synthesize a vast amount of information, including photographs, illustrations, and interviews. Developed with survivors along with nurses, doctors, social workers, and the police, the large visualization traced a survivor's journey through the system, providing workers with a shared picture of each operation, identifying service touchpoints, and affording a comprehensive overview of the overlapping and complex challenges faced by the survivor as well as medical, social, and legal care teams.

At an all-stakeholder workshop, the GIGA-map was used as a starting point for dialogue. Critical problems were reframed as opportunities, leading to three cocreated design responses: responders would provide survivors with a safety blanket complete with built-in pockets to both soothe and prevent the contamination of evi-

dence on their hands; survivors would receive a customized patient-education notebook including a journey map showing pathways through the medical, social, and legal systems, while service providers would be given tools to facilitate conversation about decisions encountered along the way; and a future sexual assault clinic would be designed to be less clinical and more calming, comforting, and dignifying, with relevant patient-focused information placed strategically in each space.

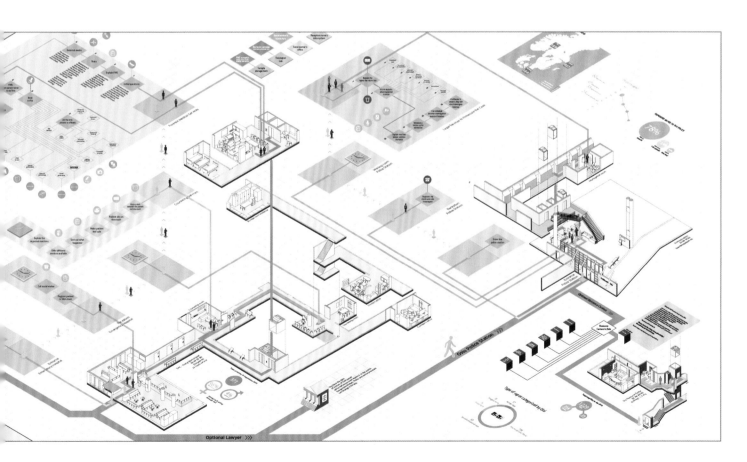

HarassMap

Designers
2010 launch: Rebecca Chiao, Sawsan Gad, Engy Ghozlan, and Amel Fahmy, with Justin Kiggins, NiJeL, and volunteers (Egypt); 2017: Rebecca Chiao, Sawsan Gad, Engy Ghozlan, Hadeer Mohamed, and Alia Soliman, with Paul Barton, Noora Flinkman, Timothy Quinn, and volunteers (Egypt)

Locations
Canada, Egypt, Mexico, South Africa, Switzerland, Turkey

Years 2010–present

HarassMap was designed by four women in response to their daily experiences with sexual harassment on the streets of Egypt. Anyone can anonymously report an incident of sexual harassment via text message, a web-based form, email, or social media. The posts are then geotagged and aggregated to reveal harassment hotspots on a digital map.

The anonymous reports allowed the team to gather data on a topic that at the time was generally taboo in Egypt, and they also provided a means by which to refer survivors to free legal and psychological support. After an incident at a large public university, the team expanded its reach, mobilizing students and engaging academic, civic, and private organizations to take a collective stand against the epidemic of sexual harassment and the assault of women.

The project's main aim is to provide evidence that sexual harassment is a serious problem and to erode its social acceptability, a factor that often prevents bystanders from intervening. HarassMap's earlier version combined the groundbreaking open-source Ushahidi mapping template and FrontlineSMS software, becoming a model for other groups. In 2017 the HarassMap team updated the reporting platform to enable any group from around the world to download it and thus to establish its own map without adding expensive staff, software, or servers. The team has assisted more than one hundred groups in anonymously tracking sexual harassment, hate crimes, and other transgressions in their own countries. An open application programming interface (API) gives researchers access to the anonymized raw data. This grassroots-generated database provides evidence to instigate social and policy changes that can lead to more secure and safe public spaces for all.

HarassMap's Safe Schools and Universities program spreads awareness about reporting and deterring sexual harassment and assault on campus, Cairo, 2015.

How can design facilitate the transition from instability to peace?

Breaking taboos, HarassMap's Open Mic events encourage inclusive dialogue on sexual violence through storytelling and experience sharing, Cairo University, 2015.

HarassMap tracks incidents of harassment and notes when intervention occurred.

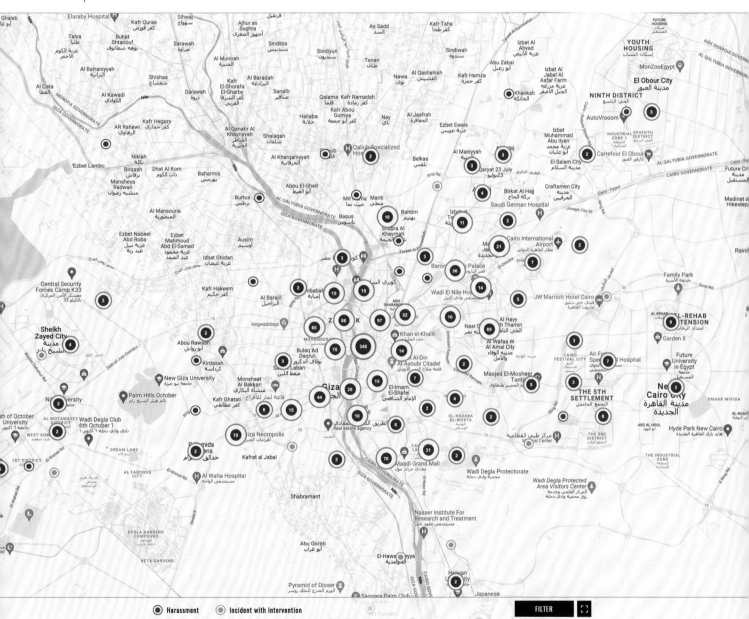

Designing for Urban Inclusivity

Chelina Odbert

"Peace is not merely the
absence of . . . tension,
but the presence of justice."
— Martin Luther King Jr.

Peace and Urbanism

From the moment it first emerged, Covid-19 has
brought a wide set of systemic inequities into sharp
focus. For those who are subject to them, these
inequities were already a defining part of daily life.
But for those at a more comfortable remove, the
pandemic was a revelation, laying bare inequity in
access to health care, to the technology needed
to learn and work from home, to jobs that allow for
flexibility, to childcare, to vaccines, and to governance structures that provide economic and
health-related support.

Another of the inequities brought into collective focus was related to public space. As health

advisories urged populations to avoid congregating
indoors and to assemble instead in outdoor public
spaces, many wondered: What public space? Access
to safe public space is deeply unequal, and it is
intertwined with the many factors that determine our
experience of community life overall, including
income, race, and, as I aim to demonstrate in this
essay, gender.[1]

Public space is not part of the community
experience for many women, since, for them, parks,
plazas, sidewalks, and transportation systems tend to
range from uninviting to potentially dangerous. This
type of pervasive gender-based exclusion should raise
the gravest of alarm. Not only does it demonstrate
that women are overlooked or forced into uncomfort-
able circumstances in their very own neighborhoods,
but it also signals a predisposition to broader cultures of violence. As Simone de Beauvoir stated in *The
Second Sex*, "All oppression creates a state of war."[2]
Since the publication of that seminal book in 1949,
her thesis has been borne out by reams of statistics
drawn from a long roster of studies that all point to
a consistent finding: the gender equity and the peacefulness of a society are directly—and measurably—
related.[3] In other words, those states that prioritize

Chelina Odbert is the cofounder and executive director
of Kounkuey Design Initiative. An urban planner by
training, she focuses on equity in the built environment
in her practice, writing, and teaching.

How can design facilitate the transition from instability to peace?

Engaging women and girls in substantive and sustained ways, Kounkuey Design Initiative designed and built a network of equitable public spaces in Kibera, Nairobi, Kenya's largest informal settlement.

gender equity—such as Austria and Sweden—create a foundation for sustainable peace. Social scientists, development experts, and others have demonstrated that gender equity is the top predictor of peace, coming in ahead of wealth, strength of democracy, and religious background.[4] It follows, then, that states in pursuit of peace ought to take a hard look at gender equity. The research also demonstrates that peace is less a stable noun than it is an active verb—something that takes deliberate focus and constant attention. As Martin Luther King Jr. knew, peace is built through a commitment to justice and equality.

This understanding of peace provides an important roadmap for those of us involved in designing and planning cities. Cities are rife with injustice. One of the foundational myths about cities is that they are a kind of springboard to opportunity—a place to unyoke from the social strictures and retrograde economics of smaller towns and rural landscapes. Going hand in hand with this myth is the dangerous assumption that opportunity is freely accessible to anyone with the drive and a dream. In reality, that springboard effect tends to work only for the narrowest demographic sliver, cut along the same lines— including gender—that regrettably carry so much

weight in determining an individual's access to opportunity in general.[5] That injustice imperils the prospect of sustaining peace. It takes more than a low crime rate to make a city a place of peace: it requires constant scrutiny and active measures geared toward achieving and expanding justice.

As cities around the world set out to address and correct longstanding social inequities, fingers are quickly pointed at social attitudes and institutional systems, giving a pass to the urban landscape as a kind of neutral backdrop. A sidewalk is a sidewalk, there to provide equal access to anyone who needs to stroll from point A to point B, or so the thinking goes. But a closer look at urban structures reveals a more pernicious fact: the urban planning and design professions have long suffered from gender inequality and because of this have created landscapes that perpetuate and sometimes even create injustice.[6] To establish peace as defined by King—which sociologists and others now call "positive peace"— cities must embody equality in three ways: in their attitudes, in their institutions, and in their structures. For this to happen, the disciplines involved with city making must fundamentally reconsider their current practices.

Plaza Aliar, the first purpose-built public space in La Favorita, suffered from underutilization because women's perspectives were not incorporated into its planning and design, Mendoza, Argentina, 2018.

Equitable and Participatory Design in Mendoza, Argentina

With women occupying just 10 percent of leadership positions in the world's principal architecture firms, and with women grossly underrepresented across all areas of the design and planning professions, it should come as no surprise that for much urban planning and design, men are the imagined end user.[7] As such, urban spaces—including streets, sidewalks, transportation networks, and parks—reflect the way men use cities. Women are an afterthought.

Take Plaza Aliar, a public space in the informal settlement of La Favorita in Mendoza, Argentina, for example. Constructed at considerable cost as part of the first phase of upgrading in this settlement just outside the city center, the plaza is the type of public space that local politicians can point to as evidence of government at work. Located squarely at the center of the barrio, the plaza is the only purpose-built open area in the district. Designed as a connective space, it links two parts of the neighborhood: the portion that has not yet been upgraded, to the south, and a district that has seen upgrades, to the north.

In 2018 my firm, Kounkuey Design Initiative, led a research and design project that focused on gender-inclusive urban planning and design in Mendoza. A collaboration with the Harvard Graduate School of Design, the work was based in barrio La Favorita and involved a study of its landscape, interviews with its residents, the collection of a range of data sets, and the provision of a framework from which to redesign the languishing plaza in a way that foregrounded women's needs and voices.

On one of our visits there, we walked with a group of women through the neighborhood. Although the half of the settlement we were traversing had been "upgraded" with paved streets, sidewalks, trash bins, and lighting, the women made their own way, using some of the streets that had yet to be improved, but to them, "felt safer"—even if that meant taking a longer route or avoiding areas altogether. Why didn't they take the easiest, most direct route? For one simple reason: the sidewalks were too narrow, making them impractical for pushing strollers or carting groceries and, more concerningly, leaving women without enough space to avoid the doorways and gates that lined the sidewalks, thus making them vulnerable to violence and intimidation from men lurking in those close spaces.

How can design facilitate the transition from instability to peace?

Though this might seem to be an incidental, even honest, oversight by a civil engineer in a small district, that sidewalk measurement exemplifies a nearly universal problem: when urban landscapes are designed predominantly by men, and when men are the default client, women are left with an inefficient and often dangerous set of options. Although Plaza Aliar has been upgraded, it has floundered as a public space, never attracting the widespread use that makes for a successful public space. There is a simple reason for this: when urban spaces are designed without input from the communities expected to use them, the result—as seen in municipalities around the world—is underutilization.[8]

In the case of Plaza Aliar, men have taken to the park, using it for circulation, socializing, and recreation. But for women it is an entirely different story. Not only is the park inhospitable to most women (because it was not designed with them in mind), but it can also be a dangerous or threatening place, something I heard from many women. In barrio La Favorita, where gender roles are all too clearly defined, and where rates of gender-based violence and discrimination are all too high, the neighborhood's landscape—even in the newly upgraded areas—is an obstacle to gender equality, and thus to positive peace.

One of the core tenets of positive peace is the existence of a feedback loop between structures, institutions, and attitudes.[9] When one becomes more equitable, the others tend to follow. For those involved in urban planning and design, the lesson is clear: to exclude women from the design and planning process is to contribute to the gender inequity of institutions and to perpetuate gender biases that have long plagued societies. But the inverse is just as true: prioritizing equity in urban space carries the real promise of changing perceptions of women's role in cities. In other words, women are trapped in a cycle that perpetuates gender inequity, imprinting it, literally, into the fabric of cities. When women are excluded from urban design and planning, the spaces created by those processes exclude women, too. The absence of women in public spaces then tends to be misinterpreted as a lack of interest, and, based on that assumption, women are excluded from consideration in future projects.

To counter this cycle in Mendoza means confronting the defined gender roles that have long existed in the local social tradition. Currently, both women and men do not think of the plaza as a place for women. To overcome that impression, designs should take into account women's existing social roles and include

Kounkuey Design Initiative and Harvard Graduate School of Design sought out and incorporated the voices and ideas of local women to reinvigorate Plaza Aliar, 2018.

From Chelina Odbert et al., *Handbook for Gender-Inclusive Urban Planning and Design* (Washington, DC: World Bank, 2020).

spaces geared toward their daily routines. This is an intermediate, stopgap measure meant to shift the discourse, supporting longer-term social transformation while integrating shorter-term changes meant to acknowledge the simple fact that women belong in public spaces. In Mendoza our design recommendations included adding to the park a washing facility, a place to deposit recyclable items, and a place amenable to watching children. Since these activities are an integral part of daily life for most women in the district, these changes will give them a reason to use the plaza. In the longer term, having women in the park and actively engaging in its life will begin to change societal attitudes about women in the public domain. If parks are the public squares of the community, and if the only people who gather in them are men, then a clear impression is created as to who is invited to participate in civic discourse (and who isn't).

Designing Gender Equity around the World

For far too long, urban landscapes have been designed and assessed based on their physical forms and on technical criteria. In recent years, however, research has brought into greater focus the role of the urban design and planning professions in reinforcing unequal gender roles and responsibilities. Following our work in Mendoza, the World Bank commissioned KDI to author what became the *Handbook for Gender-Inclusive Urban Planning Design*, published in 2020. Drawn from research and case studies from across the world, including Europe, the United States, Asia, Africa, and Latin America, the *Handbook* addresses the relationship between gender inequity and the built environment. The survey makes abundantly clear the fundamentally global nature of the problem. Across diverse contexts with different geographies, cultures, economies, and politics, we encountered the same troubling fact: even where women and men have galvanized around the expansion of women's rights, bad urban planning makes real change elusive.

In India, for example, lack of land ownership is directly correlated with physical violence directed toward women.[10] Ownership of property was found to provide women with enhanced physical security, self-esteem, and, importantly, the strength of a visible fallback position and a tangible escape route, and thus it is measurably impactful in mitigating intramarital violence. While 49 percent of women who did not own property reported some form of long-term physical violence, for women who owned land and a house, the number dropped to 7 percent.[11]

In Austria, researchers found that girls' use of city parks declined rapidly once they reached nine years old.[12]

How can design facilitate the transition from instability to peace?

After introducing recreation programming directed at girls and women, along with additional footpaths, benches, trees, and shade, the park system saw an increase of use from both women and girls. The city undertook a similar approach with its public transportation system, engaging women as active stakeholders in decision making and implementing a series of changes recommended by them, including better lighting, wider sidewalks, and ramps to improve access for people with strollers. Connecting gender-equity goals with gender-equitable spaces provides a pathway to peace. The recommendations in the *Handbook* provide cities with ways to do that.

Designing for Peace in Our Work

Since 2008 KDI has been carrying out urban design and planning in Kibera, the largest informal settlement in Nairobi, Kenya. There, with sustained and engaged input from a diverse cohort of community members, we have planned and designed a network of public spaces. While these spaces provide a forum for activities typical to parks and open areas—walking, gathering, and recreating—they also work toward a wide range of objectives, including expanding access and opportunity for women. Based on input from women, the new public spaces incorporate tangible ways by which they may gain access to economic opportunity, giving them places to create goods, vehicles through which to bring those goods to market, access to savings and loans,

and direct employment in designing and administering the construction and operations of the parks themselves. They also address a range of public health and environmental challenges that affect everyone in the community but that often disproportionately burden women. By demonstrating in real and immediate ways the valuable contributions that women offer in roles normally dominated by men—managing construction of an infrastructure upgrade, say—these gender-inclusive urban design and planning efforts have begun to tip the scale in terms of societal attitudes toward women. And in that process, these projects have created a foothold for positive peace.

As communities move toward gender equity, attention is often turned to social systems: representation in the workforce, relative income, and involvement in different areas of government. While these important standards deserve close scrutiny, so too do the spaces that comprise our cities. As we have found in our work, the acts of planning, designing, and building gender-equitable spaces expand equity across all facets of a city: positive change in urban structures is invariably linked with changes in attitudes and institutions.

1   Ming Wen et al., "Spatial Disparities in the Distribution of Parks and Green Spaces in the USA," *Annals of Behavioral Medicine* 45, no. 1 (February 2013): S18-27.

2   Simone de Beauvoir, *The Second Sex* (New York: Vintage Books, 1989).

3   Valerie M. Hudson et al., *Sex and World Peace* (New York: Columbia University Press, 2012).

4   Hudson et al., *Sex and World Peace.*

5   "Gender and Urban Planning: Issues and Trends" (Nairobi: United Nations Human Settlements Programme, 2012).

6   Susan Fainstein and Lisa Servon, *Gender and Planning: A Reader* (New Brunswick, NJ: Rutgers University Press, 2005).

7   Marcus Fairs, "Survey of Top Architecture Firms Reveals 'Quite Shocking' Lack of Gender Diversity at Senior Levels," *Dezeen*, November 16, 2007, https://www.dezeen.com/2017/11/16/.

8   Elin Andersdotter Fabre, Emelie Anneroth, and Caroline Wrangstein, "Urban Girls Catalogue: How Cities Planned for and by Girls Work for Everyone" (Stockholm: Global Utmaning, 2019).

9   "Positive Peace Report 2018: Analysing the Factors

that Sustain Peace" (Sydney: Institute for Economics and Peace, 2018), https://www.economicsandpeace.org/wp-content/uploads/2020/08/Positive-Peace-Report-2018.pdf.

10 Bina Agarwal and Pradeep Panda, "Toward Freedom from Domestic Violence," *Journal of Human Development* 8, no. 3 (November 2007): 359-88, doi: 10.1080/14649880701462171.

11 Agarwal and Panda, "Toward Freedom."

12 "Handbook for Gender Mainstreaming in Urban Planning and Urban Development" (Vienna: Urban Development and Planning, 2013).

BLUE: The Architecture of UN Peace Missions

Designers
Malkit Shoshan, Foundation for Achieving Seamless Territory (FAST) (research and design project lead, Netherlands and United States) with Irma Boom (graphic design, Netherlands)

Contributors to the *BLUE* Exhibition
Moussa Ag Assarid; Peter Chilson; Marion de Vos; Rob de Vos, Dutch Ministry of Foreign Affairs; Joel van der Beek, Economists for Peace and Security and EconoVision; Malkit Shoshan, FAST; Arnon Grunberg; LEVS architecten; Travis Bunt, One Architecture and Urbanism (ONE); Stichting Dogon Educatie; Studio Jonas Staal; David Turnbull; Erella Grassiani, University of Amsterdam; Debra Solomon, Urbaniahoeve; Laura van Santen

Helmet view of Camp Castor, United Nations Multidimensional Integrated Stabilization Mission in Mali (MINUSMA) base, Gao, Mali. Illustration by FAST, with Laura van Santen, 2016.

There are hundreds of United Nations peacekeeping missions in conflict-affected regions around the world. Their bases are generally engineered to be self-sustaining islands, walled off from their surroundings and doing little to improve the lives of local inhabitants. Growing recognition of the interplay between peace, development, and conflict prevention, coupled with mounting calls within the UN for inclusive, cross-pillar, longer-term approaches, have stimulated new ways of thinking about the physical and technological footprint of peacekeeping operations. The multi-year research and design project BLUE envisions UN camps not as temporary and closed forts but as catalysts for local development.

Camp Castor, a UN peacekeeping base in Gao, Mali, is the case study. Facing escalating violence, this ancient town on the Niger River is expected to triple in size over the next two decades due to conflict and climate migration, limiting residents' access to shelter, water, and food. Military engineers and architects, anthropologists and economists, activists, policy makers, and local inhabitants engaged with the project, informing a series of design proposals. Ranging in task and scope from the peacekeepers' first interaction with the community to the post-mission phase, these include an interface at the periphery of the base where the civilian population can receive medical treatment and access water, food, and electricity; facilities for sharing resources, education, trade, employment, and culture, as well as the joint development and execution of projects; and a design legacy strategy—use of local building techniques, so that the base's structures may be easily maintained and integrated into the city's fabric after the mission ends.

How can design facilitate the transition from instability to peace?

Policy Recommendations
FAST, with Center on International Cooperation
at New York University; Dutch Ministry of Defense;
Dutch Ministry of Foreign Affairs; Office for
Metropolitan Architecture (OMA); One Architecture and
Urbanism (ONE); UN Peacebuilding; UN Peacekeeping
Department of Field Support

Exhibitions Venice Architecture Biennale, Italy, 2016;
UN Secretariat, New York, United States, 2016; Museum
Boijmans Van Beuningen, Rotterdam, Netherlands, 2017;
Harvard University, United States, 2017

Field Research Mali, Liberia

Years 2007–present

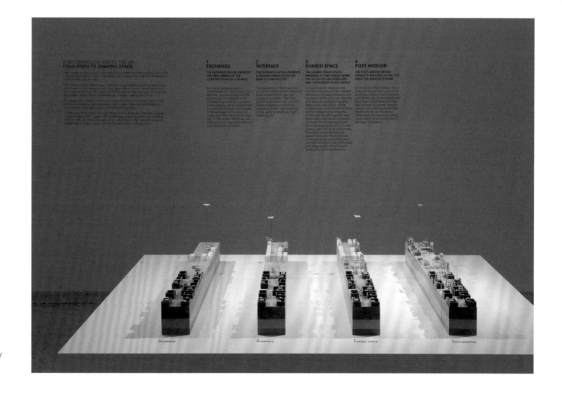

Exchange, Interface, Shared
Space, and Post-mission
models illustrate the four
steps to sharing space when
UN peacekeepers build a
base. Models in the exhibition
BLUE, Venice Architecture
Biennale, 2016. Design by
Malkit Shoshan. Production by
Studio Roel Huisman.

Gao, Mali, 2016.

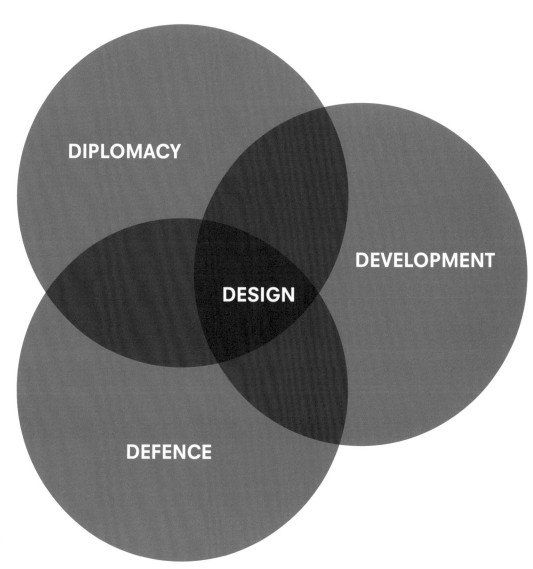

DIPLOMACY

DEVELOPMENT

DESIGN

DEFENCE

Design for Legacy proposes introducing design into the United
Nations defense, diplomacy, and
development peacekeeping
approach. Diagram by FAST/Malkit
Shoshan, 2014.

How can design facilitate the transition from instability to peace?

Nepalese care gardens at Camp Castor, Gao, Mali, 2016.

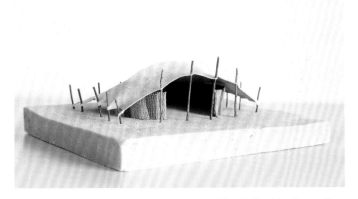

Over a dozen models and objects designed by Malkit Shoshan reflect the local conditions and experiences of journalists, architects, military engineers, missionaries, peacekeepers, and rebels.

↑ Models of a European missionary tent and a Tuareg tent, 2016. Design by Malkit Shoshan, based on sketches and depictions by L. Purssin. Fabrication by Rob Gijsbers.

↑ Models of an improvised observation post and watchtower at a Bosnian peacekeeping base, 2016. Designed by Malkit Shoshan, based on a photograph by Marcel Rot, Dutch Military Engineering Unit. Fabrication by Rob Gijsbers.

Recoding Post-War Syria

Designers
Mohamad Ziwar Al Nouri, Bilal Baghdadi, Reparametrize
Studio (Austria, China, Lebanon, Pakistan, Syria)

Location Damascus, Syria

Years 2017–present

3D scanning is used to digitally map postwar cities, providing critical data
for rebuilding efforts. Concept rendering by Reparametrize Studio, 2019.

After witnessing firsthand the destructive legacy of war in their own cities of Damascus and Beirut, two architects formed Reparametrize Studio, proposing a new methodology for transforming damaged, post-conflict cities into advanced urban environments. Their research and open-data platform, Recoding Post-War Syria, fuses state-of-the-art technology and community participation to plan, design, and rebuild war-ravaged cities, creating urban areas that are optimized with smart, connected technology and resilient systems. Their aim is to transform disaster into opportunity, supporting cities as they reinvent themselves and bringing a better life to all.

Typical post-war rebuilding approaches call for the demolition of damaged neighborhoods, but Reparametrize Studio proposes recycling the rubble and making use of existing functional buildings. Advanced 3D scanning and digital modeling of the destruction—

with lasers capturing the exact size and shape of the built environment—allow for an accurate reconstruction plan. The studio used a street in Damascus's Zamalka neighborhood as a case study. To gain insight and input from residents and from those who had fled the area, they conducted both on-the-ground and social media surveys, asking respondents about their expectations for the post-conflict city. They then generated digital models depicting their design and economic proposals. In one example, a vertical green core coupled with networked smart sensors (for a reduced carbon footprint) transforms a damaged building into a vibrant mixed-use resource for the neighborhood, offering residents the ability to grow and sell vegetables. The architects freely share their methodologies, strategies, and data, inviting architects, planners, and the private and public sectors to join them in envisioning resilient, inclusive, and peaceful communities around the world.

How can design facilitate the transition from instability to peace?

Housing units can be adapted for damaged buildings and neighborhoods, filling in gaps and reviving existing structures through simple, low-cost interventions. Concept rendering by Reparametrize Studio, 2019.

Proposed vegetation and shared public space for the central green core of the Zamalka neighborhood case study in Damascus, Syria. Concept rendering by Reparametrize Studio, 2019.

Stone Garden

Designers
Lina Ghotmeh—Architecture (France, Lebanon)

Collaborators Batimat Architects (Lebanon)

Location Beirut, Lebanon

Year 2020

The design of Stone Garden, a mixed-use residential tower located near Beirut's industrial port, is based on architect Lina Ghotmeh's experience of living in the Lebanese capital in the aftermath of war. Her "archaeology of the future," as she has termed it, seeks to uncover, reveal, and reconcile the city through architecture.

The thirteen-story mass—conceived as an inhabited sculpture rising into the sky—embodies the transformation of tumultuous events into creative potential. Carved-out asymmetrical openings echo Beirut's bulleted and blasted facades. Framing the sea, each aperture is filled with a verdant garden that invites nature into the dwelling while providing natural adaptation to the Mediterranean climate. Horizontal striations on the building's earth-and-cement facade express the accumulation of time. It took a year just to complete these surfaces, which were handcrafted by workers who had escaped wars in neighboring countries. They used a massive combing tool and computer numerical control (CNC) chisels to mark the building's thick skin in a process that was both a collaborative act of making and a quest for belonging and healing for both artisans and architect.

Stone Garden stands as a landmark to Beirut's history, a built form that materializes what the city has endured yet manifests a persistent optimism and embrace of life. Its contradictory attributes of beauty and rawness, of ephemerality and permanence, and of presence and absence embody a new way of living both the past and the future.

The texture of the facade was achieved through the use of a steel chisel comb designed specifically for this purpose by the architect.

Crafted by the hands of many workers, the building's envelope is an extension of the ground on which it stands.

Stone Garden is a sculpture drawn on an urban scale, transforming tumultuous events into creative opportunity.

Openings of various sizes hold the memory of the city and offer multiple framings of the sea from the building's interior. Stone Garden under construction in 2018.

Korea Remade

Designers
Mariel Collard Arias, Jiawen Chen, Mengting Ge,
Ran Gu, Siyu Jiang, Ann Salerno, Mengfan Sha, Xiwei
Shen, Marisa Villarreal, Na Wang, Matthew Wong,
Yiting Xi, Ziwei Ye (students), Jungyoon Kim, Niall
Kirkwood, Yoonjin Park (faculty), Graduate School
of Design, Harvard University

Location Korean Demilitarized Zone

Year 2017

The topography where the demilitarized zone bisects the Baekdu-Daegan mountain range facilitates visitors' reconnection to the north and south and to the wild. *Rewilding the Imaginary* design concept and drawing by Matthew Wong, 2018.

A long strip of land within the demilitarized zone is transformed by flora, fauna, and new landforms to create playful close and distant views. *Rescaling the Middle Ground* design concept and drawing by Ann Salerno, 2018.

Korea Remade imagines a reunified Korean Peninsula that uses landscape design to provide social, economic, and cultural opportunities for Koreans in this alternative future. The proposals consider the human habitation and natural restoration of the demilitarized zone between North Korea and South Korea—currently one of the most heavily fortified territories in the world— as well as a network of scattered observatories, abandoned military bases, minefields, subterranean tunnels, village agricultural sites, and forests, estuaries, and wetlands in the surrounding area.

The proposals erase and redraw borders and address population displacement, the presence of live land mines, and soil contamination through complex landscape reorganization and ecologies. In one scenario, detected mines are exploded to create a web of artificial bodies of water and to transform the vestiges of war— battlefield ruins, incursion tunnels, watchtowers, and tank traps—into sites of remembrance, inviting tourism while clearing the land for safe settlement. In another concept, new landforms and plantings are introduced in the middle ground between the two lines of military watchtowers; unexpected scenery and new sightlines create an attitude of curiosity and community, healing a legacy of surveillance and fear caused by the decades of military gaze. Another proposal establishes an inter-peninsula ecological spine, restoring fabled tiger passages and habitats by reconnecting Baekdu-Daegan, the 870-mile mountain ridge that runs down the entire eastern side of the peninsula. Such reimaginings of the role of the landscape in the demilitarized zone will be critical before, during, and after reunification.

How can design facilitate the transition from instability to peace?

SIBERIAN TIGER

MUSK DEER

In a reunited Korea the demilitarized zone is a testing ground for rewilding, repopulated with the bears and Siberian tigers that once roamed the peninsula. *Rewilding the Imaginary* design concept and drawing by Matthew Wong, 2018.

The design proposes reestablishing an ecological spine, the tiger's previous habitat, along the mountain range that spans the Korean peninsula, uniting north and south. *Rewilding the Imaginary* design concept and drawing by Matthew Wong, 2018.

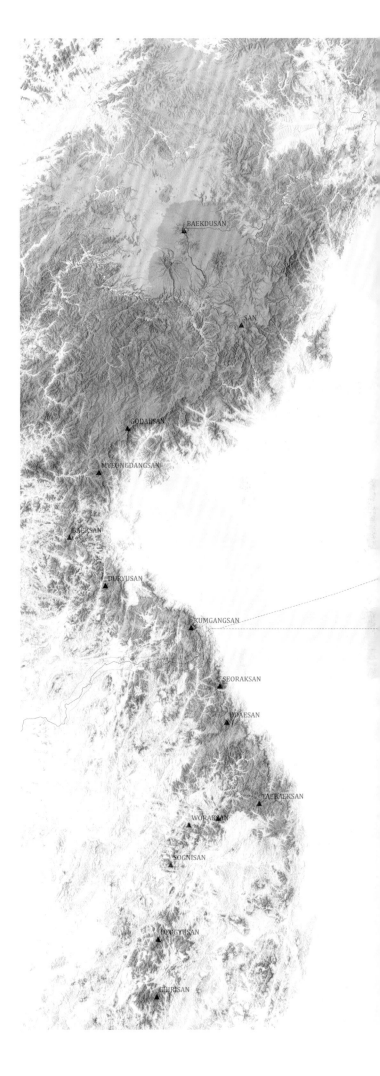

Jordan River Peace Park

Designers
EcoPeace Middle East (Jordan, Israel, Palestine),
Bezalel Academy of Arts and Design (Israel), Yale
University (United States)

Collaborators
Students and professionals (Jordan, Palestine, Israel)
with community participation (Jordan, Israel)

Location Jordan River Valley

Years 2008–present

Roman-era bridge at Old Gesher (Jisr el-Majami), 2008. The oldest of three bridges at the proposed Peace Park site, it spans the Jordan-Israel border at the lower Jordan River.

The Palestine Electric Company's former hydroelectric power plant site, Jordan, 2008. In the Peace Park design proposal the structure is transformed into a visitor and exhibition center.

To encourage cross-border cooperation in protecting a common resource—the severely depleted and polluted Jordan River and its historic valley—the environmental peacebuilding organization EcoPeace Middle East partnered with design teams from Yale University and Bezalel Academy of Arts and Design in Jerusalem, engaging the local Jordanian and Israeli communities of North Shuna and Gesher to envision a new peace park spanning both countries. Sited on one of the earliest human migration routes between Africa, Asia, and Europe, the proposed two-thousand-acre Jordan River Peace Park would safeguard the natural and cultural heritage of this shared landscape.

A series of onsite and virtual multidisciplinary design workshops resulted in site-specific design concepts for the extensive park. They incorporate existing historical structures and ancient ruins with rehabilitated landscape elements that would protect threatened habitats and provide sanctuary to millions of migrating birds, while attracting visitors to strengthen the region's economy. Designs include new bird-watching facilities and boardwalks, the reuse of long-abandoned workers' homes for eco-lodging, and the transformation of a Bauhaus-style power plant into a visitors' center where the multilayered story of the region can be told. Representing four local ecologies, four new didactic garden landscapes mark the park's entrances.

The team further proposes that access to the park be open from both sides of the border, a condition that would deliver not only tangible benefits to local communities but also hope for the future. As EcoPeace convenes regional cross-border conversations about shared resources and environmental challenges, the Jordan River Peace Park's collaborative design process embodies the search for, quite literally, common ground.

How can design facilitate the transition from instability to peace?

Constructed wetlands on the Palestine Electric Company's former hydroelectric power plant site provide new animal habitat and access to diverse ecological conditions. Rendering by Lasha Brown, Yale Urban Design Workshop, 2008.

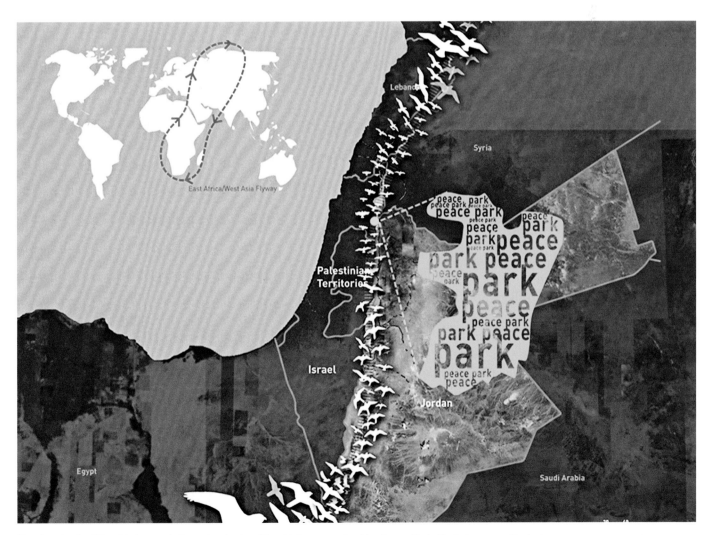

Five hundred million birds travel along the Jordan River Valley, crossing the Peace Park site twice annually during their migration through Africa, Europe, and Asia. Graphic by Diana Balmori, Yale Urban Design Workshop, 2008.

RefAid

Design Team
Shelley Taylor (creator), Keit Kollo, Mansimran Singh, trellyz (United States)

Locations
Albania, Austria, Belgium, Bosnia and Herzegovina, Bulgaria, Croatia, Czech Republic, Estonia, France, Germany, Greece, Haiti, Hungary, Ireland, Luxembourg, Malta, Montenegro, Morocco, Netherlands, North Macedonia, Romania, Serbia, Slovakia, Slovenia, Spain, Sweden, Switzerland, Turkey, United Kingdom, United States (current); Algeria, Bangladesh, Belize, Benin, Bolivia, Brazil, Burkina Faso, Cape Verde, Colombia, Costa Rica, Cote d'Ivoire, Ecuador, El Salvador, Gambia, Ghana, Guatemala, Guinea, Guinea-Bissau, Honduras, Jordan, Kenya, Lebanon, Liberia, Libya, Mali, Mauritania, Mexico, Nepal, Niger, Nigeria, Panama, Peru, Rwanda, Senegal, Sierra Leone, Togo, Tunisia (planned)

Years 2016–present

Moved by an image of the body of a Syrian child washed up on a Turkish beach, tech entrepreneur Shelley Taylor set out to create a tool that would allow migrants to find assistance where and when they need it, including basics such as medical care, food, and shelter. Understanding that people often flee conflicts with few possessions other than a mobile phone for navigation and communication with family, Taylor and her team designed a mobile application, RefAid.

The app allows migrants and those who help them to identify nearby services, geolocating them on a map through a simple interface. Available in Arabic, English, Farsi, French, and Spanish, the listed services are color coded and represented by universally understood icons, and they are sorted into seventeen categories, such as Work, Legal, Food, Health, and Shelter.

Along with migrants, aid organizations using RefAid can now see what services nearby groups are offering, allowing them to point migrants to a closer clinic or to services their organization does not offer. They can communicate with app users—who may remain anonymous—through geotargeted push notifications to a specific neighborhood or city, alerting migrants in that region, for example, that a medical unit will be arriving there the next day. Designed for people with limited internet access, RefAid can be used offline, requires minimum data updating, and takes up little space on a phone. Aggregating information into one easily accessible central repository, the app has radically transformed communication with migrants on the move and instigated a sector-wide shift to digitization.

A mother and child use the RefAid mobile app to search for nearby resources and services, Nador, Morocco, 2021.

Aid organizations, NGOs and non-profits

How can design facilitate the transition from instability to peace?

The RefAid mobile app provides migrants and refugees with access to information about available humanitarian services, including food, shelter, and medical care, Nador, Morocco, 2020.

List, map, manage services and resources and publish them to the RefAid app

Smartphone interface

Migrants, refugees and internally displaced people find help they need by type of service

Send urgent messages to people in particular locations

App users receive push notifications relevant to where they are

People on the move

User diagram: aid agencies upload and publish available services via an online web portal that enables refugees to easily view and geolocate them with their smartphones.

Casa Azul

Designers
United Nations Special Envoy for the Venezuelan
Situation, International Organization for Migration
(IOM) Panama; Institute of International Humanitarian
Affairs, Fordham University (United States); with
TAMassociati (Italy)

Locations
Venezuelan migration routes in South America, Central
America, and the Caribbean

Years 2020–present

The Casa Azul, or "Blue House," initiative is the product of a multi-year investigation by an architect and an academic into how design might improve the delivery of humanitarian aid to vulnerable migrants. Illustrated in a design playbook are a set of design actions that incorporate culture, beauty, and dignity into resource centers dedicated to the close to five million people currently fleeing Venezuela along South American, Central American, and Caribbean migration routes.

These design actions, combined with a selection of flexible modular spaces—a central plaza, a welcoming reception area, an information hub, library workstations, outdoor gardens, and spaces for resting, socializing, playing sports, enjoying culture, and receiving services—can transform an existing structure or a new building into a Casa Azul. One key action is the application of the highly recognizable logo, in its distinctive blue (Pantone 313 C), on an exterior wall,

identifying the space as safe and welcoming. Clear graphics and signage in multiple languages, which guide new arrivals within the center, communicate universal respect. Art animates the spaces, making cultural connections; color in key locations engages emotions; and natural elements signify the possibility of a new life. Doubling as resource centers and cultural hubs, the Casas aim to foster migrants' social and economic integration with local communities while recognizing and appreciating cultural difference. Applied in a variety of contexts, dependent on available space and economic resources, the same life-affirming design principles—harmony, inclusion, well-being, and sustainability—animate every Casa Azul. Unlike most refugee centers, they go beyond simply addressing basic needs, embracing a shared humanity in which beauty in architecture, food, and culture is an essential healing tool.

As they await entry to Peru, Venezuelan migrants receive humanitarian assistance from the
International Organization for Migration (IOM), border area of Haquillas, Ecuador, 2019.

How can design facilitate the transition from instability to peace?

Before and after the retrofit of an existing building. The easily recognizable Casa Azul name, logo, and color identify the resource center. Drawing by TAMassociati, 2020.

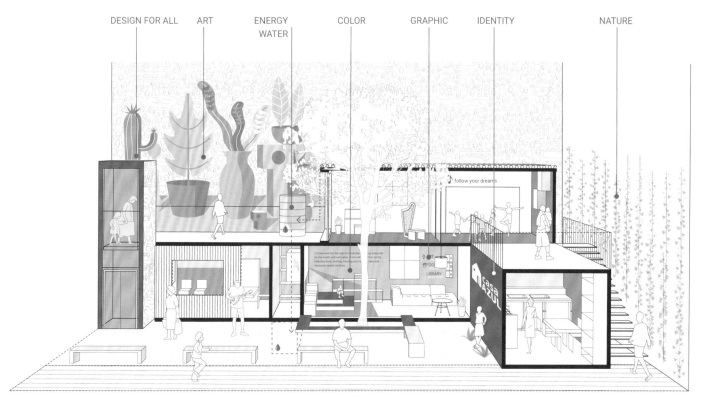

Casa Azul is a system of design actions that represent a new approach to providing basic resources, hospitality, and cultural and social support to vulnerable mobile populations. Drawing by TAMassociati, 2020.

Ideas Box

Designer
Philippe Starck (France)

Collaborators
Bibliothèques Sans Frontières (France), United Nations
High Commissioner for Refugees (UNHCR)

Locations
Australia, Bangladesh, Burundi, Colombia, Democratic
Republic of the Congo, Ethiopia, France, Germany,
Ghana, Greece, Iraq, Italy, Jordan, Lebanon, Malaysia,
Rwanda, Senegal, Tanzania, Turkey, United States

Years 2014–present

Helping to bridge the digital divide worldwide, Ideas Box provides digital access, resources, including equipment such as tablets, computers, and e-readers. Bujumbura, Burundi, 2018.

In 2010, Bibliothèques Sans Frontières (Libraries Without Borders) was building mobile libraries in Haiti when a devastating earthquake shook the island. Asked to stay on to provide books, internet access, and learning spaces in the resulting emergency camps, the organization witnessed firsthand the importance of information and cultural tools in disaster-relief efforts, particularly for children. Libraries in the camps became hubs for information about aid, family, and jobs. Books and educational activities relieved boredom and encouraged resilience.

Building on this experience, the group collaborated with French designer Philippe Starck to create Ideas Box. Designed to withstand the most difficult circumstances, these pop-up multimedia centers and portable libraries provide access to information and educational resources in places that desperately need them—camps for refugees and internally displaced persons, rural and isolated communities, underserved urban spaces, and remote Indigenous communities around the world. The easily shipped cubes are highly durable and energy independent and can be set up in twenty minutes. Their contents—books, games, art supplies, craft materials, and a stage—are tailored to each community's needs. One cube outfitted with electronic equipment connects users to digital content, including a library of more than thirty-five thousand resources in twenty-seven languages.

Deployed to twenty countries on six continents, Ideas Box programs have received over a million visits. In post-conflict and transitional justice situations, access to information, education, and culture is critical in promoting healing and building more tolerant communities. For example, in Colombia twenty Ideas Box kits were sent to guerrilla-group demobilization zones to promote reconciliation and tolerance in the country's peacebuilding process.

How can design facilitate the transition from instability to peace?

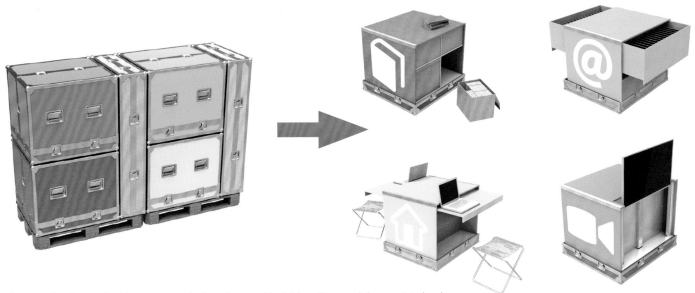

Designed to be easily shipped, unpacked, and assembled, Ideas Box modules contain books and technology as well as cases for portable tables and stools. Drawing by Philippe Starck, 2014.

Ideas Box portable library modules provide books and other resource materials for Rohingya refugees, Cox's Bazar, Bangladesh, 2020.

Ideas Box cinema modules include all the equipment necessary to show films and videos. Drawing by Philippe Starck, 2014.

Ideas Box library modules contain a selection of hardcover and paperback books tailored to each location where they are deployed. Drawing by Philippe Starck, 2014.

Safe Passage Bags Workshop

Designers
Matina Kontoleontos (initial collection) with residents and refugees, Lesvos Solidarity (Greece)

Collaborator Humade Crafts

Location Lesbos (Lesvos), Greece

Years 2015–present

In 2015 a record number of refugees arrived on the shores of Greece's easternmost islands, fleeing conflict and persecution in their homelands. The migrants traveled from Turkey across the Aegean Sea in rubber dinghies and wooden boats, nearly half landing on the island of Lesbos, discarding their orange life vests on its shores. In solidarity with the thousands of arriving migrants, local residents transformed a former summer camp into a community-run refugee camp for the most vulnerable: pregnant women, children, LGBTQ+ individuals, and people with serious medical conditions.

A local designer set up a sewing workshop at the camp to transform the discarded life jackets into bags of all sizes. The goals were to reduce and recycle the waste accumulating on the island and send an important message to the world about the refugees' right to safe passage. The Safe Passage Bags Workshop employs mostly refugees, as well as some locals—to date, thirty-six people from sixteen countries. Each bag is unique, the often faded life-jacket fabric a reminder of the experience of the migrants who wore it and who cut and sewed it. Subsequent collections incorporate discarded dinghy and tent material from the camp and are collaboratively designed by the entire workshop team: bag-makers to sales staff. The bags are available for purchase, but high labor costs require supplementary funds from Lesvos Solidarity. The workshop is now located in the organization's Mosaik Support Center in the middle of Mytilene, the island's capital city, furthering refugees' engagement in the larger community while offering them a skill they can use to start their life in a new place.

The Safe Passage Traveler bag design incorporates material from discarded life jackets, Lesbos, Greece, 2019.

How can design facilitate the transition from instability to peace?

Safe Passage Bags Workshop workers make and sell upcycled items, Mosaik Support Center, Mytilene, Greece, 2020.

Life jackets discarded by refugees who fled across the Aegean Sea on
boats and dinghies pile up on the Greek island of Lesbos in 2016 and 2017.

Selected Bibliography

Ali, Saleem H., ed. *Peace Parks: Conservation and Conflict Resolution*. Cambridge, MA: MIT Press, 2007.

Bélanger, Pierre, and Alexander Arroyo. *Ecologies of Power: Countermapping the Logistical Landscapes and Military Geographies of the U.S. Department of Defense*. Cambridge, MA: MIT Press, 2016.

Brannen, Peter. *The Ends of the World: Volcanic Apocalypses, Lethal Oceans, and Our Quest to Understand Earth's Past Mass Extinctions*. New York: Ecco, 2017.

brown, adrienne maree. *Emergent Strategy: Shaping Change, Changing Worlds*. Chico, CA: AK Press, 2017.

Bureau d'Études with Freek Lomme and Brian Holmes. *An Atlas of Agendas: Mapping the Power, Mapping the Commons*. Eindhoven, Netherlands: Onomatopee, 2019.

Coleman, Peter T., and Morton Deutsch, eds. *Psychological Components of Sustainable Peace*. New York: Springer, 2012.

Costanza-Chock, Sasha. *Design Justice: Community-Led Practices to Build the Worlds We Need*. Cambridge, MA: MIT Press, 2020.

Dávila, Patricio, ed. *Diagrams of Power: Visualizing, Mapping, and Performing Resistance*. Eindhoven, Netherlands: Onomatopee, 2019.

Elorduy, Nerea Amorós. *Architecture as a Way of Seeing and Learning: The Built Environment as an Added Educator in East African Refugee Camps*. London: UCL Press, 2021.

Hood, Walter, and Grace Mitchell Tada, eds. *Black Landscapes Matter*. Charlottesville, VA: University of Virginia Press, 2020.

Karim, Sabrina, and Kyle Beardsley. *Equal Opportunity Peacekeeping: Women, Peace, and Security in Post-Conflict States*. New York: Oxford University Press, 2017.

Killelea, Steve. *Peace in the Age of Chaos: The Best Solution for a Sustainable Future*. Richmond, VA: Hardie Grant Books, 2020.

Lederach, John Paul. *The Moral Imagination: The Art and Soul of Building Peace*. New York: Oxford University Press, 2005.

McGhee, Heather. *The Sum of Us: What Racism Costs Everyone and How We Can Prosper Together*. New York: One World, 2021.

Nepram, Binalakshmi. *Deepening Democracy, Diversity, and Women's Rights in India*. New York: New York Universal Publishing House, 2019.

Pendleton-Jullian, Ann, and John Seely Brown. "Pragmatic Imagination." Chap. 19 in *Design Unbound: Designing for Emergence in a White Water World*. Vol. 2, *Ecologies of Change*. Cambridge, MA: MIT Press, 2018.

Pinker, Steven. *Enlightenment Now: The Case for Reason, Science, Humanism, and Progress*. New York: Viking, 2018.

Smyth, Fionna, Amina Hersi, Abigael Baldoumus, and Anna Tonelli. *Transforming Power to Put Women at the Heart of Peacebuilding*. Oxford, UK: Oxfam GB, 2020.

Smyth, Sarah, Willona Sloan, Kyle Miller, and Toni L. Griffin, eds. *The Just City Dialogues: Disruptive Design*. Cambridge, MA: Just City Lab, 2021.

Tufekci, Zeynep. *Twitter and Tear Gas: The Power and Fragility of Networked Protest*. New Haven, CT: Yale University Press, 2017.

Watts, Michael J. *Silent Violence: Food, Famine, and Peasantry in Northern Nigeria*. 2nd ed. Athens, GA: University of Georgia Press, 2013.

Wendel, Delia Duong Ba, and Fallon Samuels Aidoo, eds. *Spatializing Politics: Essays on Power and Place*. New Haven, CT: Harvard University Press, 2016.

Wigen, Kären, and Caroline Winterer, eds. *Time in Maps: From the Age of Discovery to Our Digital Era*. Chicago: University of Chicago Press, 2020.

Acknowledgments

The planning and making of this publication, *Designing Peace: Building a Better Future Now*, which accompanies the exhibition *Designing Peace*, would not have been possible without the generous support and contributions of numerous individuals and organizations.

Designing Peace Advisory Committee
Yana W. Abu Taleb, Jordanian Director, EcoPeace Middle East, Amman, Jordan

Susan Chomba, Scientist, Center for International Forestry Research and World Agroforestry, Nairobi, Kenya

Thomas Fisher, Professor in the School of Architecture, Director of the Minnesota Design Center, and former Dean of the College of Design, University of Minnesota, Minneapolis

Cindy Horst, Research Professor, Peace Research Institute Oslo

Mike Jobbins, Vice President of Global Affairs and Partnerships, Search for Common Ground, Washington, DC

Justin Garrett Moore, AICP, NOMA, Executive Director, New York City Public Design Commission

Yoonjin Park, Founding Principal, PARKKIM, Seoul

Marianne F. Potvin, urban specialist and researcher, Philadelphia

Alberto Preato, Senior Regional Programme Coordinator, UN Migration Agency (IOM), Office of the Special Envoy for the Venezuelan Situation, Panama City

Support for *Designing Peace* is generously provided by Ford Foundation, Lisa Roberts and David Seltzer, Lily Auchincloss Foundation, Helen and Edward Hintz, Barbara and Morton Mandel Design Gallery Endowment Fund, Agnes Gund, Cooper Hewitt Master's Program Fund, Netherland-America Foundation, and New York State Council on the Arts, with the support of the Office of the Governor and the New York State Legislature.

Smithsonian Institution
Lonnie G. Bunch II, Secretary

Kevin Gover, Under Secretary for Museums and Culture

Richard Kurin, Distinguished Scholar and Ambassador-at-Large

Meroë Park, Deputy Secretary and Chief Operating Officer

At Cooper Hewitt
A heartfelt thank you to current and former colleagues at this incredible museum, the ever-evolving Cooper Hewitt, our nation's design museum. It has been a pleasure to collaborate with you on this project. Each of you has made it better at every stage of development, supporting our mission in the "dissemination of knowledge" by making it accessible to a wide and diverse audience.

Without the amazing talent and dedication of the following colleagues, *Designing Peace* could not have been realized: Shamus Adams, Alex Arad, Carl Baggaley, Veronica Bainbridge, Sarah Barack, Peter Baryshnikov, George Benson, Cat Birch, Laurie Bohlk, Susan Brown, Adriana Burkins, Danielle Butterly, Alexandra Cunningham Cameron, Daryl Cannon, Marites Chan, Marcy Chevali, Perry Choe, Jennifer Cohlman-Bracchi, Caitlin Condell, Alexa Cummins, Christina De Leon, Tara Dougherty, Sheila Egan, Milly Egawa, Kira Eng-Wilmont, , Debby Fitzgerald, Chris Gautier, Vasso Giannopoulos, Charlotte Gill, Rachel Ginsberg, Dana Green, Alexa Griffith, Dhan Gurung, Angela Hall, Jody Hanson, Del Hardin Hoyle, Marilu Datoli Hartnett, Kim Hawkins, Nolan Hill, Abbey Hunter, Janice Hussain, Rick Jones, Kathleen Kane, Andrea Lipps, Darnell Jamal Lisby, Maggie Lisman, Nilda Lopez, Ellen Lupton, Meagan Mahaffy, Elizabeth Matos, Matthew McEnteggart, Kirsten McNally, Phoebe Moore, Antonia Moser, Milo Mottola, Nykia Omphroy, Emily Orr, Winona Packer, Julie Pastor, Micah Pegues, Kang-Ting Peng, Angela Perrone,

Paula Pineda, Mauricio Portillo, Adam Quinn, Emily Raddant, Kimberly Randall, Kim Robledo-Diga, Wendy Rogers, Carolyn Royston, Anthony Rubert, Blake Schreiner, Julia Siemon, Mary Fernanda Alves da Silva, Larry Silver, Rona Simon, Ruth Starr, Ann Sunwoo, Kirsten Sweeney, Michael Sypulski, Ashley Tickle, Cindy Trope, Mathew Weaver, James B. Wilson, Yao-Fen You, and Paula Zamora; and interns and fellows Carlota Bamboa, Zoe Detweiler, Nejia Katica, Samuel Maddox, Macy Rajacich, Maria Salim, Roua Atamaz Sibai, and Maria Vollas.

Special thanks to
Caroline O'Connell, the project's curatorial assistant, an incredible colleague who has brilliantly assisted with every aspect of the project. It was a supreme pleasure to work with you as we organized disparate materials to bring the project into form. Your intellect, generosity, and enthusiasm have been instrumental in realizing *Designing Peace*.

Matilda McQuaid, the museum's acting curatorial director, whose thoughtful, steady leadership and experience has been critical in providing decisive creative input when it was most needed. Your support and guidance helped to distill complicated concepts into an accessible and compelling project.

Pamela Horn, head of the museum's cross-platform publishing team, who played a crucial role throughout the project—as an early sounding board, helping me to articulate the project's thesis, and as a supreme ally and partner in the development of this publication—and Matthew Kennedy, the museum's publishing associate, who brought professional integrity to the project, diligently organizing and facilitating critical elements of the publication.

Yvonne Gómez Durand, the museum's head of exhibitions, and Molly Engelman, the museum's exhibition coordinator, who brought their creativity, experience, and expertise to bear throughout the development of the project and in bringing the project to life as an exhibition.

Ruki Neuhold-Ravikumar, Cooper Hewitt's acting director, who was an early supporter of the project when I first presented it to a small group of colleagues at the museum, and who continued to provide keen insight and generous support for this publication, the accompanying exhibition, and public outreach.

The entire board of trustees, for their generous support from the very beginning of my research and at every step of the project's development, especially Karen A. Phillips, Lisa S. Roberts, Paul Herzan, Crystal Sacca, Henry R. Muñoz III, Esme Usdan, and Keith Yamashita.

Beyond Cooper Hewitt
My utmost respect and thanks go to Cara McCarty, the museum's former curatorial director, who has been a champion of this project from its earliest days. You have been a generous mentor and a kind friend and colleague, and you were instrumental in bringing this idea to life by providing me the time and space to explore and develop the project's thesis, which formed the basis for this publication and its attendant exhibition.

Thank you to John Davis, the museum's interim director, who stepped in and kept the museum moving forward when we most needed it. You made certain that this project would happen when everything seemed uncertain.

A full-throated thank you to my friends and family, who brighten my world and who urged me on when I was in the midst of research and writing. You fed my soul and brought a smile to my face when I most needed it.

Finally, my unwavering gratitude to my beloved spouse, Laura A. Berenson, who supported the idea of "designing peace" during its germination and actively discussed its development, peppering me with questions about key concepts at every stage. Your intellect, empathy, and love has enabled me to do this work. It has been especially joyful to share this daily journey with you during these uncertain times. You provide me with inspiration and hope for a better future.

Designing Peace Works
Art the Arms Fair: Sally Oliver, War Boutique, Ali Mehmet, Shepard Fairey, Tristan Oliver
Astropolitics: Depletion of Terrestrial Resources and the Cosmic Future of Capitalism: Xavier Fourt, Léonore Bonaccini
Black Lives Matter Harlem Street Mural: Nikoa Evans-Hendricks, Valerie Wilson, LeRone Wilson, Thomas Heath, Omo Misha McGlown, Guy Stanley Philoche, Joyous Pierce, Dianne Smith, Jason Wallace; Black Lives Matter Online Census: Kim Albrecht, Steven Larrick, Justin Garrett Moore
BLUE: The Architecture of UN Peace Missions: Malkit Shoshan, Elza van den Berg, Aric Chen
Body Mapping: Jocelyn Kelly
Casa Azul: Alberto Preato, Brendan Cahill, Laura Candelpergher, Raul Pantaleo, Virna Di Schiavi, Federica Cevasco
Christmas Operations: Jose Miguel Sokoloff, Juan Pablo Garcia, Danielle Hayes, Jaime Duque
Conflict Kitchen: Jon Rubin, Dawn Weleski, Brett Yasko
CONIFA: Per-Anders Blind, Loïck Blouet, Alejandra Calderon, Jason Heaton, Aaron Johnsen, David Marino-Nachison, Francesco Zema

Designing for Dignity: Manuela Aguirre Ulloa, Jan Kristian Strømsnes

Extinction Symbol: ESP, Christina See, Gareth Morris, Ward Ogden

HarassMap: Rebecca Chiao, Angie Abdelmonem

Hate Speech Lexicons: Sheldon Himelfarb, Samantha Dols, Grant Castle, Deirdre Saunder

House of Peace: Junya Ishigami, Laura Pasquier, Masayuki Asami, Héloïse Darves, Kasper Winding, Johnny Svendborg

Ideas Box: Manuella Bitor, Mahaut Champetier de Ribes, Edouard Delbende, Aaron Greenberg, Manon Carbonne, Abel Sollier, Peter Sahlins, Patrick Weil, Jérémy Lachal, Adam Echelman

Island Tracker: Gregory B. Poling, Harrison Prétat, Paul Franz

Jordan River Peace Park: Andrei Harwell, Alan Plattus, Yana W. Abu Taleb, Mohammad Bundokji, Abdelrahman Sultan, Michael Turner

Korea Remade: Jungyoon Kim, Yoonjin Park, Niall Kirkwood, Jiawen Chen, Ann Salerno

Maps (Bullet Rug Series): Raúl Martínez

My Ancestors' Garden: Walter Hood, Paul Peters, Azja Alvarenga, Regine Ong

New World Summit—Rojava: Jonas Staal, Nadine Gouders, Franziska Bigger, Nadia Schneider Willen, Catherine Reymond

Oceanix City: Julie May, Emily Cones-Browne, Camilla Filtenborg Borggaard, Kai-Uwe Bergmann, Joshua McLaughlin, Morgan Day

Paper Monuments: Bryan C. Lee Jr., John Ludlam, Mahalah Lewis, Suzanne-Juliette Mobley, Mary Mitchell, Kathryn O'Dwyer

Papers, Please: Lucas Pope

Peace Pavilion: Mujib Ahmed, Lalita Tharani, Mihir Mistry

Positive Peace Index: Kiera Mitchell, Charlie Allen, Aaron Castle, Michael Collins, Jessica Duque, Darren Lewis, Laurie Smolenski

Rare Earthenware: Liam Young, Kate Davies, Laura Maccarelli

Recoding Post-War Syria: Mohamad Ziwar Al-Nouri, Bilal Baghdadi

RefAid: Shelley Taylor, Betty Porter, Kiri Kitano

Regreening Africa: Susan Chomba, Tor-Gunnar Vagen, Leigh Winowiecki, Mieke Bourne, Muhammad Nabi Ahmad, Constance Neely, Winnie Achieng, Sabrina Chesterman, May Muthuri, Marion Aluoch

Safe Passage Bags Workshop: Nicolien Kegels, Diana Dias, Efi Latsoudi, Stella Balouka

Social Emergency Response Centers: Lori Lobenstine, Kenneth Bailey, Ayako Maruyama

Stalled!: Joel Sanders, Seb Choe, Lee Onbargi, Marco Li, Martin Carrillo

Startblok Elzenhagen: Wouter Veldhuis, Giacomo Gallo, Veerle Simons

Stone Garden: Lina Ghotmeh, Anna Checchi, Theia Flynn, Amanda Compaoré, Alessandro Colli

Teeter-Totter Wall: Ronald Rael, Virginia San Fratello, Nancy Bateman

The Adventures of Daly Graphic Novels: Hendrick Townsley, Imen Belhedi, Mike Jobbins, Hilde Deman, Bouraoui Ouni, Moez Tabia, Abir Guesmi

The Chronic: Ntone Edjabe, Chantal Bouw, Graeme Arendse

The Murder of Halit Yozgat: Eyal Weizman, Christina Varvia, Sarah Saraj, Sarah Nankivell, Elizabeth Breiner

Universal Declaration of Human Rights Posters: Martha Rich, Esther Pearl Watson, Jennifer May, Steven Butler, Garret Scullin, Mariana Amatullo, Christopher Kosek, Cindy Chen, Benny Chu

World Peace Symbol: Amijai Benderski, Yabel Guerra, Max Phillips, Rosana Malaneschii

Designing Peace Research

American Constitution Society: Kara Stein

The Arctic University of Norway (UiT): Gunhild Hoogensen Gjørv (Center for Peace Studies), Thomas Juel Clemmenson (Art Academy), Aileen Aseron Espiritu, Bjarge Schwenke Fors (The Barents Institute)

Armory of Harmony: Cameron Sinclair

BAK, basis voor actuele kunst: Eva Postema

Barents Secretariat: Lars Georg Fordal, Marit Egholm Jacobsen

John Bicknell

ByBi: Ragna Ribe Jørgensen, Camilla Brox, Ane Johnsen, Rune Kristian Dale-Andresen

Campfire Innovation: Joanna Theodorou

Change Labs: Heather Fleming

Columbia University: Cassim Shepard, Sarah Beth Stone

Conflict Textiles: Roberta Bacic, Breege Doherty

Conservation International: Lydia Cardona

Consulate General of the Netherlands in New York: Robert Kloos

Criteria Architects: Jerry Allan

Curry Stone Foundation: Eric Cesal, Emiliano Gandolfi

Dahl & Uhre Architects: Kjerstin Uhre

Design and Architecture Norway (DOGA): Ingerid Helsing Almaas, Ingvil Aarholt Hegna, Jannicke Hølan, Ellen Magrethe Skilnand

Design Museum Den Bosch: Timo de Rijk

Designing Justice + Designing Spaces: Deanna Van Buren

Dominican Republic Department of Planning and Projects: Shaney Peña-Gómez

Envelope A+D: Douglas Burnham, Nathan John

Equal Justice Initiative: Sia Sanneh

Forward Union: Julia Clark, John D. Freyer
Gates Discovery Center: Charlotte Beall
Georgia Institute of Technology: Michael Elliott
Global Alliance for Urban Crises: Håvard Breivik-Khan
Global Peace Foundation: Gail Hambleton
Harvard University: Marianne F. Potvin, Naomi Woods, Diane E. Davis, Susan Nigra Snyder, George Thomas, Rosetta Sarah Elkin, Megan Marin, Malkit Shoshan (Graduate School of Design); John Peterson (Loeb Fellowship)
The Hauge Humanity Hub: Jill Wilkinson
Het Nieuwe Instituut: Kim Bouvy, Rosalie Witte, Klaas Kuitenbrouwer, Marina Otero Verzier, Guus Beumer
Hope School: Abdulghani Dehhan, Deyaa Orfali
Humanity House: Lisette Mataar
Impact Justice: Sia Henry, Michela Bowman, Ashlee George, Alex Busansky
Interface Studio Architects: Brian Phillips
International New Town Institute: Michelle Provoost
INTERPRT: Nabil Ahmed
JR Studio: Marc Azoulay
Kati Collective: Anitha Moorthy
Kennesaw State University: Maia Carter Hallward, Susan S. Raines
KORO (Public Art Norway): Truls Ramberg
LATRA Innovation Lab: Aris Papadopoulos, Georgina Finou
LeapFrog Enterprises: David Perkinson, Mari Sunderland
Lesvos Solidarity: Carmen Dupont, Matina Kontoleontos, Efi Latsoudi, Chryssa Panoussiadou, Stratis Valamios
MacArthur Foundation: Laura Scholl
Maidan Tent: Bonaventura Visconti di Modrone
Massachusetts Institute of Technology: Amy Smith, Martha Thompson (D-Lab); David Dolev (International Science and Technology Initiatives); Delia Duong Ba Wendel (Urban Studies and International Development; Azra Akšamija (Future Heritage Lab); Joy Buolamwini (Media Lab, Algorithmic Justice League); Silvia Danielak (Urban Studies and Planning)
Middletown Restorative Justice Center: Justin Carbonella
MUST Urbanism: Wouter Veldhuis, Giacomo Gallo
National Endowment for the Arts: Joan Shigekawa (former acting chair)
The New School: Diana Duque, Shannon Mattern, Sarah Lichtman
New York University: Natasha Iskander
Norwegian Consulate General in New York: Ginni Wiik, Kelly Tigera
Norwegian Polar Institute: Jack Kohler
Norwegian Refugee Council: Jørn-Casper Owre

Olso Architecture Triennial (arkitekturtriennale): Hanna Dencik Petersson, Nabil Ahmed, Dámaso Randulfe
Oslo Biennial (osloBIENNALEN): Eva González-Sancho Bodero, Per Gunnar Eeg-Tverbakk, Ed D'Souza (UK, Migrant Car), Mônica Nador (Brazil, Another Grammar for Oslo)
Oslo National Academy of the Arts (KHiO): Apolonija Šušteršič
Oslo School of Architecture and Design (AHO): Morgan Alexander Ip, Janike Kampevold Larsen, Peter Hemmersam, Tone Selmer-Olsen
The Overhead Wire: Jeffrey Wood
Peace Innovation Lab Stanford: Mark Nelson
Peace Research Institute Oslo: Cindy Horst, Kristian Hoelscher, Jason Miklian
Peace Science Digest: Kelsey Coolidge
PeaceTech Lab: Kelly Hoye, Zeluis Teixeira
Pikene på Broen: Franziska Kraiczy, Luba Kuzovnikova
Pratt Institute: Harvey Bernstein, Constantin Boym, Amanda Huynh, Mary McBride, Karol Murlak, Matte Nyberg, Alex Schweder
The Ray: Allie Kelly
Rhode Island School of Design: John Caserta, Raina Wellman
Royal College of Art: Dámaso Randulfe
Rutgers University: Jack Tchen
The Salt Project: Eric Geboers
Santa Fe Art Institute: Jamie Blosser, Toni Gentilli, Nuttaphol Ma, Kourtney Andar (staff); Tamara Ann Burgh, Peggy Diggs, Jay Critchley, Robert Garcia, Veronica Jackson, Jessica Lawless, Cara Levine, Israel Francisco Haros Lopez, E. Oscar Maynard, Eliza Myrie, Gil Arnaud Ngolé, Heather Robinson, Reveca Torres, Huang Yi-ying (artist residents)
SAYA/Design for Change: Karen Lee Bar-Sinai, Yehuda Greenfield-Gilat
Search for Common Ground–Asia: Tereza Grünvaldová
Specialist Operations: Jan Willem Petersen
Stanley Center for Peace and Security: Jessica Kline, Kelsey Shantz
Stavros Niarchos Foundation: Kira Pritchard
Studio Jeanne van Heeswijk
Studio O: Liz Ogbu
Superuse: Jos de Krieger
Sustainable Ports: Roberta Weisbrod
Svalbard Global Seed Vault: Hannes Dempewolf, Åsmund Asdal
TAMassociati: Raul Pantaleo
Topio 7 Landscape Architects: Thanasis Polyzoidis, Katerina Andritsou, Panita Karamanea
Tromsø City Planning: Anniken Romuld
Tufts University: Paul Arthur Berkman
UN Women for Peace Association: Melissa Mannis

United Nations Foundation: Chandrima Das
Universidad Católica de Chile: Mónica Flores
University of Arkansas: Ethel Goodstein-Murphree,
    Peter MacKeith
University of Oxford Refugee Studies Centre:
    Mark E Breeze
University of South Australia Museum of Discovery:
    Kristin Alford, Natalie Carfora, Daniel Lawrance
Urban-a: Synne Bergby
Manon Van Hoeckel
Vardø Restored: Svein Harald Holmen, Brona Keenan
Vera Institute of Justice: Jennifer Trone
Winterhouse Institute: Mariana Amatullo, Charlie
    Cannon, Lee Davis, Liz Gerber, Deborah Johnson,
    Chris Kasabach, Marcia Lausen, David Mohney,
    Laura Penin, Natacha Poggio, Eduardo
    Staszowski, Mike Weikert, Andrea Wollensak
WXY Studio: Jhordan Channer, Amina Hassen
Yale School of Architecture: Emily Abruzzo, Trattie
    Davies

Exhibition and Book Design
Book design: Practise: Shan James, James Goggin
Exhibition design: Höweler + Yoon: Jonathan Fournier,
    Karl Heckman, Eric Höweler, Caroline Shannon
Exhibition graphic design: Common Name:
    Yoonjai Choi, Ken Meier
Editorial: Connie Binder, Jessica Leaman, Rebecca
    Roberts

Publication
Amanda Williams Studio
Beautiful Trouble: Chelsea Byers
Bold Alliance: Mark Hefflinger
Humanitarian Tracker: Hend Alhinnawi
MASS Design Group: Lauren DiLoreto
Karen Nickell
Permanent Mission of Norway to
    the United Nations: Astrid Sehl
Tom Olin Collection: Dan Wilkins

Extreme gratitude to John Paul Lederach for penning a
beautiful and evocative set of verses that reflect the
ethos of the work explored and expounded upon in this
book. Thank you for envisioning the multitude of ways
we might embrace creativity and imagination in
working for peace.

Cynthia E. Smith

Index

Image Credits

Cover: © Martin Reis

Frontmatter sequence: SSP3 / Juan Pablo Garcia, Carlos Andrés Rodriguez; © BSF & Philippe Starck; Mark Claudio for New Kingston Media; © Conflict Kitchen; HarassMap

8, 10, 13: Cynthia E. Smith © Smithsonian Institution; 15: Jocelyn Kelly; 16 (top): Ruben Hamelink © Jonas Staal; 16 (bottom) & 17 (both): Along Sicherman for New Kingston Media; 18: © Conflict Kitchen; 19, 21: Cynthia E. Smith © Smithsonian Institution

How can design support humane forms of peace and security?
24: Ronald Rael and Virginia San Fratello; 25: © MUST Urbanism, Amsterdam; 27: © Bill Bachmann / Alamy Stock Photo; 28: Courtesy of the artists—Olalekan B. Jeyifous and Amanda Williams, 2019; 29: Joyfull / Shutterstock.com; 30–31: The Southern Poverty Law Center; 32: Elman Studios; 34 (left): Photo by Anselmo Cassiano; 34 (right): Photo by Lori Lobenstine; 35 (top): Ayako Maruyama, Courtesy of Design Studio for Social Intervention; 35 (bottom): Photo by Lori Lobenstine; 38 & 39 (bottom): Moez Tabia and Abir Guesmi, Lab619 © Search for Common Ground; 39 (top left & right): Emna Elloumi, Search for Common Ground Project Officer © Search for Common Ground; 40: © David Kelly; 41: © Kaja Strand Ellingson TK; 42: © Kevin Benny Kuriakose, Victor Carpintero Ferran, and Heini Hiukka TK; 43: © Ingrid Hove Viljoen and Olav Bog Vikan; 44: Rufus de Vries © MUST Urbanism, Amsterdam; 45 (top & bottom), 46–47: © MUST Urbanism, Amsterdam; 48–49 (all): © BIG-Bjarke Ingels Group and Oceanix City; 50–53 (all): SSP3; 54: Jocelyn Kelly; 55 (all): Mothers of former child soldiers participating in the body mapping session (anonymous participation due to ethical considerations); 56 (all): CSIS Asia Maritime Transparency Initiative / Maxar Technologies; 57 (top): CSIS Asia Maritime Transparency Initiative; 57 (bottom): CSIS Asia Maritime Transparency Initiative / Maxar Technologies; 59–62: Google Earth, image © 2020 Maxar Technologies; 63: Courtesy Borders and Boundaries; 64 (top): Courtesy of Rael San Fratello; 64–65: Drone photography by Ronald Rael and Virginia San Fratello; 65 (top): © Ronald Rael and Virginia San Fratello; 66–67 (all): © 3909 LLC. Used with permission; 68: Nawneet Ranjan, courtesy of PeaceTech Lab; 70: Joy Buolamwini; 71 (top): Syria Tracker, a project of Humanitarian Tracker; 71 (bottom): Cynthia E. Smith © Smithsonian Institution

How can design address the root causes of conflict?
72: Kyle Johnson + Renzy Reyes; 73: Regreening Africa / Brian Gathu; 75: Photo: Nieuwe Beelden Makers © Jonas Staal; 77: © Jonas Staal; 78: Photo: Lidia Rossner © Jonas Staal; 79: Photo: Ernie Buts © Jonas Staal; 80: Remco van Bladel, Dilar Dirik, and Jonas Staal © Jonas Staal; 82: © Jonas Staal; 83 (top & bottom): Photo: Ruben Hamelink © Jonas Staal; 84–85 (bottom, top & left): CONIFA; 85 (right): Kyle Johnson + Renzy Reyes; 87: ClassicStock / Alamy Stock Photo; 88–91 (all): Courtesy of Michael Adlerstein / Capital Master Plan Archives; 92 (all): Regreening Africa; 93 (top): Regreening Africa/Kelvin Trautman; 93 (bottom left): Regreening Africa / Brian Gathu; 93 (bottom right): Joshua Adombire; 95–97: Bureau d'Études; 98–101 (all): Photography © Toby Smith/Unknown Fields; 102–103 (all): Courtesy of PeaceTech Lab; 104 (left): Whitney Keller / The Herald-Sun via AP; 104 (right): Tom Olin Collection, Ward M. Canaday Center, University of Toledo © Tom Olin; 105 (all): Drawing by JSA / MIXdesign, 2018; 106–107 (all): © Collaborative Architecture; 108–109 (all): Courtesy of junya.ishigami+associates, 2014; 110 (left): © 2008 Design by Cindy Chen for Designmatters at Art Center College of Design; 110 (middle): © 2008 Design by Christopher Kosek for Designmatters at Art Center College of Design; 110 (right): © 2008 Design by Cindy Chen for Designmatters at Art Center College of Design; 111: © 2008 Design by Christopher Kosek for Designmatters at Art Center College of Design; 112–13 (all): IEP

How can design engage creative confrontation?
114: Courtesy of Raúl Martínez; 115: JessicaGirvan / Shutterstock.com; 116: National Nurses United, Alyssa Schukar; 117 (all) & 118 (cards): Beautiful Trouble; 118–19: Mary Anne Andrei / Bold Nebraska; 119 (top right): Jim Lo Scalzo / EPA-EFE / Shutterstock.com; 119 (cards): Beautiful Trouble; 120: Mark Claudio for New Kingston Media; 121 (top): Sekou Luke for New Kingston Media; 121 (bottom): Rendering courtesy of DOT; 122–23: Alon Sicherman for New Kingston Media; 124: Courtesy of Tristan Oliver; 125 (top left & right): Rosie Litterick; 125 (bottom): UNCLE; 127: Names Project Foundation / National AIDS Memorial; 128 (both): Photo Colin Peck © Conflict Textiles; 129: AP / Shutterstock.com; 130: Raúl Martínez; 131 (top): Rodrigo Pereda; 131 (bottom): Courtesy of Raúl Martínez; 133 (both): Margaret Mead Papers and South Pacific Ethnographic Archives, Library of Congress Manuscript Division, Washington, DC; 134: Courtesy of The National Museum of Natural History Library, Smithsonian Libraries and Archives; 135: Image courtesy of Dover Publications; 136, 137 (top left & right): © Amijai Benderski; 137 (bottom left): Rosana Malaneschii; 137 (bottom right): Design: Max Phillips © Signal Type Foundry Limited; 138: Jessica Girvan / Shutterstock.com; 139 (top left): Extinction Rebellion UK; 139 (top right): Keen to be Green / Alamy Stock Photo; 139 (bottom): Extinction Rebellion UK

How can design embrace truth and dignity in a search for peace and justice?
140: Chris Daemmrich; 141: © Forensic Architecture; 144 (left): © Trustees of the British Museum; 144 (right) & 145 (all): © Hood Design Studio, Inc.; 146–47 (bottom): Forensic Architecture, 2017 © Forensic Architecture; 147 (top): Forensic Architecture and Dr. Salvador Navarro-Martinez, 2017 © Forensic Architecture; 148 & 149 (top): Chris Daemmrich; 149 (bottom left): Colloqate Studio; 149 (bottom right): Chris Daemmrich; 150: Women's International League for Peace and Freedom (WILPF); 152: Manipur Women Gun Survivors Network; 155: Juliet Prie; 157–59 (all): Iconoclasistas; 160–63 (all): © Chimurenga; 164–65 (all): © Conflict Kitchen; 167–69: Courtesy of Merve Bedir

How can design facilitate the transition from instability to peace?
170: © All rights reserved to Reparametrize Studio; 171: Image © Jiawen Chen; reproduced courtesy of Jungyoon Kim, Niall Kirkwood, Yoonjin Park, and Harvard University Graduate School of Design and the President and Overseers of Harvard College; 172 (top): Photo by Alex Asensi; 172 & 173 (bottom): Visualization by Jan Kristian Strømsnes and Manuela Aguirre Ulloa; 173 (top): Photo by Alex Asensi; 174: HarassMap © Mostafa Abdel Aty; 175 (top): HarassMap; 175 (bottom): HarassMap; 178–79: Courtesy of Kounkuey Design Initiative; 182–83: FAST with Laura van Santen © FAST / Malkit; 183 (bottom): Iwan Baan © FAST / Malkit; 184 (top): Malkit Shoshan © FAST / Malkit; 184 (bottom): FAST / Malkit Shoshan © FAST / Malkit; 185 (top): Malkit Shoshan © FAST / Malkit; 185 (grid): Rob Gijsbers © FAST / Malkit; 186–87 (all): © All rights reserved to Reparametrize Studio; 188 (left): © Lina Ghotmeh — Architecture, Photo © Lina Ghotmeh; 188 (right): © Lina Ghotmeh — Architecture, Photo © Takuji Shimmura; 189: © Lina Ghotmeh — Architecture,

Photo © Iwan Baan; 190–91: © Lina Ghotmeh — Architecture, Photo © Takuji Shimmura; 192 (left): Image © Matthew Wong; reproduced courtesy of Jungyoon Kim, Niall Kirkwood, Yoonjin Park, and Harvard University Graduate School of Design and the President and Overseers of Harvard College; 192 (right): Image © Ann Salerno; reproduced courtesy of Jungyoon Kim, Niall Kirkwood, Yoonjin Park, and Harvard University Graduate School of Design and the President and Overseers of Harvard College; 193 (both): Image © Matthew Wong; reproduced courtesy of Jungyoon Kim, Niall Kirkwood, Yoonjin Park, and Harvard University Graduate School of Design and the President and Overseers of Harvard College; 194–95 (all): Urban Design Workshop, Yale School of Architecture 2008; 196, 197 (top): Alvar Sánchez © trellyz, inc.; 197 (bottom): Shelley Taylor © trellyz, inc.; 198: © International Organisation for Migration; 199 (all): TAMassociati; 200: © Astrid Bellon & Philippe Starck; 201 (all): © BSF & Philippe Starck; 202: Knut Bry; 203 (top): Lesvos Solidarity; 203 (bottom): Knut Bry

Backmatter sequence (starting 224 opposite): Joanna Tam; Photo: Ruben Hamelink © Jonas Staal; Gallery 51; © Hood Design Studio, Inc.; Alvar Sánchez © trellyz, inc.; © Lina Ghotmeh — Architecture, Photo © Laurian Ghinitoiu

Image Credits

Design Note

When beginning work on a new book project, we often hear descriptions from curators, publishers, and editors regarding what kind of book it is and their ambitions for it. We carefully analyze these descriptions, often seizing the opportunity to reappraise ostensibly familiar terms or, sometimes, take them more literally than intended. Early in the design process for *Designing Peace*, curator and author Cynthia E. Smith talked about the distinction between a field guide, which this book isn't, and a guidebook, which we hoped it could be. While field guides aid observation—helping readers identify wildlife, for example—guidebooks are compendia of information designed, crucially, to be put into action.

With this in mind, we wanted to emphasize that the projects in this book are a form of collective action, what we think of as a simultaneous flow of work being done across the world. This flow starts on the cover, with Extinction Rebellion's prompt to "act now" pulling readers in and connecting them with a variety of people, places, and movements.

The color overlays on the cover, in the front matter, and on the section dividers act as filters, an attempt to honestly acknowledge the role of curators, writers, editors, the publisher, and Cooper Hewitt itself as subjective moderators. *Designing Peace* brings together a wide variety of works by diverse practitioners with myriad perspectives—from activists and policymakers to designers, artists, and community members—and connects them within sections framed by provocative curatorial questions. These questions are repeated at the bottom of every left-hand page as a consistent critical orientation for the reader, printed in thematic colors chosen more for contrasting section identification than from any conceptual rationale. There is already a deliberate and charged use of color in the works on display, by turns joyous, urgent, defiant, and just plain beautiful.

To accord with our concept of the publication as a tool for action—if not a field guide, it is designed for potential use in the field—we borrowed for its cover jacket the tough linen-embossed lamination you often find on old guidebooks or atlases. Not just on the cover but throughout the whole book, we hope readers will sense our respect for this collection of remarkable international projects and recognize this publication as the guidebook for peace we intended to make. May this flow of inspiring work prompt us all to join in and make a contribution.

James Goggin and Shan James, Practise

Designing Peace

ISBN: 978-1-942303-32-9
Library of Congress Control Number:
2022931646

Published by

Cooper Hewitt,
Smithsonian Design Museum
2 East 91st Street
New York, NY 10128
United States
cooperhewitt.org

Distributed (North America) by
Artbook | D.A.P.
75 Broad Street
Suite 630
New York, NY 10004
United States
artbook.com

Distributed (Worldwide) by
Thames & Hudson, UK
181A High Holborn
London, WC1V 7QX
United Kingdom
thamesandhudson.com

Author: Cynthia E. Smith
Publisher: Pamela Horn
Cross-Platform Publishing Associate:
Matthew Kennedy
Curatorial Assistant: Caroline O'Connell
Book Design: Practise
Color Preparation: Embassy Graphics
Printer: Rotolito S.p.A.

Front cover jacket: © Martin Reis
    (see image below)
Back cover jacket: Drone photography by
Ronald Rael and Virginia San Fratello

2022 2023 2024 2025 / 10 9 8 7 6 5 4 3 2 1
Printed in Italy

Paper: Sappi Magno Volume 250gsm, 130gsm

Type: LL Brown Narrow (Aurèle Sack, Lineto,
2022), LL Brown Mono (2020), and
LL Brown Arabic (2019, with Titus Nemeth)

Facebook.com/CooperHewitt
Twitter: @CooperHewitt
Instagram.com/CooperHewitt
Youtube.com/user/CooperHewitt

This book is published in conjunction with the exhibition *Designing Peace* at Cooper Hewitt, Smithsonian Design Museum, New York, June 10, 2022–September 4, 2023.

Designing Peace is made possible with lead support from

FORD
FOUNDATION

Major support is provided by Lisa Roberts and David Seltzer.

Generous support is also provided by the Lily Auchincloss Foundation, Helen and Edward Hintz, and the Barbara and Morton Mandel Design Gallery Endowment Fund.

Additional support is provided by Agnes Gund, the Cooper Hewitt Master's Program Fund, the Netherland-America Foundation, and the New York State Council on the Arts with the support of the Office of the Governor and the New York State Legislature.

COOPER HEWITT
Smithsonian Design Museum

Front cover jacket © Martin Reis,
Extinction Symbol ▶ 138

Social Emergency Response Centers ▶ 34